BEN GOLDSTEIN
CERI JONES

The BIG Picture

A2 ELEMENTARY Student's Book

CONTENTS UNITS 1–6

1 ONE WORLD

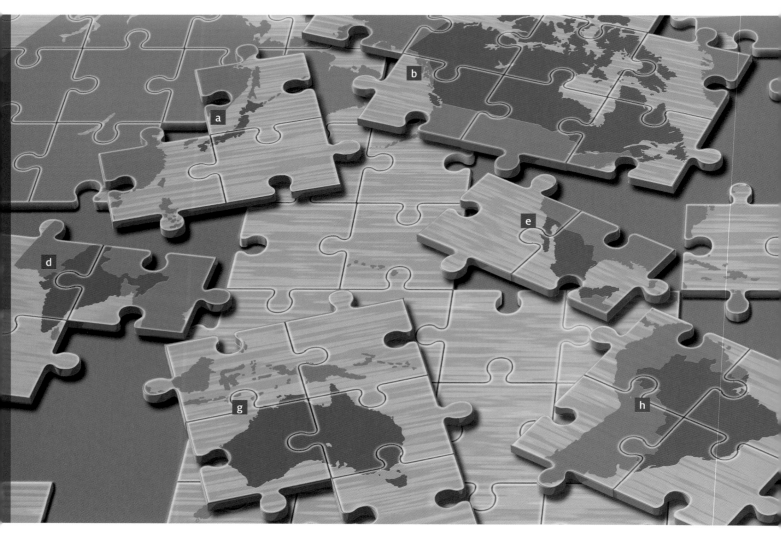

1 Look at the table in the KEY VOCABULARY PANEL ▪▪ .
   Work in pairs to complete A.

2 a 🔊)) 1.1 Listen to the countries and nationalities.
   Mark the stress on the words in A.

   b Listen again and repeat. Are your country and
   nationality in the table in A? If not, add them.

3 a 🔊)) 1.2 Listen and complete the dialogue.

   Q What's your name?
   A My name's ....
   Q Where are you from?
   A I'm .... I'm from ....

   b 💬 Change the dialogue so it is true for you.
   Practise it with a partner.

4 💬 Stand up. You have five minutes. Introduce yourself
   to as many students as possible.

5 Look at the map in the KEY VOCABULARY PANEL ▪▪ .
   Work in pairs to complete B.

6 a Which of the countries in A and B are in
   1 Africa?   3 Asia?   5 the G8?
   2 America?   4 the EU?

   b Write one more country for each category in 6a.

7 a Look at the photos. What countries do you think they
   are from?
   I think number 1 is Germany.
   No, I think it's Japan.

   b 🔊)) 1.3 Listen and check.

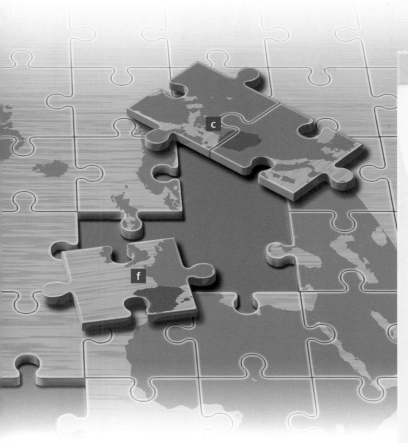

■ KEY VOCABULARY

Countries & nationalities

A Match the countries in the table to the puzzle pieces, a–h. Is the name of each country the same in your language?

Country	Nationality
Aus<u>tra</u>lia	Aus<u>tra</u>lian
Bra<u>zil</u>	Bra<u>zil</u>ian
Canada	Canadian
India	Indian
Japan	Japanese
Mexico	Mexican
Poland	Polish
Spain	Spanish
....	....

B Match the countries in the box to the numbers on the map. Then answer the questions.

Argentina   Bulgaria   China   Colombia
Egypt   France   Germany   Italy   Kenya
Thailand   Turkey   the UK   the USA

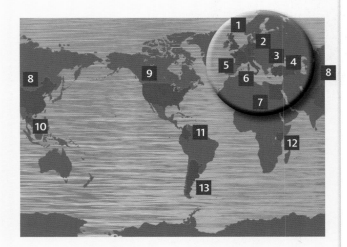

- What do the letters UK mean? And USA?
- What are the nationality adjectives for these countries? Use a dictionary to help you. Mark the stress.

READING & LISTENING

1 Work in pairs. Look at the photos. Match them to the sentences.

   1   Come in! Welcome to my house.
   2   Hello. Welcome! Nice to meet you.
   3   Goodbye! Take care!
   4   Hi there, everybody!

2   **a**   Complete the dialogues for photos b and c with the phrases in the box.

> Nice to meet you.   What's your name?
> Where are you from?

BAN	Hello. Welcome! (1) .... This is your room.
ERIC	Thanks.
BAN	(2) ....
MARIE	We're from France… Paris.
BAN	Ah, a beautiful city!
MARIE	Yes, it is.
BAN	Have a nice stay!
ERIC/MARIE	Thank you.

SONIA	Come in! Welcome to my house.
DAVE	Thanks. I'm Dave and this is Jen. (3) ....
SONIA	Sonia. (4) ....
JEN/DAVE	And you.
SONIA	Are you American, Jen?
JEN	No, I'm not. Dave's American. I'm Canadian.
SONIA	Canadian? (5) ....
JEN	Vancouver.

b 🔊 1.4 Listen and check.

3 💬 Work in groups of three. Practise reading the dialogues. Act out the two scenes.

4   **a** 🔊 1.5 Listen to the dialogues for photos a and d. <u>Underline</u> the words you hear.

A	Who's he?
B	He's a friend. His name's (1)*Sam / Tom*. He's very nice. He says hello to everybody!
A	Where's he from? Is he from round here?
B	No, he isn't. He's (2)*Australian / German*, I think.
A	It's a great (3)*photo / picture*.
B	Thanks!

A	And who are they?
B	They're my best friends, Luis and Carmen. They're (4)*Mexican / Spanish*. They're from (5)*Puebla / Seville*.
A	Are they (6)*married / in love*?
B	No, they aren't, but they're (7)*married / in love*!
A	I can see!

b 💬 Work in pairs. Practise reading the dialogues.

5 💬 Act out the scenes in **4a** without looking at the dialogues. Use the photos to help you remember.

GRAMMAR

1 Work in pairs. <u>Underline</u> all examples of the verb *to be* in the dialogues in READING & LISTENING 2a and 4a. Which forms are

1 affirmative?
2 negative?

2 Complete 1–9 in the GRAMMAR PANEL ▪ with the correct forms of the verb *to be*.

3 Work in pairs. Replace the words in **bold** using *he*, *she*, *it* or *they*. Use contracted forms of the verb *to be*.

His name is Tom. (1)~~Tom's~~ _He's_ very nice.
(2)**Tom's** _____ Australian. I like the photo –
(3)**the photo's** _____ great.

He's Luis. (4)**Luis is** _____ from Spain. She's
Carmen. (5)**Carmen is** _____ Spanish. (6)**Luis
and Carmen are** _____ in love.

4 💬 Read the dialogues in READING & LISTENING 2a and 4a again. Work in pairs. Answer these questions with short *yes/no* answers.

1 Is Tom American?
   No, he isn't.
2 Are Carmen and Luis in love?
3 Are they married?
4 Is Eric English?
5 Is Marie from Paris?

5 **a** Put the words in the correct order to make questions.

1 your what's name ? *What's your name?*
2 you are from where ?
3 you are Italian ?
4 surname your what's ?
5 your who's teacher ?
6 are married you ?

b 💬 Work in pairs. Ask and answer the questions.

PRESENT SIMPLE: *TO BE*

Affirmative

Full form	Contracted form	
I am	I' (2) _____	French.
You (1) _____	You're	
He/She/It is	He'/She'/It' (3) _____	
We/They are	We'/They' (4) _____	

Negative

Full form	Contracted form	
I am not	I'm not	Mexican.
You/We/They are not	You/We/They aren't	
He/She/It is not	He/She/It (5) _____	

I'm not Mexican, I'm Brazilian.

Questions
In questions the verb comes before the subject:
Where (6) _____ *you from?* (7) _____ *he Spanish?*

Yes/No answers
Yes, I (8) _____ . /No, I'm not.
Yes, she (9) _____ . /No, she isn't.

We do not use contracted forms in short *yes* answers.

See page 140 for grammar reference and more practice.

SPEAKING

1 💬 Work in pairs. Tell your partner about three of your friends. Talk about

• name
• nationality
• where they're from.
This is João. He's Brazilian.
He's from São Paulo.

IMPORTANT TRIP DETAILS

Call 0871 286 0808 for customer support

Main contact: José Luis Castillo Fdez   Traveller(s): 1
Email: castillo777@hotmail.com   Traveller(s): José Luis Castillo
Home phone: 222 485 2972   Itinerary number: 12283274680

ITINERARY

Thursday, June 9, 2011   My Account   Change/Cancel trip

FLIGHT   Airline confirmation code: TZMV9

Depart: 17:05   Mexico City (MEX)   FLIES UP AIRLINES
Arrive: 20:15   Chicago (ORD)   Flight 1073

33K, Economy/Coach Class, Boeing 737-800

VOCABULARY: Money & documents

1 Work in pairs. Find the items in the box in the photos.

> money   a credit card   an ID card   a travel card
> receipts   a passport   a plane ticket

2 Look at the documents and answer the questions about José.

1 What's his full name?
2 Is he American?
3 How old is he?
4 What's his address and phone number?

LISTENING

3 🔊 1.6 Listen to José talking about the items in the photos. Number them in the order you hear them.

4 Listen again and complete the sentences.

1 These are my two .... – my .... passport and my
   .... passport.
2 This is my Mexican ID ....
3 This is my .... – these are the .... dollars, here,
   and those are the .... pesos, there.
4 Well, this is my plane .... , this is my .... and
   that's my .... for when I arrive in Chicago.
5 And those? Those are .... I don't need them now.

SPEAKING

1 Read the questions in VOCABULARY 2 again. Rewrite them using *you* and *your*.

2 💬 Work in pairs. You are at passport control in an airport. Student A, you are an immigration officer. Ask student B the questions and complete the arrival card for him/her. Change roles and repeat.

ARRIVAL CARD

1 Name *(as in passport)* [   ]

2 Nationality [   ]

3 Date of birth
  Day [ ] Month [ ] Year [   ]

4 Address [   ]
  [   ]
  [   ]

5 Phone number [   ]

GRAMMAR & VOCABULARY:
Personal possessions

1 Work in pairs. Match the pictures to the sentences.

1 Hey! **Those** are my books!
2 No, it isn't. **That's** my book.
3 No, they aren't. **These** are my books.
4 **This** is my book.

2 Complete the GRAMMAR PANEL ■ with *this, that, these* and *those*.

3 a Match the words in the box to the items in the photo.

> camera   glasses   iPod   keys   mobile phone
> newspaper   sunglasses   wallet

b Which are singular? Which are plural?

4 a Complete the sentences and questions with the correct option.

1 *This / These* are nice sunglasses.
2 Is *that / those* your mobile phone?
3 Sorry, but *that / those* are my keys.
4 Whose wallet is *this / these*?
5 *This / These* is my new iPod.
6 Is *that / those* your newspaper?

b 🔊 1.7 Listen and check.

■ THIS, THAT, THESE, THOSE

	Here ⬇	There ↗
Singular	(1) .... is my book.	(2) .... is your book.
Plural	(3) .... are my books.	(4) .... are your books.

See page 140 for grammar reference and more practice.

PRONUNCIATION: /ɪ/ & /iː/

1 🔊 1.8 Listen and repeat.

/ɪ/ This is a kiss.   /iː/ These are my keys.

2 a Mark the words in the box /ɪ/ or /iː/.

> me   he   she   it   three   is   thirteen
> receipts   isn't   six   ticket

b 🔊 1.9 Listen and check. Then listen and repeat.

3 a 🔊 1.10 Listen and <u>underline</u> the word you hear.

1 this / these   3 this / these
2 this / these   4 this / these

b Listen again and write the complete sentences.

SPEAKING

1 Work in small groups. What objects can you find in your bag? Put them on the table and name them. Use a dictionary to help you.

2 💬 Move some of the objects to the other side of the table. Tell your group about your objects.

This is my new mobile phone. This is my wallet. This is my ID card. Those are my sunglasses and those are my car keys.

Our Turkish Holidays

1   2   3   4

READING & VOCABULARY: Adjectives

1   Work in pairs. Match the photos to the captions.

a Here we are at the airport. Our plane is **late**! We're **bored**!

b In Istanbul at last! We're at the taxi rank. These are our bags. My bag is the **small** bag. Kate has a **big** bag – it's REALLY big.

c This is the bus station at Ankara. It's really **early**. It's 5 a.m. We're **tired**! But the coffee is **good**! ;)

d Here we are – at last! Cappadocia. It's **beautiful**. We're VERY **happy** to be here.

2   Match the words in **bold** in **1** to the pictures. One adjective does not match a picture.

1   2   3   4   5   6   7   8

GRAMMAR (1)

1   Work in pairs. Complete 1–3 in the GRAMMAR PANEL with examples from the captions in READING & VOCABULARY **1**.

2   Complete the sentences with the words in brackets.
   1   Her house is big. *(very)*
   2   It's a really house. *(beautiful)*
   3   And we're happy to be here. *(really)*
   4   But it's very and we're really. *(late/tired)* It's time for bed!

3   Underline the best adjective to make these sentences true for you.
   1   I'm *happy / bored / tired*.
   2   My classroom is *big / small*.
   3   I'm usually *early / late* for class.
   4   I'm *hungry / thirsty*.

4   Add *very* or *really* to the sentences in **3**. Then compare your sentences with a partner.

NOTICE   *REALLY/VERY + ADJECTIVE*
We can use *really* or *very* before an adjective to make it stronger: *It's a really big bag. We're very happy.*

■ POSITION OF ADJECTIVES

We use adjectives with the verb *to be*:
We're tired. It's early. (1)........................

We use adjectives with nouns. The adjective comes before the noun:
good coffee ✓ ~~*coffee good*~~ ✗
(2)........................ ✓ ~~*the bag small*~~ ✗

Adjectives do not have a plural form:
We're tired. ✓ ~~*We're tireds.*~~ ✗
(3)........................ ✓ ~~*We're boreds.*~~ ✗

See page 140 for grammar reference and more practice.

GRAMMAR (2)

1 Work in pairs. <u>Underline</u> all the possessive adjectives in the captions in READING & VOCABULARY 1. Complete 1–4 in the GRAMMAR PANEL ▪▪ .

2 🔊 1.11 Complete the descriptions with possessive adjectives. Listen and check.

> These are photos of (1) _our_ holiday.

> This is Tim and this is (2) _____ best friend, Hans. They live together. We're in (3) _____ flat in Istanbul. (4) _____ flat is very big and beautiful.

> Here I am again. I'm in the station with Tim and Hans. (5) _____ train is late.

> This is a friend from the train. (6) _____ name's Tina. She's a student.

<table>
<tr><th colspan="2">POSSESSIVE ADJECTIVES</th></tr>
<tr><td>I</td><td>my</td></tr>
<tr><td>you</td><td>your</td></tr>
<tr><td>he</td><td>(1) _____</td></tr>
<tr><td>she</td><td>(2) _____</td></tr>
<tr><td>we</td><td>(3) _____</td></tr>
<tr><td>they</td><td>(4) _____</td></tr>
</table>

See page 140 for grammar reference and more practice.

3 💬 Work in pairs. Student A, you are a visitor to the classroom. Student B, tell your visitor about the classroom and your classmates. Then swap roles.

This is our classroom. This is my teacher. These are my classmates. That's Kim. He's from Korea. That's Jean. She's from...

LISTENING

1 a 🔊 1.12 Listen and match the situations, 1–3, to the photos.

b Listen again. Complete the extracts.

1

A All watches, money, _____ and _____ phones in the plastic tray, please. Take your computer out of your _____ . Thank you. Next, please.

2

A Passports or _____ cards, please. Thank you. _____ are you _____ ?
B Poland.
A Are you _____ ?
B Yes, we're on holiday.
A Thank you.

3

KATE	Look. It's Leyla.
BEN	_____ ?
KATE	That's her _____ .
BEN	Oh, yes! Hi, Leyla! _____ over here!
LEYLA	Hi! I'm really _____ to see you! Are these your _____ ?
KATE	Yes, they are. So, how's your family?

2 💬 Work in groups of three. Act out dialogue 3 in 1b.

Greetings Different people greet in different ways.

Some people **kiss on the cheeks**.

Other people prefer to **shake hands**.

Some people **bow**.

And others **hug**.

When I say hello to my friends and family we _____ or _____ .

TUNE IN

1 Read the text. Use the words in **bold** to complete the last sentence about you. Use a dictionary to help you.

2 💬 Work in pairs to answer the questions.
- Are your answers similar?
- Are they typical of other people in your country?
- Are they the same in other countries? Give examples.

FOCUS ON LANGUAGE (1)

3 Look at photos b–d in **1**. Choose the best description for each one.
1 This is their first meeting.
2 They are good friends.
3 She is his boss.

4 a 🔊 1.13 Read and listen to three dialogues. Match them to photos a–c.

1
  A Hello! Pleased to meet you.
  B And you.
2
  A Hello, Hiro, how are you?
  B Fine, thanks, Mrs Sato. And you?
3
  A Hi! How are you? You look great!
  B Thanks. You too.

b 💬 Work in pairs. Practise the dialogues.

5 Match the answers to the faces.

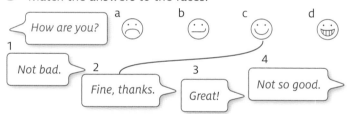

How are you?   a   b   c   d

1   Not bad.   2   Fine, thanks.   3   Great!   4   Not so good.

66 Intonation 99

🔊 1.14 Listen to the speakers. Notice how they use their voice to show if they're happy ☺ or sad ☹. Practise repeating the sentences using the right intonation.

OVER TO YOU

6 💬 Say *Hello* and *How are you?* to your classmates. Change your answer each time.

FOCUS ON LANGUAGE (2)

7 a 🔊 1.15 Listen to five people saying goodbye. Number them in the order you hear them.
  a Have a good weekend!   d See you on Monday.
  b See you tomorrow.   e See you later.
  c Bye. Take care.

b Listen again and repeat. How do you say each one in your language?

OVER TO YOU

8 💬 You are at a party. It's time for you to go home. Say goodbye to all your classmates.

TUNE IN

1 **a** Work in pairs. Write *a* or *an* in front of the words in the box.

> .... actor   .... singer   .... sports star
> .... politician   .... artist   .... writer

b Match the words to the photos.

2 **a** 💬 Work in pairs. Ask and answer the questions for each photo.

1 Who's he/she?
2 Where's he/she from?

b 🔊 1.16 Listen and check.

3 Work in groups. Think of three famous people for each category in **1**. Compare your lists with the class.

4 💬 Work in pairs. Talk about your favourite actor/singer/politician/sports star.

Lionel Messi. He's great!
Beyoncé. She's beautiful. And her voice is incredible.

a Angela Merkel
b Daniel Craig
c Fernando Botero
d Isabel Allende
e Usain Bolt
f Christina Aguilera

PREPARE FOR TASK

5 🔊 1.17 Listen to a role-play between a fan and one of his favourite celebrities. Who is the celebrity? Is he an actor?

6 **a** Listen again. Put the sentences in the correct order.

1 PEDRO   Thanks!
2 ANA   Jan, I'd like to introduce you to a friend. Jan, this is Pedro. He's a film director. Pedro, this is Jan.
3 JAN   Hi, Mr Almódovar! Nice to meet you, too. I'm a big fan. I love your films!
4 PEDRO   Hi, Jan. Nice to meet you.

b 💬 Practise reading the dialogue in threes.

7 **a** 💬 Work in groups of three.

Student A: introduce student B to a celebrity from your list in **3**.
Student B: you are a big fan of the celebrity.
Student C: you are the celebrity.

b Repeat the dialogue two more times. Change your role each time.

TASK

8 **a** 💬 Work in pairs. Choose a new celebrity from the list.

Student A: you are the celebrity.
Student B: you are his/her friend.

Together decide how best to introduce student A to the class.

b Introduce your celebrity partner to your classmates.

REPORT BACK

9 Work with a new partner. Write a list of the 'celebrities' in your class. Include their occupations.

10 💬 Read the list of celebrities in your class. Take a vote. Who is the number one favourite celebrity for the whole class? Why?

➡ Go to Review A, Unit 1, p. 34   ➡ Go to Writing bank 1, p. 152   **13**

2 MY LIFE

a Sierra Leone

b Romania

c China

d Germany

1 **a** Look at the photos. Find examples of the words in the box.

> dad   daughter   husband   kids   mum   son   wife

b Work in pairs to complete A in the KEY VOCABULARY PANEL ■.

2 Read the descriptions of the four families. Match the speakers to the photos.

1
> **Li:** This is my <u>mother</u> and father. I'm an only child. That's me on the right. We're on a train in Tibet.

2
> **Corina:** We are a big family. Those are my parents and that's my uncle Vasile, my mother's brother, and my cousin Mirela – she's his daughter! I have three little brothers and sisters.

3
> **Anna:** This is me with my three children and husband, Karsten. We have two sons and a daughter. The kids are very happy because it's dinner time – they love hamburgers!

4
> **Mohammed:** I'm Mohammed and these are my two sons. Little Ibrahim is my only nephew – he's three years old. His mum's dead. He lives with his grandparents – my mum and dad.

3 Work in pairs. Look at the photos again. Point to Li, Corina, Anna and Mohammed.

4 **a** <u>Underline</u> all the family words in the texts. Which are not in the table in A? Add them to the table.

b Work in pairs to complete B in the KEY VOCABULARY PANEL ▪▪.

5 Match the dialogues to two of the photos.
1 **A:** Do you have any brothers or sisters?
  B: No. I'm an only child.
2 **A:** Do you have any brothers or sisters?
  B: Yes. I have one sister and two brothers.

6 💬 Discuss these questions with a partner.
- Do you have any brothers or sisters?
- What are their names?
- How old are they?

▪ KEY VOCABULARY

Family members

A Use the words in 1a to complete the table.

👫	👩	👨
parents	mother/..........	father/..........
married couple	....	....
children/..........	....	....
....	sister	brother
....	aunt	....
....	niece	....
....	grandmother/ grandma	grandfather/ grandad
grandchildren	granddaughter	grandson
cousins	....	cousin

- 🔊 **2.1** Listen and check your answers. Then listen again and repeat.

B Look at the picture. It shows three generations of the same family. Label the people with words from the table.

1 *daughter, sister, granddaughter*
2 _____
3 _____
4 _____
5 _____
6 _____

■ PRACTISE THE VERB *HAVE* & POSSESSIVE *'S*
■ TALK ABOUT YOUR FAMILY

GRAMMAR

1   Work in pairs. Read the descriptions in **2** on pages 14–15 again. Match the names in the box to the sentences.

> Anna and Karsten   Corina   Ibrahim
> Li   Li's parents   Mohammed

1   I **don't have** any brothers or sisters.
2   I **have** a big family.
3   He **doesn't have** a mother.
4   We **have** one child.
5   They **have** three children.
6   He **has** two sons.

> **NOTICE**
> *one child*
> *two children*

2   Complete 1–3 in the GRAMMAR PANEL ▪ with the verbs in **bold** in **1**.

3   **a**   Complete the sentences.

1   I _have_ two brothers.
2   I .... have any sisters.
3   My brother .... three kids.
4   My sister .... have any kids.
5   I'm married. We .... have any children yet.
6   My aunt .... five children, two girls and three boys.

b 💬 Are any of the sentences true for you and your family?

4   **a**   Put the words in the correct order to make questions.

1   a family big have you do ?
2   do have aunts or uncles you any ?
3   have you do nieces or nephews any ?
4   your father any does brothers or sisters have ?
5   any grandchildren your parents have do ?
6   any great-grandchildren does have your grandmother ?

b 💬 Work in pairs. Answer the questions with short answers.

Yes, I do./No, I don't.   *Yes, he does./No, he doesn't.*
Yes, they do./No, they don't.   *Yes, she does./No, she doesn't.*

▪ PRESENT SIMPLE: *HAVE*

We use *have* to talk about families and possessions.

+

I/You/We/They	have	
He/She/It	(1)	three sisters.

−

I/You/We/They	(2)	
He/She/It	doesn't have	any sisters.

?

Do	I/you/we/they	(3)	
Does	he/she/it		any sisters?

See page 141 for grammar reference and more practice.

LISTENING & READING

1   🔊 2.2 Listen to Anna talking about a video of her family. Tick the family words that you hear.

> brother   children   daughter   father   husband
> mother   nephew   niece   sister   son

2   **a**   Listen again and complete the description with the names in the box.

> Karolina   Daniel   Gus   Janet
> Julia   Karsten   Theo   Tobias

> *This is my family. I have three children – two boys and a girl –* (1) .... , (2) .... *and* (3) .... *In the video you can see Julia and Tobias. My husband,* (4) .... , *and Daniel are in the park. My father is dead but my mother is still alive. Her name is* (5) .... *I have a brother called* (6) .... *He's married to* (7) .... *and they have a son called* (8) .... *He's my nephew.*

b 💬 Work in pairs. Cover the description and look at the names in the box. Can you remember who the people are?

Karolina is her sister-in-law.

GRAMMAR

1 Read Anna's description in LISTENING & READING 2a again. Choose the correct word to complete the sentences.

1 Gus is Karolina's *brother / son / father.*
2 Theo and Karolina are Gus's *children / parents / grandparents.*
3 Daniel is Janet's *son / grandson / brother.*
4 Anna is Julia's *daughter / sister / mother.*
5 Karsten is Tobias's *father / brother / son.*
6 Karolina is Theo's *sister / daughter / wife.*

2 Complete 1–5 in the GRAMMAR PANEL ◼◼ .

3 Complete the definitions with the words in the box.

> cousins   grandmother   nephew
> niece   uncles

1 Your brother's son is your ....
2 Your parents' brothers are your ....
3 Your mother's mother is your ....
4 Your sister's daughter is your ....
5 Your uncle's children are your ....

NOTICE   APOSTROPHE S

's can mean two things:
1 *is*: Anna's German.
2 the possessive: Anna's brother

---

4 💬 Write the names of five people who are important to you. Tell your partner about them. Use the possessive 's.

Latif – he's my boyfriend's brother.
Analisa – she's my husband's sister.

◼◼ POSSESSIVE 's

We use **name + 's** to show possession:
Anna is Daniel's mother. (the mother of (1) ....)
Daniel is Julia's brother. (the (2) .... of (3) ....)

For names ending in -s you can add:
's: *Gus's friend* or
': *Gus' friend.*

For plural nouns that end in -s add **'**:
his parents' family. (the (4) .... of his (5) ....)

See page 141 for grammar reference and more practice.

PRONUNCIATION: Schwa /ə/

1 🔊 2.3 Listen to the words. The stress is on the first syllable. The vowel in the second syllable has no stress. It is a schwa /ə/.

O o	O o
mother	children
ə	ə

2 a 🔊 2.4 Listen to more family words. Mark the syllables and main stress (O o o), and the schwa (ə).

O o	....	....
parents	father	cousin
ə	....	....
....	....	....
uncle	daughter	sister
....	....	....
....	....	....
brother	grandmother	grandfather
....	....	....

b Listen again and repeat.

SPEAKING

1 💬 Work in pairs. Ask your partner questions about his/her family and write the names in the family tree.

What are your mum and dad's names?
Do they have any brothers or sisters?
What are their names?

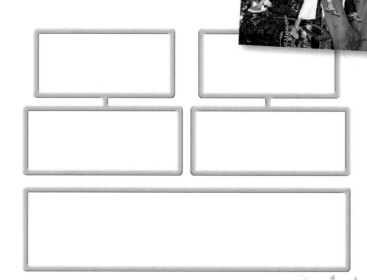

2 💬 Work with a new partner. Explain your previous partner's family tree.

LISTENING

1 a Match the photos to the expressions.

1 get married   2 have children   3 leave home

b 💬 At what age, on average, do people do these things in your country?

People get married at about 30 in Poland.
We have children very late in Brazil.

2 🔊 2.5 Listen to a news report about the average age people do these things in different countries. Complete the table with countries and ages.

The average age people…		
1 leave home	Women	Men
UK	………………	22
Italy	27	………………
………………	32	34
2 get married	Women	Men
USA	………………	………………
UK	………………	31
………………	31	33
3 have children		
All countries: between 30 and ………………		

3 Listen again and complete the sentences.

1 In the UK, young people leave home very ……………… .
2 In ……………… , men don't leave home until they're 30.
3 Mexicans like ……………… life!
4 In Spain, people get married ……………… – 31 for women and 33 for men.

4 💬 Are any of the sentences true for your country, too? Change them if not. Compare your answers with a partner.

GRAMMAR

1 a Work in pairs. Read the sentences in LISTENING 3 again. <u>Underline</u> all the verbs.

b Complete 1–3 in the GRAMMAR PANEL ■ with a suitable verb.

2 Complete the sentences so that they are true about you.

1 I *live / don't live* with my family.
2 I *have / don't have* a job.
3 I'm / 'm not married.

3 a Make questions from the sentences in 2.

1 Do you live ……………………………… ?
2 Do you ……………………………… ?
3 ……………………………… married?

b 💬 Work in pairs. Ask and answer the questions with short answers.

Yes, I do./No, I don't.   Yes, I am./No, I'm not.

■ PRESENT SIMPLE: *I, YOU, WE, THEY*

We use the present simple to talk about facts – things that are generally true.

+

I live with my friends.
Young people (1)………………………… *home very late in Mexico.*

–

I/you/we/they don't + verb (infinitive)
I don't live with my friends.
Young people (2)………………………… *home very late in the UK.*

?

Do + I/you/we/they + verb (infinitive)
Do you live with your friends?
(3)………………………… *home very late in Mexico?*

See page 141 for grammar reference and more practice.

YOUR ANSWERS Topic: Leaving home?

Open

Sort by: ▶ Newest   ▶ Most Popular   ▶ Fewest Answers

Manu How old are you? Where do you live? Who do you live with? Do you live at home with your parents? Do you share a flat with friends? How many friends do you share with? My friends want to leave home. I don't. I love family life! What do you think?

Steven K Hi, Manu! I'm 29. I'm from Singapore. I live with my mum and my aunt. I love my family. I have a good relationship with them and I'm still a student.
Answer #1

Claudia Hello, everybody! I'm 18. I'm an only child. I study Medicine at university. I live at home with my mum and dad in Mendoza. I work in a restaurant at the weekend, but I don't have enough money to leave home.
Answer #2

Renée Hi! I'm 25. I have three brothers. They live at home with my parents, but I share a flat with friends. We don't have a lot of money. But we're independent and we like it.
Answer #3

READING & VOCABULARY:
Common verb collocations

1 Read the first paragraph of the text and answer the questions.

2 Read answers 1–3 in the text. Is any of the information true for you? Are you similar to any of the people?

3 Work in pairs. Cover the text. Match 1–7 with a–g to make sentences.

1 I share	a my job.
2 I work	b Medicine.
3 I study	c a flat with friends.
4 I love	d with my parents.
5 I want	e my family.
6 I live	f in a restaurant.
7 I like	g to be a doctor.

4 **a** If the sentences are not true for you make them negative.

I don't share a flat with friends.

b Compare your sentences with your partner.

GRAMMAR

1 **a** Work in pairs. Read the questions in the first paragraph of the text again. <u>Underline</u> the question words.

b Match 1–5 with a–e in the GRAMMAR PANEL ▪▪.

2 Complete the questions with a question word. Add a preposition where necessary.

1 .... brothers do you have?
2 .... old are you?
3 .... do you live?
4 .... is your address?
5 .... do you live .... ?

3 **a** 💬 Work in pairs. Ask and answer the questions.

NOTICE *TO BE FOR AGE*

When we ask about age we use *to be*:
How old are you? NOT ~~How many years do you have?~~
Is it the same in your language?

b Ask other students in your class. Does anyone have the same answers as you?

Juan and I have two brothers. We're both 21.

▪▪ *WH-* QUESTIONS

Wh- questions start with a question word (*what, who,* etc.).

1 who		a	age
2 what		b	a place
3 where		c	a person
4 how many		d	a thing or idea
5 how old		e	a number

When we use a preposition in a question it usually goes at the end:

Who do you share with?

See page 141 for grammar reference and more practice.

VOCABULARY: Free-time activities

1 Work in pairs. Read the sentences. Match them to the people in the pictures.

Fiona: In my free time I play tennis.
Xavi: I go to the cinema in my free time.
Jon: I go shopping when I want to relax.
Lin: When I want to relax I play computer games.

2 a Match 1–6 with a–f to make free-time activities.

1	watch	a	dancing
2	go	b	sport
3	go	c	to music
4	listen	d	to the gym
5	spend	e	TV
6	do	f	time with friends

b 🔊 2.6 Listen and check.

3 💬 Read the activities in 2a again. Tick the activities you do in your free time. Ask your partner what he/she does in his/her free time.

What do you do in your free time?
I go to the gym, I spend time with friends, I do sport.

4 💬 Write three more activities people do in their free time. Use a dictionary to help you. Find out how many students do these activities.

Do you play with your children?
Do you go for a walk?

Hi, my name's Simon. I have two lives: my real life and my virtual life. This is me in my real life. I'm a student. I love university life. I have a lot of friends and I spend a lot of time with them. In my free time I do a lot of sport – I play basketball, I go to the gym and I spend hours and hours on my computer. I play games and I visit virtual worlds.

This is me in my virtual life. This is my avatar. Avatars are virtual people. They live in virtual worlds. My avatar's name is Bo Lecker. In my virtual life I go skiing and I dance the tango!

READING

1 Look at the photos of Simon in his real life and his virtual life. What do you think his favourite free-time activities are?

2 Read the text and complete the table.

	Real life	Virtual life
Name	Simon	....
Interests	....	....

3 💬 Work in pairs. Read the text again. <u>Underline</u> all the expressions about free-time activities. Answer the questions.

● Do you do any of these activities?
● Who are you more similar to – Simon or his avatar?

LISTENING

1 🔊 2.7 Listen to two more people talking about their avatars. Complete the tables.

	Real life	Virtual life
Name	*Ruth*	....
Occupation	....	....
Interests	....	....

	Real life	Virtual life
Name	*Tony*	....
Occupation	....	....
Interests	....	....

2 Listen again and complete the extracts.

1

Hi, (1)............. Ruth. (2)............. a doctor.
We walk in the park and we (3)............. to the cinema.
In the evening, I (4)............. on the computer.
In my virtual life my (5)............. Bel. (6)............. a famous singer. I also (7)............. as a DJ in a local club.

2

Hi, (1)............. Tony. (2)............. a student. In my free time I (3)............. sport.
In my virtual life my (4)............. Zack. I (5)............. in a bar. It's very cool and beautiful people (6)............. there. In my free time I (7)............. to funk and soul music, and I (8)............. dancing. I meet a lot of people.

READING & WRITING

1 a Put the sentences in the correct order to complete the instant messaging dialogue.

a	Hi, I'm Zack. What's your name?
b	You too, Bel. Do you like the park?
c	I do sport, I listen to music and I go dancing.
d	I love the bar. It's great. And what do you do in your free time?
e	Yes, I do. I come for a walk every day. And you?
f	Hi, I'm Bel. Nice to meet you, Zack.
g	I work here. In the bar.
h	That's funny! Me too!

b 🔊 2.8 Listen and check.

2 Choose a virtual identity for yourself and complete the table.

	Virtual life
Name	....
Interests	....

3 a Work in pairs. You are online in a virtual park.
Student A: write a short message to student B. Use your new virtual identity.
Student B: answer student A in your virtual identity.
Continue the conversation for as long as possible.

b 💬 Tell the class about your partners' avatars. Who has the most interesting avatar?

TUNE IN

1 Work in pairs. Read the survey question. What do you think the three most common questions are?

Today's survey asks:

What are the three most common questions people ask when they first meet?

1 What _____ _____ _____ ?
2 Where _____ _____ _____ ?
3 What _____ _____ _____ ?

2 a 🔊 2.9 Listen to a short conversation between two strangers. Complete the top three questions.

b 💬 Discuss the questions with a partner.

• Are these the three most common questions in your language?
• What other questions do you ask?

FOCUS ON LANGUAGE

3 Match answers a–g to the top three questions in **1**.

a Jennifer, but my friends call me Jen.
b I'm a student. I study Medicine.
c I don't have a job at the moment.
d Call me J.J.
e I'm from Rio, but I live in New York.
f I work in an office.
g Paris. This is my home town.

4 a Match the words in the box to the pictures.

designer   photographer   reporter
shop assistant   model   engineer

b Is your occupation here? If not, how do you say your occupation in English? Use a dictionary to help you.

NOTICE   *A/AN* + OCCUPATION

To say what someone's job is we use *to be + a/an*:
I'm a teacher. I'm an engineer.

5 💬 Work in pairs. Ask and answer the top three questions in **1**.

6 a Read the questions. Which can you ask a student (S), a person with a job (J), or both (B)?

1 What do you do?
2 What do you study?
3 What school/college/university do you go to?
4 Where do you work?
5 What year are you in?
6 Who do you work for?

b 🔊 2.10 Listen and check.

❝Intonation: *wh-* questions❞

🔊 2.11 Listen to the questions again. Do the speakers' voices go up ↗ or down ↘ ?

Listen again and repeat.

7 💬 Work in pairs. Turn to page 162. Act out the conversations in transcript 2.10.

OVER TO YOU

8 Choose a person from the photos below. Complete the table with information about that person.

Name	
Nationality	
Occupation	

9 a 💬 Work in pairs. Imagine you are the person you wrote about in **8**. You meet at a friend's house. Use the questions in **1** to start a conversation. Ask other questions to get more information.

b Can you guess which photo your partner chose?

TUNE IN

1 **a** Read Alberto's student profile from the *English To Go* website. Tick the topics he mentions.

- his family
- his job
- his home
- his English classes
- his town

b 💬 Work in pairs. What do the photos show?

2 Complete the information in the table for Alberto.

	Alberto	You
Age		
Family	Not married, girlfriend: Renata	
Home town		
Occupation		
English studies		
Why English is important		

3 Match summaries a–d to paragraphs 1–4 in Alberto's profile.

a why English is important to him
b a general introduction
c why the blog is important
d a description of the photos

```
○ ○ ○
```

ENGLISH TO GO

Student blog

1 Hi, readers, let me introduce myself. I'm Alberto Costa. I come from Rio de Janeiro and I'm 42. I'm not married, but I have a girlfriend, Renata, and she has two kids.

2 Here's a photo of Renata in Rio, on the famous Copacabana beach. You can see it's a beautiful place. Here's another photo of me and my English teacher, Ray. We're in a bar where we have conversation classes.

3 I'm an engineer. It's very important to know English for my work. I use it every day, but I'm not a confident speaker.

4 I want to practise my English and learn about other English students around the world. I want to learn about other cultures because I think this is very interesting. Thanks for reading!

PREPARE FOR TASK

4 **a** Complete the sentences with the correct option.

1 I come from Rio de Janeiro *and* / *but* I'm 42.
2 I'm not married, *and* / *but* I have a girlfriend.

b Check your answers in the profile. Complete the explanations with *but* or *and*.

We use .... to give extra information.
We use .... to contrast two facts.

5 **a** Join the two sentences using *but* or *and*.

1 I write in my blog every day / I get a lot of messages
   and
   from other English students.
2 I want to learn to speak English. I want to work in an English-speaking country.
3 I live at home. I want to share a flat with friends.
4 I study hard. My English isn't very good.
5 In my free time I go to the beach. I spend time with my friends.

b 💬 Are any of the sentences true for you? Compare with a partner.

TASK

6 Write your own profile for a blog. Follow the steps.

1 Complete the table in 2 with your own information.
2 Decide on two photos to include.
3 Organise your ideas into three or four paragraphs.
4 Write your profile.
5 Don't forget to link your ideas with *and* and *but*.

REPORT BACK

7 💬 Work in groups of three. Read your partners' profiles. Find two things you have in common. Tell the class.

We all live in...
We all like...
We all want to...

➜ Go to Review A, Unit 2, p. 35   **23**

3 DAYS TO REMEMBER

a LONDON

b KATHMANDU

c SYDNEY

d VANCOUVER

e CARACAS

1 Look at the photos 1–5. Match them to cities a–e.

2 Work in pairs to complete A in the KEY VOCABULARY PANEL ▉.

3 Match the times to the city clocks above.

1 half past seven in the morning
2 twelve o'clock midday
3 quarter to six in the evening
4 four o'clock in the morning
5 eleven o'clock at night

4 Read what different people do at the same time around the world. Match each person to a city in 1.

1 I finish work at this time. Sometimes I go to the market on the way home. I get home at about 7 o'clock.
2 I usually watch TV at this time and then I go to bed at about midnight.
3 This is the time I have lunch. I go to a café near my office. I go back to work at one o'clock.
4 I'm in bed at this time. I don't get up until 8 o'clock. I start work at 10.
5 I'm usually on the bus at this time. I work in a bank. I start work at 8.

5 When it's 12 o'clock midday in London, what time is it in your country? What do you usually do at this time?

6 **a** Work in pairs. Complete B and C in the KEY VOCABULARY PANEL ▉.

b 🔊 3.2 Listen and complete the times.

1 07 : .... 2 08 : .... 3 .... : 15 4 13 : .... 5 .... : 45 6 .... : 15

◾ KEY VOCABULARY

Telling the time

A Match the times, 1–4, to the clocks below.

 a
 b

 c
 d

1 twelve o'clock 3 quarter past twelve
2 half past twelve 4 quarter to one

B Look at the clocks and complete the times.

1 five past _____ 5 twenty-five to _____

2 ten past _____ 6 twenty to _____

3 twenty past _____ 7 ten to _____

4 twenty-five past _____ 8 five to _____

● 💬 Practise asking for and telling the time using the clocks above.

NOTICE
To ask the time say:
What's the time? OR *What time is it?*
To answer use *It's...:*
It's half past five.

C ◀))) 3.1 Listen and complete the notes.
There are two ways of telling the time:
8.10 ten past eight or _____ _____
8.15 quarter past eight or _____ _____

7 a ◀))) 3.3 Match the times in 6b with the activities below. Then listen and check.

a get home e have breakfast
b get up f have a coffee
c go to bed g have lunch
d go to work/school h take a break

b 💬 Work in pairs. Ask and answer questions about the activities in 7a.
What time do you get up? I get up at about 8 o'clock.

NOTICE *AT & ABOUT*
Use *at* + time: *at 9 o'clock.*
Use *about* with an approximate time: *at about 9 o'clock.*

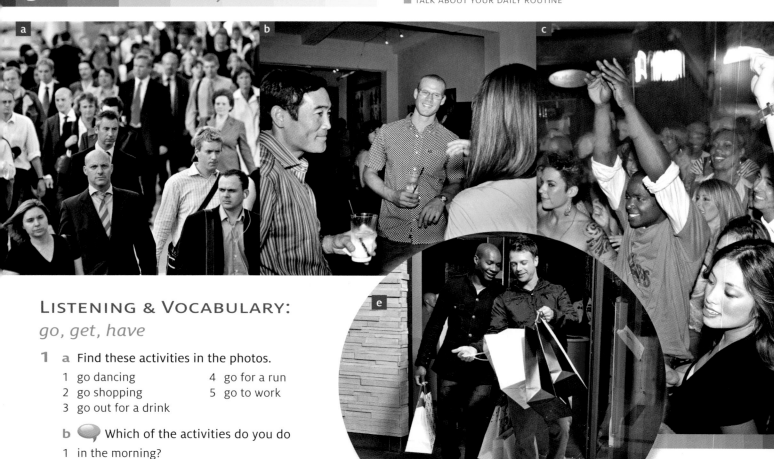

LISTENING & VOCABULARY:

go, get, have

1 a Find these activities in the photos.

1 go dancing
2 go shopping
3 go out for a drink
4 go for a run
5 go to work

b 💬 Which of the activities do you do

1 in the morning?
2 in the afternoon/evening?
3 at night?

2 🔊 3.4 Listen to Michelle (M) and Veronica (V) talking about their daily routines. Match them to the pictures.

3 a Listen again and complete the sentences with the correct times.

Michelle
1 During the week I get up at ....
2 I start work at ....
3 At the weekend I get up at ....

Veronica
4 I get up at ....
5 I start work at ....
6 I finish work at ....

b 💬 Work in pairs. Answer the questions. Are you more similar to Michelle or Veronica? Why?

I'm more similar to Michelle because I get up early. I get up at about seven o'clock.

4 a Write the words in the box after the correct verb.

| ~~a shower~~ | a coffee | a bus | up early |
| dressed | breakfast | lunch | |

1 **have**: *a shower* ....
2 **get**: ....

b Check your answers in transcript 3.4 on page 162. What words can you find that follow the verb *go*?

5 Choose the correct verb and complete the sentences so that they are true for you.

1 At the weekend I *get / go* up *early / late*.
2 I *go / have* a shower *before / after* I *go / have* breakfast.
3 During the week I *have / go* to bed at about .... o'clock.
4 I *have / go* to *school / work* at about ....

6 a Write three more sentences about yourself using phrases with *go*, *get* and *have*.

b 💬 Work in pairs. Compare your sentences with your partner. Are your daily routines similar?

GRAMMAR

1 a Match Michelle (M) or Veronica (V) to the sentences. Use the notes in the GRAMMAR PANEL ■ to help you.

1 I **usually** get up early.
2 I **never** get up early.
3 I'm **always** in the office at 8 a.m.
4 I **often** go dancing.
5 I **hardly ever** go out for a drink.
6 I **sometimes** watch a DVD in the morning.
7 I don't go to the gym **very often**.
8 I clean the house **once a week**.
9 I go to church **every Sunday**.

b Read the sentences in 1a again. Complete 1–5 in the GRAMMAR PANEL ■ .

2 a Look at the pictures and write sentences using the adverb in brackets.

1 *(always)* I .... at six o'clock.
2 *(once a week)* I ....
3 *(always)* I .... before breakfast.
4 *(usually)* I .... tired after work.
5 *(never)* I .... in the morning.
6 *(every day)* I ....

b 💬 Are the sentences true for you? Compare with a partner.

3 a Read the quiz. Decide if the sentences are true (T) or false (F) for you.

Are you a night person or a day person?

Do our quiz and find out.
1 I never get up before 8 a.m. at the weekend. ☐
2 I always go to bed before midnight. ☐
3 I usually stay in and watch DVDs on Saturday night. ☐
4 I'm often tired on Sunday morning. ☐
5 I watch TV after midnight every night. ☐
6 I go to the late show at the cinema about once a month. ☐

b 💬 Compare your answers with a partner. Are you night people or day people?

4 a Write five questions using *What time...?* or *How often...?* and the activities in the box.

get up   go to bed   have breakfast   have lunch
have dinner   start work   finish work
go out with your friends   go to the cinema
go dancing   go shopping   go to church
go for a run   get to work   get home

What time do you usually get up on Saturday?
How often do you go out with your friends?

b Write answers to the questions.

5 💬 Talk to at least three students in your class. Ask them the questions. Who is most similar to you?

■ FREQUENCY ADVERBS

We use frequency adverbs to say how frequently we do things.

100%	*always*
	usually
	often
	sometimes
	not very often
	hardly ever
0%	*never*

Position of frequency adverbs
Frequency adverbs go ⁽¹⁾<u>before / after</u> most verbs.
But they go ⁽²⁾<u>before / after</u> the verb *be*.

Expressions with *once* & *every*
We say ⁽³⁾<u>once / every</u> + day/week/month/year/Sunday.
We say ⁽⁴⁾<u>once / every</u> + a day/a week/a month/a year.
These expressions normally go ⁽⁵⁾<u>at the beginning / at the end</u> of a sentence.

See page 142 for grammar reference and more practice.

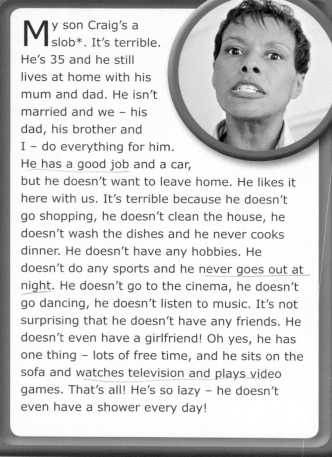

My son Craig's a slob*. It's terrible. He's 35 and he still lives at home with his mum and dad. He isn't married and we – his dad, his brother and I – do everything for him. He has a good job and a car, but he doesn't want to leave home. He likes it here with us. It's terrible because he doesn't go shopping, he doesn't clean the house, he doesn't wash the dishes and he never cooks dinner. He doesn't have any hobbies. He doesn't do any sports and he never goes out at night. He doesn't go to the cinema, he doesn't go dancing, he doesn't listen to music. It's not surprising that he doesn't have any friends. He doesn't even have a girlfriend! Oh yes, he has one thing – lots of free time, and he sits on the sofa and watches television and plays video games. That's all! He's so lazy – he doesn't even have a shower every day!

*slob = a lazy person

READING

1 🗨 Work in pairs. Look at the photo of Craig and guess the answers to the questions.

1 How old is he? *35*
2 Is he married? *No*
3 Does he have a job? *Yes*
4 Is he a day person or a night person?
5 What are his hobbies and interests?

2 Read what Linda, Craig's mother, says about her son. Check your answers to the questions in 1.

3 Is Craig's mother happy with her son? Why/Why not?

GRAMMAR

1 <u>Underline</u> the verbs in the sentences.

1 He lives at home.
2 He watches TV all day.
3 He doesn't go shopping.
4 His mother does the cleaning.
5 Does he do sports? No, he doesn't.
6 Does he play video games? Yes, he does.

2 Complete 1–9 in the GRAMMAR PANEL ■ with -s, -es, *does* or *doesn't*.

3 a Work in pairs. Write questions in the present simple about Craig.

1 Who/live with? *Who does he live with?*
2 have a good job?
3 do any of the work in the house?
4 do any sports?
5 listen to music?
6 What/do in his free time?

b 🔊 3.5 Listen and check.

4 🗨 Ask and answer the questions with a partner.

1 *He lives with his parents.*

■ PRESENT SIMPLE: 3RD PERSON SINGULAR

In present simple **affirmative** sentences with *he/she/it* we add (1) _____ to the verb:
He sits on the sofa and plays video games.

With verbs that end in *-s*, *-sh*, *-ch* and *-x* we add (2) _____ :
He watches television.

In **negative** sentences we use (3) _____ + infinitive:
He (4) _____ *go shopping.*

In **questions** we use (5) _____ + subject + infinitive:
(6) _____ *he do any sports?*

In **short answers** we use *does* and (7) _____ :
Yes, he/she/it (8) _____ .
No, he/she/it (9) _____ .

See page 142 for grammar reference and more practice.

VOCABULARY: Activities

1 Match verbs 1–8 with nouns a–h to make activities.

1	clean	a	the house
2	cook	b	to music
3	do	c	TV
4	listen	d	video games
5	play	e	football
6	play	f	sports
7	wash	g	dinner
8	watch	h	the dishes

2 a 💬 Work in pairs. Ask and answer questions using *How often* and the activities in 1.

How often do you wash the dishes?
I usually wash the dishes every day.

b Tell a new partner about your previous partner. Which of your partners is most similar to you?

Maria washes the dishes every day. She never cooks dinner. She always listens to music.

3 a 🔊 3.6 Listen to Craig talking about his hobbies and daily tasks. Look at your answers in GRAMMAR 4 and change them if necessary.

b 💬 Do you have any friends like Craig? Tell a partner about them.

PRONUNCIATION: Third person & plural endings

1 a 🔊 3.7 Listen to the third person forms of *do* and *go*. In which verb does the sound of the *o* change?

I *do* a lot of sport.
She *does* a lot of sport.
We often *go* dancing.
She often *goes* dancing.

b Listen again and repeat.

2 a 🔊 3.8 Listen to the words. Which have an extra syllable after adding the final *-s*? Which are verbs and which are nouns?

live – lives
hobby – hobbies
watch – watches
game – games
dish – dishes

b Listen again and repeat.

SPEAKING

1 Look at the photos. Which of these activities can you see?

a visit social networking sites
b play video games
c watch TV
d listen to music
e surf the internet
f blog/chat online
g read a book/newspaper/magazine
h chat or send text messages on your phone

2 a 💬 Work in pairs. Read the activities in 1 and answer the questions.

● Which activities do you do in your free time at home?
● When do you do these activities?
● How much time do you spend on each activity every week?

b Tell the rest of the class about your partner.

Luigi spends a lot of time on the internet. He chats on Messenger every day for about an hour.

LISTENING

1 Work in pairs. Look at the photos. Choose a caption for each one.

1 My favourite place
2 A happy moment
3 A Sunday walk
4 Happy days
5 Me and my music
6 A sunny afternoon

I think number 1 is a, or maybe it's b. Or maybe d – that's a place, too.

2 Look at the photos again. Which photographer do you think likes

1 eating out?
2 going to the beach?
3 relaxing in the sun?
4 listening to music?
5 playing with his/her kids?
6 going for a walk in the mountains?

3 a 🔊 3.9 Listen to six people talking about what makes them happy. Match them to the photos.

b Listen again. Complete the extracts.

1 **Benedict:** *My five-year-old .... She's beautiful! I love being with her.*

2 **Mie:** *Having .... or dinner in a good restaurant. **I really like eating out!***

3 **Ali:** *I really love going to the .... and seeing a beautiful sunset.*

4 **Paulo:** ***I love listening to music** and I love my .... It's great! I always take it with me everywhere I go.*

5 **Raquel:** ***I really love relaxing in the sun** in my .... 's garden. **I really hate winter!***

6 **Renata:** ***I love walking** in the .... The city is OK, but I really prefer the countryside.*

4 💬 Look at the expressions in **bold** in 3b. Are they true for you? Work in pairs. Ask and answer questions about the activities.

Do you like eating out?
Yes, I do. I love eating out with my friends.

GRAMMAR

1 Work in pairs. Match the verbs in the box to the faces.

> I hate   I really like   I love   I don't like
> I quite like   ~~I really love~~   I really hate

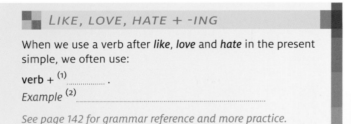

☺☺☺☺	*I really love*
☺☺☺	....
☺☺	....
☺	....
☹	....
☹☹	....
☹☹☹	....

2 **a** Find four of the verbs in **1** in the extracts in LISTENING 3b. Underline the word that comes after each verb.

  b Complete 1–2 in the GRAMMAR PANEL ▪ .

> ### ▪ LIKE, LOVE, HATE + -ING
>
> When we use a verb after *like*, *love* and *hate* in the present simple, we often use:
>
> **verb +** (1) ....
>
> *Example* (2) ....
>
> *See page 142 for grammar reference and more practice.*

3 💬 Work in pairs. Make true sentences with the verbs in **1** about these things. Are any of your sentences the same?

1 shopping
2 Monday mornings
3 politicians
4 loud music
5 working on your computer
6 cleaning the house

4 💬 Work in groups. Ask and answer the questions.

● What's your favourite month? Why?
● What's your favourite day of the week? Why?
● What's your favourite time of day? Why?

My favourite month is July because I'm on holiday and I like going to the beach.

VOCABULARY: Adjectives

1 **a** Work in pairs. Underline the adjectives in LISTENING 1 and 3b. How many can you find?

  b Complete the sentences with the adjectives.
1 Happiness for me is g................... food. I love eating and cooking.
2 I love looking at a b................... view of the sea or the mountains.
3 I really love football. It's g...................!
4 My f................... food is pizza.
5 I'm really h................... when I'm with my friends.
6 I love s................... days. They make me feel good.

2 **a** Read the sentences in **1b** again and complete the rules.
1 We put adjectives *before / after* the **noun**.
2 Adjectives *change / don't change* in the **plural**.

  b Correct the mistakes in the sentences.
1 My food favourite is chocolate.
2 I love reading goods books.
3 I really like the view from my window. It beautiful is.
4 I don't really like music classical.

3 💬 Read the sentences in **1b** and **2b** again. Are they true for you? Tell a partner.

Number 1 in exercise 2 is true for me – I love chocolate.

> ### NOTICE REALLY + VERB
> Add *really* to verbs and adjectives to be more emphatic:
> *I really like walking in the mountains.*
> *The mountains are really beautiful in winter.*

TUNE IN

1 a Work in pairs. Match the photos to the special days.

1 Women's Day
2 Valentine's Day
3 New Year's Day
4 Halloween
5 World AIDS Day
6 Carnival
7 Labour Day
8 International Peace Day

b 💬 Answer the questions.

1 Which days are
   a religious? b political? c commercial?
2 Which do you celebrate in your country?
3 Which are public holidays?

FOCUS ON LANGUAGE (1)

2 a Work in pairs. Match the special days in the photos to the dates.

1 1 January
2 14 February
3 Some time in February or March
4 March 8
5 1 May
6 21 September
7 October 31
8 1 December

b 🔊 3.10 Listen and check.

NOTICE DATES

We can write the date in two ways:
1 May or *May 1*.
We can say the date in three ways:
the first of May, May the first, May first.

3 Match the numbers to the dates.

| 1 | 2 | 3 | 4 | 5 | 8 | 14 | 22 | 29 | 31 |

twenty-second ....
third ....
thirty-first ....
twenty-ninth ....
second ....

fourteenth ....
fifth ....
eighth ....
first ....
fourth ....

OVER TO YOU

4 💬 Write the date of your birthday. Practise saying it. Ask other students when their birthday is. Write the dates.

5 💬 Work in pairs. Compare your lists of birthdays. Does anybody in the class have the same birthday as you or someone you know?

FOCUS ON LANGUAGE (2)

6 a What special day or occasion are these people celebrating? Use a dictionary to help you.

- *Happy birthday!*
- *Have a good holiday!*
- *Congratulations!*
- *Enjoy!*
- *Good luck!*
- *Happy anniversary!*
- *Merry Christmas!*
- *Happy New Year!*
- *Well done!*

b What do you say in your language?

66 Sounding happy 99

🔊 3.11 Listen to the phrases. Do the speakers' voices go up ➚ or down ➘ ?

🔊 3.12 Listen to other speakers saying some of the phrases. Do they sound happy?

OVER TO YOU

7 💬 Work in pairs. Practise saying the phrases in a happy way.

TUNE IN

1 Read the list of activities. Which do you think are

1 popular?
2 unpopular?

washing the dishes
going online
getting up early
doing sport
spending time with friends
cleaning the house
watching TV
studying

2 Read an article about a survey of people aged 18–25 in northern Europe. Do they agree with your answers in 1?

A survey in the news today shows that young people prefer going online to doing sport. They also like watching TV, spending time with friends and shopping. Most young people between the ages of 18 and 25 say they love surfing the internet, and only 20% say they prefer doing sport to sitting in front of the computer. They all agree about the top three most unpopular activities: getting up early, cleaning the house and washing the dishes. But most people say they do these things at least once a week. Some people, about 40%, also say they hate cooking. Only 5% say they hate studying.

3 Underline the words *some*, *most* and *only* in the article.

1 Which talks about
   a a big percentage (%)?
   b a small percentage?
   c a percentage that's not big or small?
2 Which can you use before the word *people*?
3 Which can you use before a %?

4 💬 Do you think the answers to the survey are the same for young people in your country? Why/Why not?

PREPARE FOR TASK

5 a 🔊 3.13 Listen to Hannah answering some questions in a similar survey. Which question does the interviewer **not** ask?

1 How often do you go out with your friends?
2 What's your favourite free-time activity?
3 How much time do you spend watching TV every night?
4 What programmes do you like watching?
5 What's your favourite programme?

b Listen again and make a note of Hannah's answers.

6 a Match the interviewer (I) or Hannah (H) to the questions and answers.

1 Can I ask you a few questions?
2 I don't know.
3 more or less every night.
4 it depends...
5 OK, that's it. Thanks a lot.
6 You're welcome.

b Check your answers in transcript 3.13 on page 162.

TASK

7 a Work in groups. You are going to write some questions for a survey. Choose two topics from the box.

using the computer   going to the cinema
eating out   helping in the house   studying
spending time with friends and family
free-time activities at home

b Write three questions for each topic. Use the examples to help you.

How much time do you spend...?
Do you prefer... or ...?
How often do you...?
Do you like...?
What's your favourite...?

8 💬 Ask as many students as possible your survey questions. Write their answers.

REPORT BACK

9 💬 Work with the same group. Compare your answers. Prepare to tell the class about your survey. Use *some*, *most* and *only* to report your results.

10 💬 Tell the class about your results. Do any of the results surprise you?

➡ Go to Review A, Unit 3, p. 36 ➡ Go to Writing bank 2, p. 153

VOCABULARY

Personal possessions

1 Work in pairs. Look in your bags and pockets. Write down the names of eight things you find.

Countries & nationalities

2 a Write the name of
  1 a country with a very famous capital city.
  2 a very cold country.
  3 a very hot country.
  4 a big country.
  5 a small country.

  b 💬 Compare your answers with a partner. Are your countries the same?

3 a Write the nationalities for all the countries in 2.

  Italy → Italian

  b Mark the correct stress on both words.

  Italy   Italian

Adjectives

4 a Write the letters in the correct order.
  1 rdeti   *tired*
  2 yppha   ....
  3 gbi   ....
  4 lmsal   ....
  5 alte   ....
  6 dogo   ....

  b Think of three more adjectives. How do you say them in your language?

GRAMMAR

Present simple: *to be*

1 Add an apostrophe (') to each sentence.
  1 Hes Paul.
  2 His surnames Stevens.
  3 Hes from Cape Town.
  4 His telephone numbers 7783451.
  5 Hes married.

2 Write questions for the answers in 1.
  What's his name?

3 Change the questions. Use *you/your* not *he/his*.
  What's your name?

4 💬 Work in pairs. Ask and answer the questions in 3. Make a note of the answers.

5 💬 Change pairs. Tell your new partner about your partner in 4. Is any of the information the same for all of you?

This, that, these, those

6 a 🔊 R1 You are at security in an airport. Complete the dialogue with *this/that/these/those*. Listen and check.

> A .... is my wallet and .... are my keys. And ....
>   are my sunglasses, over there, on the table.
> B Is .... your mobile phone, too?
> A Where?
> B There, on the table with the glasses.
> A No, ... is my mobile, here, in my pocket.

  b 💬 Work in pairs. Act out the dialogue. Use real objects if possible.

FUNCTIONAL LANGUAGE

Saying hello & goodbye

1 Write the words in the correct order.
  1 look you great !
  2 I'd introduce like you a to friend to
  3 meet you to pleased
  4 are you how ?

2 a Complete the mini-dialogues. Use the expressions in 1.
  1

  > A Eva, this is Dani.
  > B ....

  2

  > A ....
  > B You too.

  3

  > A ....
  > B Fine, thanks. And you?

  4

  > A .... This is Sue.
  > B Nice to meet you, Sue.

  b 🔊 R2 💬 Listen and check. Then stand up and introduce yourself to five people in your class.

■ LOOKING BACK

- Think of three things you can say about yourself.
- Think of three ways to say hello and three ways to say goodbye.
- Which lesson or activity in this unit is your favourite? Why?

VOCABULARY

Family members

1 a Work in pairs. Do you know these famous people? Can you complete the sentences? Use the family words in the box to help you.

cousin uncle sister mother daughter son

1 Isabella Rossellini is Ingrid Bergman's ....
2 Sean Lennon is John Lennon's ....
3 Hillary Clinton is Chelsea Clinton's ....
4 Venus Williams is Serena Williams' ....
5 Francis Ford Coppola is Nicolas Cage's ....
6 Whitney Houston is Dionne Warwick's ....

b R3 Listen and check.

2 Do you know of any other celebrity family relations?

Free-time activities

3 Think of five free-time activities you do every weekend. Work in pairs. Ask your partner about his/her interests.

Do you go the cinema at the weekend?

4 Find three free-time activities you and your partner **never** do.

GRAMMAR

Present simple

1 a Work in pairs. Write eight questions using the words in the box. Use each word at least once.

How many How old What
Where Who Why

b Ask and answer the questions.

2 a Work with a new partner. Write questions beginning *Do you...?* Use the verbs in the box.

live have listen play go watch

1 .... a brother?
2 .... to the radio?
3 .... tennis?
4 .... to work?
5 .... television every day?
6 .... in a flat?

b Answer the questions using short *yes/no* answers.

FUNCTIONAL LANGUAGE

Asking about occupations

1 Work in pairs. Think of six occupations. Do you know anyone who has these jobs?

Doctor – my uncle's a doctor.

2 Write the words in the correct order to form questions.

1 do you what do ?
2 work you do where ?
3 for you who do work ?
4 job your like you do ?

3 Choose a job from your list in **1**. Decide where you work or who you work for. You can describe your own job if you want.

I'm a reporter. I work in Japan. I work for CNN...

4 Stand up. Ask the questions in **2** to at least four students in your class. Use your answers from **3**.

■ LOOKING BACK

● What is your favourite part of this unit? Why?
● Do you want to look at something again? If yes, what?
● Write down five new things you can say about yourself and your family.

VOCABULARY
Telling the time

1 **a** 🗨 What time is it now? What time is it in London? And in Sydney?

b Add a) *10 minutes*, b) *quarter of an hour*, c) *20 minutes*, d) *half an hour* to the time. Practise saying the times in two different ways.

Go, get, have

2 Work in pairs. Think of at least five phrases with each verb.

3 🗨 Work in pairs. Look at the phrases you wrote in **2**. Answer the questions.
Which activities are
1 daytime activities?
2 night-time activities?
3 things you do at home?
4 things you do outside?
5 things you never do?

Other activities

4 Complete the phrases with the verbs in the box.

cook   do   listen   play (x2)   wash   watch (x2)

1	.... to music	5	....	TV
2	.... video games	6	....	DVDs
3	.... football	7	....	dinner
4	.... the dishes	8	....	sports

5 🗨 Ask your partner.
Which activities do you do
a every day?
b once a week?

Adjectives

6 Work in pairs. Think of five adjectives and write a sentence for each one.

7 Write the sentences again without the adjective. Show them to another pair. Can they guess the missing adjective?

GRAMMAR
Frequency adverbs

1 Complete the list of frequency adverbs.

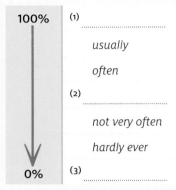

100%
(1) ....
 usually
 often
(2) ....
 not very often
 hardly ever
0%
(3) ....

2 **a** Look at the activities in VOCABULARY **4**. Write questions about three of them using *How often...?*

b 🗨 Work in pairs. Ask and answer the questions. Remember to use frequency adverbs in your answers.

Present simple

3 Write three sentences about your partner's answers in **2b**.

Like, love, hate + -ing

4 **a** Think of one thing you
1 really love doing. 2 really hate doing. 3 quite like doing.

b 🗨 Tell a partner. Do you have the same tastes?

FUNCTIONAL LANGUAGE
Special days

1 🗨 Work in pairs. What are the next three special days on the calendar for you? What do you usually do on those days?

2 **a** 🔊R4 Listen to the phrases and match them to the dates and special occasions below.
1 1 January
2 25 December
3 a wedding
4 a graduation ceremony

b 🗨 How many other phrases for special occasions can you remember? Can you say them in a happy way?

◼ LOOKING BACK

Think of five useful expressions or phrases from this unit.
● Where or when can you use them?
● How do you plan to remember them?
● Which section do you want to know more about?

LISTENING

1))R5 Listen to two people introducing themselves. Complete the information opposite.

2 a Complete the texts with the correct verbs. Use contractions where possible.

Hello. My name (1) .... Yukiko. I live in Osaka, in Japan. I (2) .... an English student. I (3) .... two brothers. They (4) .... English students, too. We all (5) .... English at school and in the evening we (6) .... to conversation classes. We (7) .... a lot of speaking in class – speaking English (8) .... difficult. At home I (9) .... English clips on YouTube and sometimes I talk to other English students on the computer. I (10) .... meeting new people and I like using English. It (11) .... difficult but it (12) .... lots of fun!

Hi, nice to (1) .... you. My name's Fernando. I (2) .... in São Paulo and I (3) .... in a hotel. I (4) .... English every day with the people in the hotel. I love speaking English. I (5) .... watching English movies, too, and reading English books. I (6) .... grammar and vocabulary at home with my son – he's 14. He (7) .... English at school. He (8) .... a good student. We talk to each other in English sometimes – just for fun! But I think Portuguese (9) .... more beautiful!

b Listen again and check. Do you have anything in common with Yukiko or Fernando? Tell a partner.

Name: ....
Nationality: ....
Occupation: ....
Use of English: ....

Name: ....
Nationality: ....
Occupation: ....
Use of English: ....

SPEAKING

3 a Think of three questions to ask Yukiko and Fernando.

b Work in pairs. Student A, you are Yukiko. Student B, you are Fernando. Ask and answer your questions. Then swap roles.

WRITING

4 a Write a short text about yourself and your English studies. Practise reading it out loud. Then read it to the class.

b As you listen to your classmates, make a note of anything you have in common.

▪ QUICK CHECK

Complete the checklist below.

Can you...	Yes, I can.	Yes, more or less.	I need to look again.
1 name ten countries and nationalities?	☐	☐	☐
2 ask for people's names?	☐	☐	☐
3 talk about your family and friends?	☐	☐	☐
4 talk about things you like and don't like?	☐	☐	☐
5 talk about things you do every day?	☐	☐	☐
6 tell the time?	☐	☐	☐
7 greet people in different ways?	☐	☐	☐
8 introduce yourself and other people?	☐	☐	☐

Compare your answers with a partner.

- What else do you know now after studying units 1–3?
- Do you need to look again at any of the sections?
- Do you need any extra help from your teacher?

4 HOME LIFE

Näckros Villa, Sweden

Container City, UK

1 **a** Look at the photos of two unusual homes. Choose adjectives in the box to describe them. Use a dictionary to help you.

> comfortable   modern   traditional
> beautiful   big   small   light   dark
> quiet   noisy

b Look at the table in the KEY VOCABULARY PANEL ▓. Work in pairs to complete A.

2 Read what the people who live in the two homes say. Match the descriptions to the homes. Which adjectives in 1a do they use?

1 I love my new home. It's a big house with lots of light and a beautiful view of the river. It has three bedrooms and two bathrooms. My favourite thing is the terrace. We eat out there in summer – I love listening to the sound of the water.

2 This is my flat. It's on the third floor. It's not very big. There's only one bedroom and a living room, which is also my study. It has a very small balcony and sometimes it's a bit noisy.

KEY VOCABULARY

Talking about homes

Adjectives to describe homes

A Complete the table with the opposites of the adjectives.

big	small
light	....
quiet	....
traditional	....
ugly	....
uncomfortable	....

Rooms & spaces

B Complete the sentences with the words in the box

> bedroom   bathroom   kitchen   dining room   garden
> living room   hall   study   garage   balcony

1 You have a shower in the ....
2 You sleep in the ....
3 You eat in the ....
4 You work in the ....
5 You cook in the ....
6 You watch TV in the ....
7 The first place you walk into is the ....
8 You park your car in the ....
9 Children like playing outside on the grass in the ....
10 You sit on the .... and watch people in the street.

C 💬 Which home from the photos does the floor plan show? Where do you think the rooms and places are?

I think number 4 is the bathroom.

• 🔊 4.1 Listen and check.

Furniture & fittings

D Which of the words in the box can you see in the photos?

> table   chair   sofa   bed   wardrobe   TV   cooker   sink   toilet
> bookshelves   shower   mirror   cupboard   microwave   fridge   desk

---

3 **a** Work in pairs to complete B in the KEY VOCABULARY PANEL ◼️ .

b How many sentences are true for your home?

4 Look at the floor plan in the KEY VOCABULARY PANEL ◼️ . Work in pairs to complete C.

5 💬 Turn to page 162. Read transcript 4.1, then practise describing the plan.

6 **a** Look at the furniture and fittings in the KEY VOCABULARY PANEL ◼️ and complete D.

b Which of the furniture and fittings can go in the

1 living room?
2 kitchen?
3 bedroom?
4 bathroom?

7 **a** 💬 Draw a simple floor plan of your home. Show the plan to a partner and describe your home. Explain what you like and don't like about it.

b Are your homes similar or different? Tell the class.

■ PRACTISE *THERE IS/THERE ARE + A/AN, SOME, ANY*
■ TALK ABOUT HOMES

LES ENFANTS DE DON QUICHOTTE

a   b   c

> Most people in the world have a roof over their head. But other people are not so lucky. They have no homes. They are homeless. The children of Don Quixote want to help.

LISTENING

1 **a** Work in pairs. Look at the photos and find the words in the box. Use a dictionary to help you.

> street   square   river   tent   protester   camp

b Name five more things in the photos.

2 💬 Discuss the questions.
- Who is Don Quixote? Why is he famous?
- How do you say his name in your language?
- What do you think the Children of Don Quixote want?

3 **a** 🔊 4.2 Listen to Patrick, one of the protesters, talking to a reporter. Number the photos in the order Patrick talks about them.

b Listen again and correct the statements.

1 The protest is about homeless people in Paris.
2 Hundreds of people are homeless in France.
3 They have 50 tents in the camp.
4 Leonor has one bed in her tent.
5 The camp has toilets and bathrooms.
6 Life isn't difficult on the streets.

4 💬 Discuss the questions.
- Do you think the protest is a good idea? Why/Why not?
- Do you ever protest against anything?

GRAMMAR

1 **a** 🔊 4.4 Listen again to the last part of the recording. Complete the description of Leonor's tent and the camp.

> L: **There are** two (1)............. and **there's** a light, and that's it. It's a small tent. **There are** (2).............. of us in this tent – and our bags, that's all.
>
> H: **Are there any** (3)................ ?
>
> L: **No, there aren't**, but **there are** some (4)................ .
>
> H: **Is there a place** where you can wash?
>
> L: No, **there isn't**, but **there are** hostels for a (5)............. – you pay (6)............. or (7)............. euros.

b Look at the words in **bold** in 1a and complete 1–7 in the GRAMMAR PANEL ▪▪.

2 💬 Work in pairs. Answer the questions with short answers. Give more details.

1 Is there a problem like this in your country?
   Yes, there is.   *No, there isn't.*

2 Are there any protests in your country to help the homeless?
   Yes, there are.   *No, there aren't.*

> **NOTICE**
>
> | 100 | one hundred |
> |---|---|
> | 1000 | one thousand |
> | 100s | hundreds |
> | 1000s | thousands |
> | 300 | three hundred |
> | 4000 | four thousand |
>
> 🔊 4.3 Listen and repeat.

3 Work in pairs. Write five sentences about your classroom. Compare them with the rest of the class. Score one point for each original sentence.

There are two windows.

4 Complete the questions using *is/are* and *a/an* or *any*.

1 _____ there _____ blackboard or _____ whiteboard?
2 _____ there _____ pictures on the wall?
3 _____ there _____ bags on the floor?
4 How many students _____ there?
5 How many tables _____ there?
6 _____ there _____ TV or _____ DVD player?

5 💬 Look at the photo on page 158 for one minute. Then turn back to this page. Work in pairs. Answer the questions in 4 from memory.

PRONUNCIATION: Sentence stress

1 a 🔊 4.5 Listen to the two sentences. Notice the stress.

There's a <u>chair</u> in the <u>tent</u>.
There <u>isn't</u> a <u>chair</u> in the <u>tent</u>.

b Listen and repeat.

2 a 🔊 4.6 Listen to four more sentences. Are they affirmative or negative?

b Listen again and write them down. Repeat the sentences. Remember the stress.

SPEAKING & LISTENING

1 💬 Work in pairs. Look at the photos below. What can you see in Marco's camper van? What else do you think there is in the van?

2 a 🔊 4.7 Listen to Marco talking about his van and check your answers in 1. Answer the questions.

1 Why does Marco live in a van?
2 What does he do?
3 Does he want to live in a house one day?

b 💬 Do you like the idea of living in a van? Why/Why not?

THERE IS/THERE ARE

Talking about one thing:

+	(1) _____ a sofa in the street.
–	There isn't a kitchen.
?	(2) _____ a shower?
Yes/No	Yes, there is./No, (3) _____ .

Talking about more than one thing:

+	(4) _____ some tables and chairs.
–	(5) _____ any bathrooms.
?	(6) _____ any toilets?
Yes/No	Yes, there are./No, (7) _____ .

We often use *a/an* with *There is/isn't* and *Is there?*
We often use *some* with *There are*.
We use *any* with *There aren't* and *Are there?*

In conversation, some people use *There is* with plural nouns: *There's lots of chairs.*
When we talk about a group of people we use *There are*: *There are two of us.*

See page 143 for grammar reference and more practice.

I don't have a house or a flat. I live in my camper van. Do you like it? There's everything you need!

READING

1 Look at the photos. What do they show? Read the website article and check your answers.

| Home | Hotels | Flights | Restaurants | Holiday Rentals | Cruises | Ferries | Car Hire |

Hotels   Search

A bed for the night?

This week we look at a new hotel concept: mini-hotels. They're easy on the pocket, but still offer a good night's sleep.

The first photo shows a Japanese-style capsule hotel. The room really is this small! But there's a satellite TV, a reading light and free Wi-Fi if you want to check your email.

The room in the second photo is huge in comparison! There's space for three people, with a double bed below and a small single bed above, and a shower room in the corner.

Both hotels are cheap, clean and modern. They are usually in airports or near motorways and are perfect when all you need is a bed for the night.

2 Read the article again. <u>Underline</u> all the words for furniture and fittings. Find them in the photos.

3 💬 Work in pairs. Find three similarities and three differences between the two hotel rooms. Which do you think is better for a good night's sleep? Why?

4 Read the two website reviews. Match them to the photos. Do the reviewers agree with your opinions in 3?

1

Great little hotel! It's in the airport next to all the shops, restaurants and bars. Perfect when you have a long wait between flights. It's very clean and comfortable… but watch your head when you get out! There's a TV on the ceiling, and a cupboard for your bags under the room. It's all very clever. There are showers in the corridor and there's even a sauna and a swimming pool for hotel guests only!

2

OK, but not great. There's a free car park in front of the hotel and it's very easy to find – it's just off the motorway. But that's the problem. It's right next to the motorway, so it's really, really noisy! The room's OK. The bed's comfortable, there's a small shower room in one corner and a satellite TV on the wall. All very clean and simple, but no character. Fine to break a journey, but not good for a long stay.

5 Read the reviews again and answer the questions.
1 What do the reviewers like and dislike about the hotels?
2 Are their opinions generally positive or negative? <u>Underline</u> the positive and negative words in each.

6 💬 Which hotel do you prefer now? Why?

GRAMMAR

1 Match the hotel rooms in READING 1 to the sentences.

1 It's in the airport.
2 There's a car park in front of the hotel
3 There's a table under the TV.
4 The bed is on the floor.
5 It's next to the motorway.
6 The single bed is above the double bed.

2 Underline the prepositions of place in 1. Then match the prepositions and pictures in the GRAMMAR PANEL ▪▪ .

3 💬 Work in pairs. Answer the questions about your classroom.

1 What's next to the window?
2 What's next to the door?
3 What's above the board?
4 What's in front of the board?
5 What's on the floor?
6 What's in the corner?
7 What's on your table?
8 What's under your table?
9 Who's next to you?
10 Who's in front of you?

4 Work in pairs. Look at the image of a hotel room below. Write a review for the website in READING 4.

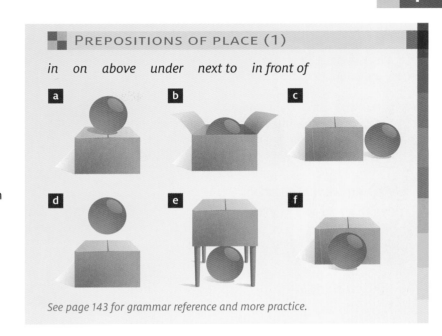

PREPOSITIONS OF PLACE (1)

in   on   above   under   next to   in front of

a **b** **c**

d **e** **f**

See page 143 for grammar reference and more practice.

5 💬 Look at the photo of a similar hotel room on page 158. Find six differences.

SPEAKING & VOCABULARY: Urban places

1 a Work in pairs. Match the words in the box to the places in the photos. Use a dictionary to help you. Which four words aren't in the photos?

> park   bus stop   train station   local shop   bar   café
> sports centre   swimming pool   cinema   theatre   museum
> art gallery   shopping centre   supermarket   news-stand
> police station   market   restaurant   car park   post office

b 💬 Answer the questions.

1 Which places do you go to
  a every day?
  b about once a week?
  c not very often?

2 Which places
  a can you walk to?
  b do you need to get on a bus, or in a car, to go to?

2 🔊 4.8 Listen to three people talking about where they live. Which places in 1 do they mention?

3 a Listen again. Match the people, 1–3, to the extracts.
  a I live in a flat in the centre of town.
  b I live in a small village.
  c I live in a quiet street in the suburbs.
  d It's very quiet.
  e It's got everything you need.
  f Every morning I go out to buy a newspaper at the local news-stand.
  g There's a shopping centre not far away.
  h When I want to go out I get a bus to town.

b 💬 Are any of the sentences true for you?

4 💬 Work in pairs. Tell your partner about where you live and the places in your neighbourhood.

GRAMMAR

1 a  4.9 Listen to five dialogues. Complete the questions with the places that the people are looking for.

1 Is there a .... near here?
2 Where's the nearest .... ?
3 Is there a .... near here?
4 Is there a .... near here?
5 Where's the .... ?

❝ Excuse me ❞

4.10 Listen again to one of the people asking for directions. Notice how he says *Excuse me* to get the other person's attention. Does his voice go up ⬈ or down ⬊ ?
Excuse me, can you help me?
Listen again and repeat.

b Listen again to the five dialogues. Match the places to the descriptions.

1 It's over there, **on** the other side of the road.
2 There's one over there, **at** the end of the road.
3 It's over there, **behind** the park.
4 See? **Opposite** the supermarket.
5 There's one at the end of the road. It's **on** the left.
6 See? **Between** the café and the cinema.

2 Look at the prepositions in **bold** in **1b**. Match the prepositions and pictures in the GRAMMAR PANEL ▪ and complete 1–4 with *on* or *at*.

3 💬 Work in pairs. Practise reading the dialogues in transcript 4.9 on page 163.

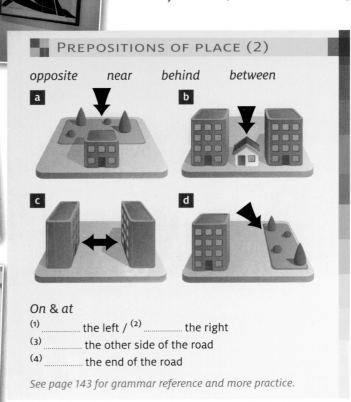

PREPOSITIONS OF PLACE (2)

opposite   near   behind   between

a   **b**

c   **d**

On & at

(1) .... the left / (2) .... the right
(3) .... the other side of the road
(4) .... the end of the road

See page 143 for grammar reference and more practice.

SPEAKING & WRITING

1 💬 Ask other students about places near your school.

- A news-stand
- A café with Wi-Fi
- The best place to have a coffee
- The best place to listen to good music

Is there a...?
Where's the nearest...?

2 a Work in pairs. Write a short description of the location of your school. Use as many prepositions of place as possible.

b Read your description to the class. Which description has the most details?

NOTICE *ONE*

We use *there's one* when we don't want to repeat a word:
Is there a café near here?
Yes, **there's one** over there.

one = a café

TUNE IN

1 **a** Work in pairs. Match the actions to the photos.

1 look at a map
2 find it on the internet
3 use satnav
4 stop a person on the street
5 phone a friend

b 💬 When you want to know how to get to a particular place, what do you usually do? Why?

2 🔊 4.11 Listen to three conversations. Answer the questions.

a Where do the people want to go?
b How do they get directions?
c Who gets the best directions?

FOCUS ON LANGUAGE

3 Listen to the conversations in **2** again. Complete the directions with the words you hear.

1 Cross the road (a) *at / before* the post office and then turn (b) *right / left*. That's Old Street. The café's at the (c) *beginning / end* of the street on the (d) *right / left*.

2 Go straight on for (a) *100 / 300* metres. Turn in approximately (b) *one minute / two minutes*. Take the (c) *first / second* street on the left.

3 Turn right (a) *at / on* the traffic lights… the car park's on the (b) *right / left*. You can't (c) *miss / see* it!

4 Match the directions to the pictures.

1 turn left
2 turn right
3 go straight on
4 take the first street on the left
5 take the second road on the right
6 cross the road at the traffic lights

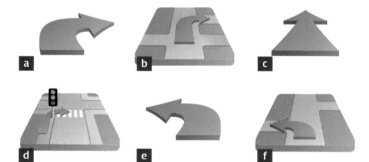

5 💬 Work in pairs. Practise giving directions to the following places from your school.

- the nearest bus stop
- the nearest news-stand
- the nearest bank
- the nearest taxi rank

OVER TO YOU

6 **a** 💬 Work in pairs. You want to go out with the other students in your class after the next lesson. Decide where to go. Practise giving directions to get there.

b Speak to other students. Tell them your idea and listen to their suggestions. Ask them for directions.
Where do you suggest? Where is it? How do you get there?

7 💬 Discuss all the suggestions with the class and decide on the best one.

8 Work in pairs. Write a short note to your teacher. Explain where you want to go and how to get there. Compare notes with other students. Which note gives the best directions?

TUNE IN

1 💬 Work in pairs. Look at the photos. Answer the questions.

- Do you think this is a good place for a summer holiday? Why/Why not?
- Do you like camping?
- Are there any good places to camp near your town?

2 Kim and her friends want to go on holiday for two weeks to the Lago Azul campsite. Read her email and answer the questions.

1 Which place does Kim want to book?
2 What extra information does she want?

To: reception@lagoazul.es

Subject: Request for information

We're interested in booking a cabin on your campsite for two weeks in July. We'd like some more information about the campsite and the cabins, please.

Is the swimming pool free or do we need to pay? Is there Wi-Fi access in the cabins, or only in the bar? You say you have kayaks to rent. Are there bikes to rent, too?

Thank you for your help,

Kim

3 Read the information on page 158. Find the answers to Kim's questions.

PREPARE FOR TASK

4 a Put the words in the correct order to make sentences.

1 campsite We're your in interested
2 information more like some We'd
3 you help for Thank your

b Read Kim's email again and check your answers. Which phrase means *we want*?

5 Which do you think is more polite, *we want* or *we'd like*? How do you say *we'd like* in your language?

6 💬 Work in pairs. Read the list. Which three things are most important for you when you go on holiday? Why? What else is important?

- restaurants and bars
- a satellite TV and a DVD player
- Wi-Fi access
- a children's playing area
- bikes or kayaks to rent
- nightlife

TASK

TorreBianca campsite

7 Work in pairs. You want to go to this campsite in Italy for a week. Write an email asking for more information. Use the phrases in 4 and your answers in 6 to help you.

REPORT BACK

8 Exchange emails with another pair. You work at Torre Bianca campsite. Write a reply to their email.

9 💬 Exchange replies. Do you still want to book the cabin this summer? Why/Why not? Tell the class.

➡ Go to Review B, Unit 4, p. 68 47

5 A REAL ACHIEVEMENT

1 a Work in pairs. Match the sports and pastimes in the box to the photos.

chess   crossword   cycling   football   skateboarding   sudoku

b 💬 Look again. What is unusual about each photo?

People don't usually play football on top of buildings.

2 a Work in pairs. Complete the descriptions with the activities in 1a. Which photo does each sentence describe?

1 In Japan they **play** .... on top of tall buildings.
2 Some people **go** .... in very dangerous places, like this rock high above a canyon in Africa.
3 People don't usually **go** .... in business suits.
4 It takes all day to **do** this .... in Ivov, Ukraine. The clues are in the town and the answers show up on the wall at night.
5 In Hungary people often **play** .... in outdoor swimming pools.
6 Some people **do** giant .... on the street, like these ones in New York.

b 💬 Where do people usually do these activities in your country?

People usually play chess at home or in a bar – or maybe in the park.

3 a Work in pairs to complete A in the KEY VOCABULARY PANEL ▩ .

b Answer the questions about the activities in A.

- Which do you usually do a) indoors, b) outdoors?
- Which are a) physical, b) mental or c) both?
- Which do you usually do a) on your own, b) in a team?
- Which is your favourite? Why?

48

4 Look again at the descriptions in 2a. Then work in pairs to complete B in the KEY VOCABULARY PANEL █ .

5 💬 Work in small groups. Discuss the questions.
- Do you do any of these activities on a regular basis?
- Where do you do them?
- Who do you do them with?

I love cycling. I go out on my bike every day. I cycle to work and at the weekend I go cycling with friends in the country.

■ KEY VOCABULARY

Sports & pastimes

Activities

A Complete the lists with the words in 1a.

Sports
surfing, jogging, tennis, judo, gymnastics, Pilates, basketball, golf, climbing, horse riding, ... , ... , ...

Pastimes
cards, dominoes, salsa, ... , ... , ...

- Add three more sports or pastimes to the lists.

Collocations

B Match the verbs in the box to the activities in A.

do   play   go

do: *judo...*
play: *tennis...*
go: *surfing...*

- We can also use *go for* + noun to describe some activities. Complete the notes.
  1 go cycling/horse riding – *go for a ride*
  2 go running/jogging – *go for a run /* ....
  3 go swimming – *go for* ....
  4 go walking – ....
  5 go driving – ....

NOTICE *GO FOR A*

We use *go for a* in common expressions with food and drink:
go for a coffee/a drink/a meal
as well as with other expressions:
go for a break/a holiday/a weekend away.

READING

1 💬 Work in pairs. Look at the photos. Which activities do you think are

1 easy to learn?
2 difficult to learn?

2 a Look at the photo of identical twins in the newspaper article below. How old do you think they are? Which of the activities in **1** do you think they do?

b Read the article to find out.

3 a Read the article again. Are the statements true (T) or false (F)?

1 The twins have nothing in common.
2 Marcia isn't good at sports.
3 Marcia gets top marks in Maths and English.
4 Madeleine plays two musical instruments.
5 Their different abilities often cause problems.

b 💬 Do you know any children the same age as Marcia and Madeleine? Are they sporty or academic?

They look alike, but…!

On the outside they look exactly the same, but on the inside they're very different children. Meet identical twins Marcia and Madeleine Carlisle, 5 years old. All they have in common, it seems, are their looks and the fact they can both speak Spanish and English!

Marcia is the academic one. She finds it easy to learn languages, she gets top marks in Maths and English and she can read for hours and hours without getting bored. But when it comes to physical activity, she just can't compete with her sister.

Madeleine doesn't like reading and studying. She can't sit still for one second. But she can swim, she can ski, she can ride a bike and now she wants to try other sports.

Their parents can't believe it. 'They're so different,' says mother Charlene. 'Madeleine can do all these sports and she can play the guitar. Marcia can't do those things yet, but she's really good at the academic side. The great thing is that there's no conflict or arguments. They both know that they are good at different things.'

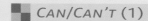

CAN/CAN'T (1)

We use **can/can't** + infinitive to talk about [1]*ability / preferences*.

+	I can ski.	Madeleine can ski.
−	I can't ski.	Marcia can't ski.
?	Can you ski?	Can Marcia ski?
Yes/No	Yes, I can./No, I can't.	No, she can't.

We [2]*add / don't add* **-s** for the third person singular: *Marcia can read.*

We [3]*use / don't use* **to** after **can**: *I can sing.*

See page 144 for grammar reference and more practice.

GRAMMAR

1 Work in pairs. Look at the article again and <u>underline</u> all the examples of *can* and *can't*.

2 Choose the correct option to complete 1–3 in the GRAMMAR PANEL ■ .

3 a Look at the picture of Marcia and Madeleine's brother Max. He is 2. What can he do? Write sentences using the verbs in the box.

> ~~walk~~ read write talk
> run ride a bike sing

He can walk.

b ◀))) 5.1 Listen to Max's mother discussing what he can and can't do and check your answers.

NOTICE *(NOT) VERY WELL*

We often use *very well*, *quite well* and *not very well* in short answers with *can*:
Can you ski? Yes, but *not very well.*
Can Madeleine ski? Yes, *very well.*
How do you say these words in your language?

4 💬 Work in pairs. Look again at the photos above. Ask and answer questions about the abilities.

Can you play the guitar? Yes, I can.

PRONUNCIATION

1 a ◀))) 5.2 Listen to the dialogue. Notice when *can/can't* are stressed and how the pronunciation of *can* changes.

> A Can /ə/ you ski?
> B Yes, I can /æ/. I can /ə/ ski really well, but I can't /ɑː/ snowboard. Can /ə/ you snowboard?
> A No, I can't /ɑː/.

b Listen again and repeat.

2 ◀))) 5.3 Listen to four more sentences. Are they affirmative or negative? Write down what you hear.

3 Practise the stressed and unstressed forms of *can* in these sentences.

Can /ə/ you touch your toes? Yes, I *can /æ/.*
Can /ə/ you touch the floor as well? No, I *can't /ɑː/.*

SPEAKING

1 a Write five questions to ask your classmates using *Can you...?* Think about different abilities.

b 💬 Work in groups of four. Ask and answer the questions.

2 a Write five sentences about your discussion using the phrases below.

> Only one of us can/can't...
> Two/Three of us can/can't...
> All of us/None of us can...

All of us can ride a bike. None of us can speak Italian.

b 💬 Report back to the class. Which group is the most sporty, the most artistic, the most academic?

GRAMMAR

1 ◀))) 5.4 Listen to three conversations. Match them to three of the signs.

2 **a** Work in pairs. Complete the extracts using *can/can't*.

1

> A Excuse me, sir, I'm sorry you .... smoke here. This is a no-smoking area.
>
> B Oh, sorry.
>
> A There's a smoking area over there. You .... smoke there.

2

> A .... I drink this water?
>
> B Ah, no, sorry, you .... It isn't drinking water.

3

> A .... I pay in dollars?
>
> B No, sorry, you .... use dollars here, only pesos.
>
> A Ah, OK. .... I pay by credit card?

b Listen again and check. Where do you think the people are?

3 Complete 1–8 in the GRAMMAR PANEL ▢ .

4 💬 Write three more questions to ask about your classroom. Ask and answer the questions with your partner.

CAN/CAN'T (2)

We use (1) .... to talk about what is **OK** or **possible**.

We use (2) .... to say that something is **not possible**.

You (3) .... *smoke here* = It's OK/possible to smoke here.

You (4) .... *smoke here* = It isn't possible to smoke here.

Write the words in the correct order to form questions.

a you here smoke can ? (5) ....

b eat you can here ? (6) ....

Answer the questions for your classroom.

a *Yes/No, you* (7) ....

b *Yes/No, you* (8) ....

See page 144 for grammar reference and more practice.

NOTICE *YOU*

We can use *you* to talk about people in general:

You can't sell food here = No one can sell food here.

What do you say in your language?

SPEAKING

1 Work in pairs. Think of a sentence for each sign in GRAMMAR 1 using *can't*. Use a dictionary to help you.

d *You can't smoke.*

2 **a** 💬 Change partners. Compare your answers. Where do you think you can see these signs? Use the places in the box to help you.

> on the street   in a shop   in a station   in a church
> in a swimming pool   in a museum   on a plane
> in a square   in a shopping centre   on a beach
> on the door to a restaurant   in a hospital   in a hotel
> in a park   in a theatre   in a cinema   near a computer

b Which signs are common in your country? Which are not? Can you think of any more signs?

3 💬 Draw four signs that you can see in your town. Give them to another pair. Ask them to say

1 what they mean.

2 where you can see them.

READING

1 **a** Work in pairs. Match the words in the box to the images.

> plastic ball   roll   jump   wall
> trampoline   hill   acrobatics

b Do you know where these sports come from?

2 💬 Read the descriptions and check your answers in 1. Which sports would you like to try?

3 Read the descriptions again and match one sport to each statement.

1 you can't do this alone
2 you can do it on water
3 you can do it on the beach
4 you can do it in the city
5 you can invent your own rules

NOTICE CAN/CAN'T IN RULES

We often use *can/can't* to talk about rules:
The players can't touch the ball with their hands = a rule
We also use *can/can't* to say that something is, or isn't, possible:
You can play on the beach = this is possible

LISTENING & WRITING

1 🔊 5.5 Listen to the description of a sport. What is it?

2 **a** Complete the paragraph with the words in the box.

> ball   park   hands   teams   street

> You can kick the (1)............... but you can't pick it up with your (2)............... . You can play this sport on the (3)..............., on the beach or in a (4)............... . You can see professional (5)............... play it in special stadiums.

b Listen again and check.

3 **a** Work in pairs. Think of the rules of a sport you know and write them using *can* and *can't*. Use a dictionary to help you.

b Read out the rules to the class. Can they guess the sport?

Bossaball: You can only play this on a special court. It's similar to beach volleyball. It's a team game and there are strict rules. It comes from Slovakia and it's very popular in Eastern Europe.

Parkour: This comes from France. You can do what you like, there are no rules and no teams. The idea is to get across the city without touching the ground. It's really acrobatic, but you need to be careful!

Zorbing: This is great fun! You roll down a hill in a big plastic ball called a zorb. Two or three people can do it together. You can even do it on water! The idea comes from New Zealand.

VOCABULARY (1):
Parts of the body

1 Match the words in the box to the parts of the body in the picture. Use a dictionary to help you.

> arm   back   stomach   foot/feet
> hand   head   leg

2 Work in pairs. Draw the parts of the face on the head. Use the words in the box.

> ears   eyes   hair   lips
> mouth   nose   teeth

3 a 🔊 5.6 Listen to eight people answering the question *When you meet someone for the first time, what do you notice first?* Make a note of their answers.

b 💬 Work in pairs. Check your answers in transcript 5.6 on page 163. Who do you agree with most? What is your answer to the question?

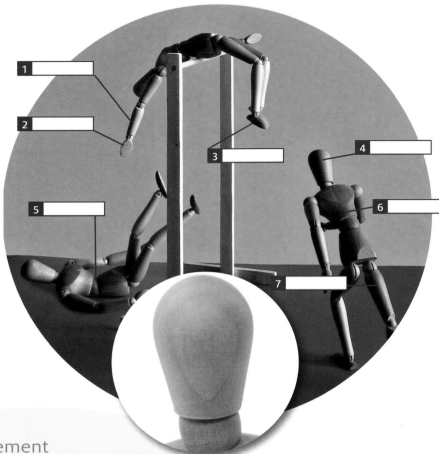

VOCABULARY (2): Verbs of movement

1 a Work in pairs. Complete the labels with a part of the body or face.

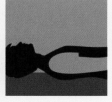

1 clap your
....

2 dance with your ....

3 wink (with your ....)

5 touch your
....

6 stretch your
.... and
....

7 lie on your
....

4 breathe in through your
.... ,
breathe out through your
....

b Mime the actions.

2 💬 Work in pairs. Look at the photo of an acrobat. What do you think she can do?

3 a 🔊 5.7 Listen and complete the sentences.

1 She can .... her nose with her ....

2 She can dance on her ....

3 She can put her .... behind her ....

4 She can .... with her feet.

b Can you do any of these things?

4 🔊 5.8 Listen to the instructions. Stand up and do the actions.

GRAMMAR (1)

1 Work in pairs. Read the instructions. <u>Underline</u> all the verbs. How many negative verbs are there?

1 Touch your *nose* with your *left hand*.
2 Stretch your *right arm* to the *right*.
3 Stand on *one leg* and wink with your *left eye*.
4 Sit down and put your *hands* on your *head*.
5 Open and close your *mouth*. Now open and close your *eyes*. Repeat and don't stop!

2 Choose the correct option to complete 1–2 in the GRAMMAR PANEL ▪ .

3 a Read the instructions in 1 again. Change the body parts to make new instructions.

Touch your left ear with your right hand.

b 💬 Work in pairs. Ask your partner to do the actions.

4 a 🔊))5.9 Choose two of the photos. Write instructions for them. Then listen and check.

b Work in pairs. Read your instructions. Your partner guesses which photo they describe.

▪ IMPERATIVES

We often use the imperative to give instructions.

The imperative form [(1)]*has / does not have* a subject pronoun:
Touch your toes.

We form the negative with [(2)]*not / don't* :
Don't stop!

See page 144 for grammar reference and more practice.

GRAMMAR (2)

1 Work in pairs. Read transcript 5.9 on page 163. Find two words that end in *-ly*. Complete 1–2 in the GRAMMAR PANEL ▪ .

2 Match the adverbs in the box to make four pairs of opposites. Which adverb is irregular?

> well   quickly   happily   sadly
> quietly   badly   slowly   loudly

3 🔊))5.10 Listen to eight people doing different actions. Write the adverb that you think best describes the way they do the action.

1 He always speaks ....
2 She sings .... in the shower.
3 She always laughs ....
4 He usually speaks .... when we don't understand.
5 He speaks English very ....
6 He always laughs very ....
7 I speak English very ....!
8 She always sings so .... but she's a really happy person.

4 💬 Work in small groups. Think of an action and an adverb. Use the verbs in the box to help you. Perform your action to the class. Can they guess your action?

> dance   eat   drink   walk   jump
> laugh   sing   whistle   breathe

▪ -LY ADVERBS

-ly adverbs describe a verb. They tell us **how** we do an action.

We form *-ly* adverbs by adding *-ly* to an adjective:
careful → [(1)]...............
slow → [(2)]...............

For adjectives that end in *-y*, change *-y* to *-ily*:
happy → *happily*

See page 144 for grammar reference and more practice.

TUNE IN

1 💬 Work in pairs. Answer the questions.

- How many text messages do you send every day?
- How many phone calls do you make?
- Are you a texter or a talker?

2 a Read the text messages and answer the questions.

1 What do Ted, Dan, Ali and Steve want to do this evening?
2 What does Dan ask Ted to do?
3 What does Ted ask Ali to do?

a Hi Ted. Football tonight?

b 8 p.m. Can u give Ali & Steve a lift? Dan

c Hi Dan. No problem. Ted

d Hi Ali. Meet you on the corner at 7.30? Can u tell Steve? Ted

e Great! Thanks, Ted. Steve knows. C u @ 7.30. Ali

b 🔊 5.11 The friends decide to phone each other. Listen to their conversations. Who are the two people in each conversation?

1 *Jo and*...   3 ....
2 ....

3 💬 Work in pairs. Compare your answers in **2b**. Match the conversations to the pictures.

FOCUS ON LANGUAGE

4 a Read the questions. Which conversation do they come from? Who is speaking, Jo (J), Dan (D), Ted (T) or Ali (A)?

1 Is Ted there?
2 Can I take a message?
3 Can you tell him it's about football tonight?
4 Can you ask him to call me?
5 Is that you, Dan?
6 Can you give Steve and Ali a lift in your car?
7 Can you call Steve?

b Listen to 5.11 again and check your answers.

❝ Hello? ❞

🔊 5.12 Listen to Jo when she answers the phone. Notice how her voice goes up ↗ when she says *Hello?*

🔊 5.13 Listen to four people saying hello. Are they a) on the phone? b) saying hello to a friend?

5 💬 Work in groups of four. Turn to page 163. Read the telephone conversations in transcript 5.11.

OVER TO YOU

6 a Work in pairs. Read the instructions for your part of the conversation. Decide what to say. Use the questions in **4a** to help you.

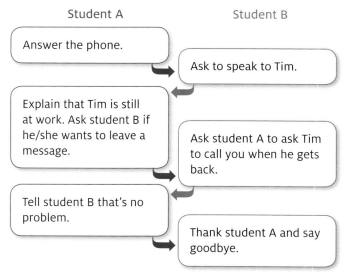

Student A	Student B
Answer the phone.	
	Ask to speak to Tim.
Explain that Tim is still at work. Ask student B if he/she wants to leave a message.	
	Ask student A to ask Tim to call you when he gets back.
Tell student B that's no problem.	
	Thank student A and say goodbye.

b 💬 Act out the conversation. Then change roles and repeat the conversation.

TUNE IN

1 a Read the descriptions, 1–3, and match them to the photos.

b 💬 Work in pairs. Compare your answers in **a** and answer the questions.

1 What is a childminder?
2 Why does Nia want a childminder?

PREPARE FOR TASK

2 a Nia wants to interview Martina and Brad for the job of childminder. Write seven questions that Nia can ask them in the interview. Use the prompts to help you.

1 Drive? A car? *Can you drive? Do you have a car?*
2 Swim?
3 What sports/do?
4 What other interests/have?
5 What languages/speak?
6 Sing? Play a musical instrument?
7 Work at weekends?
8 Like animals?

b Think of three more questions Nia can ask.

3 🔊 5.14 Listen to a job interview. How many of the questions in **2** did you hear?

4 Work in two groups. Group A is Brad. Group B is Martina. Complete the form for your character. Answer *no* to at least two items.

Home   Links   Archives   Search

Holiday playmates
The website that cares about your children

1 Hi, I'm Brad. I'm an engineering student. During the holidays I work as a childminder. I love my job. It's a great excuse to play sports and games of all types.

2 My name's Martina. I'm a childminder. I really like working with children of all ages. I also cook and clean and look after the house. It isn't a bad job, and I learn to speak English at the same time.

3 Hi, I'm Nia. I'm a doctor. I work full time. I don't have a lot of time to spend with my two boys, Jake (6) and Josh (9). I need a childminder to help me in the summer holidays.

Name: ....
Age: ....
Nationality: ....
Languages: ....

Tick the things you can do:
☐ cook
☐ drive
☐ swim
☐ play a musical instrument (which?)
....

What sports do you do regularly?
....

What other interests do you have?
....

Do you have a car? ....
Do you have a bike? ....
Do you like animals? ....

TASK

5 a Work in pairs – one student from group A and one student from group B.

Student A: you are Nia. Use the questions in **2** to help you.
Student B: you are Martina. Use the notes in the form in **4** to help you.

b 💬 Act out the interview between Nia and Martina. Make notes.

6 💬 Now act out the interview between Nia and Brad.

Student A, you are Brad. Student B, you are Nia.

REPORT BACK

7 💬 Look at page 159 and decide who is the best person for the job.

8 💬 Report back to the class. Do you all agree? Why/Why not?

→ Go to Review B, Unit 5, p. 69   → Go to Writing bank 3, p. 154

6 SHOPPING AROUND

1 a Look at the photo. What does it show?

1 a department store
2 a local market
3 a mall or shopping centre

b Is there a place like this near where you live?

2 💬 Discuss the questions in pairs.

● Do you like shopping?
● Where do you usually go shopping? To a mall, the town centre, markets or the local shops?
● Who do you go with?

3 🔊 6.1 Listen to Kirsten and Tom. Where do they like shopping?
a) At local shops and markets or b) at the mall? Why?

4 a Listen again. Decide if the statements are true (T) or false (F).

1 Kirsten buys everything at the mall.   2 Tom thinks the mall is stressful.
3 She doesn't spend a lot of time there.   4 He never buys anything at the mall.

b 💬 Do you think malls are bad for local businesses in your town? Why/Why not?

5 Work in pairs to complete A and B in the KEY VOCABULARY PANEL 🔲. Use a dictionary to help you.

6 💬 Work in pairs. Where do you usually buy the things on the list?

trainers *sports shop*   meat
magazines   medicine
pasta   bread
software   tomatoes
jeans   football

■ KEY VOCABULARY

Shops & amenities

A 💬 Which of the places in the box can you find in a mall? Which can you find in the town centre?

> bakery   bookshop   boutique   butcher's
> café   chemist's   cinema   clothes shop
> computer store   convenience store
> department store   grocer's   market stall
> music store   news-stand   restaurant
> shoe shop   sports centre   sports shop
> supermarket

NOTICE *SHOP OR STORE?*

We can often say *shop* or *store* with no difference in meaning:

a music shop or *a music store.*

But we always say *convenience store* and *department store*, NOT *convenience shop* or *department shop*.

B Write the places in **A** in the correct circles. How many shops and amenities go in more than one circle? How do you say these places in your language?

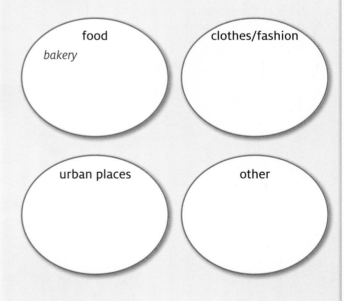

food
bakery

clothes/fashion

urban places

other

7 Work in pairs. Look again at the list of shops and amenities in the KEY VOCABULARY PANEL ■.
Which do you go to

1 every day?
2 once or twice a week?
3 almost never?

8 a 💬 Discuss the questions with a partner.

- How often do you go shopping in your local mall?
- Which shops and amenities do you visit there?
- What do you buy?
- What else do you do there?

b Are your answers similar or different?
Tell the class.

NOTICE *SHOP OR BUY?*

We can say *shop* or *go shopping*:
I shop/go shopping at the market/the mall.
We use *buy* to talk about the things we get:
I buy all my food at the market.

READING

1 Look at the photos of Langham Place mall in Hong Kong and read the text. Match the different parts of the mall to the photos.

   1 the Spiral   2 the Grand Atrium   3 the O-Zone

2 What can you do in each part of the mall? Match the places in 1 to the activities.

   a meet people   d relax
   b buy things   e look at clothes
   c have a meal   f watch videos

3 Work in pairs. Underline the positive words in the text. Why are there so many?
great, paradise...

4 💬 Do you like the look of Langham Place? Why/Why not?

A MALL WITH A DIFFERENCE

Langham Place is a shopping paradise with more than 200 stores, cafés and restaurants on 13 floors.

The Grand Atrium is the entrance to the mall. It's a great meeting point. There's an enormous screen. You can watch music videos and movie clips while you wait to meet your friends. From here, the enormous escalators take you to the top of the building. There you can see amazing panoramic views of the city.

Do you want to shop? Walk down the Spiral, a long spiral-shaped corridor, and visit all the stores and fashion boutiques selling the latest designs for young people.

The O-Zone is at the top of the mall on floors 12 and 13. There are lots of cool bars and places to eat. It's the perfect place to chill out, listen to music and spend time with your friends.

Langham Place is *the place* to be in HK!

LISTENING

1 🔊 6.2 Look at the pictures. What part of the mall are the people in? Listen to three conversations and match them to the pictures.

2 Listen again. Where are the people they are talking to?

GRAMMAR

1 In which conversation do you hear the sentences?

a I'm not shopping – I'm just looking.
b Are you having a drink with Alex?
c He's just coming through the door.
d I'm standing at Information.
e What are you doing?

2 Underline the verbs in the sentences in 1 and complete 1–10 in the GRAMMAR PANEL ▪.

3 🔊 6.3 Listen to two short conversations and answer the questions. Use *He* or *She* in your answers.

1 a What's the man doing? b And the woman?
2 a Where's the woman going? b What's the man doing?

4 a Work in pairs. Complete the conversations.

1

A Hi, what _____ ?
B Nothing special, I'_____ . And you?
A I'_____ to the _____ . Do you want to come, too?
B No, thanks. I need to finish this.

2

A Hi, how are you? Where _____ ?
B I _____ to my _____ . And you?
A I _____ for Ivan. He _____ .
B OK. See you later!

b Listen again and check.

5 💬 Work in pairs. Read the conversations in 4a. Give different answers to the questions.

6 Complete the sentences in three different ways.

1 I'm going...
2 I'm doing...
3 I'm playing...
4 I'm eating...
5 I'm having...

NOTICE *JUST*

We often use *just* with the present continuous to explain what we are doing **right now**, at the time of speaking:

I'm just walking through the doors.
He's just coming in now.

We also use *just* to mean 'only': *I'm just looking.*

▪ **PRESENT CONTINUOUS**

We use the present continuous tense to talk about what is happening *now*.

To form the present continuous we use:

be + verb + (1) _____ .

+ I'(2) _____ shopping; you'(3) _____ shopping; she's shopping.

– I'(4) _____ shopping; you aren't shopping; she (5) _____ shopping.

? (6) _____ you shopping? (7) _____ she shopping?

Y/N Yes, I (8) _____ ./No, I'(9) _____ .
Yes, she (10) _____ ./No, she isn't.

See page 145 for grammar reference and more practice.

SPEAKING

1 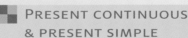 Work in pairs. Look at the people in the photos. Discuss the questions.

- Where are they?
- What are they selling?
- Do people sell things on the street in your town? If yes, what do they sell?
- Do you ever buy anything from people on the street? If yes, what do you buy?

GRAMMAR

1 Work in pairs. Match the photos to the sentences.

1 I usually sell my bread near the market.
2 Today I'm selling sunglasses.
3 I'm a high school student, but I don't go to school very often!
4 I'm talking to a customer.
5 I'm waiting for a customer.
6 I sell all kinds of things.
7 I'm getting my things ready.

2 a Read the sentences in 1 again. Match them to the questions.

1 What do you do?
2 What are you doing?

b Which question is in the present continuous and which is in the present simple?

3 Underline the time expressions in the sentences in 1. Complete 1–2 and a–g in the GRAMMAR PANEL ■ .

4 a Complete the questions.

1 What .... (you/do) at the moment?
2 What .... (you/do) at this time on other days?

b Work in pairs. Ask and answer the questions.

5 a Work in pairs. Invent a situation for each of the sentences.

1 Who's speaking, please?
2 Are you reading that newspaper?
3 Do you come here every day?
4 I'm just getting off the bus.

b Choose one of the situations and continue the conversation.

PRESENT CONTINUOUS & PRESENT SIMPLE

We use the present [(1)]*continuous / simple* to talk about actions that are happening at the moment.

We use the present [(2)]*continuous / simple* to talk about things that are generally true:

I study Medicine.

I'm studying for my final exams.

Which words/phrases do we usually use with the **present simple** (PS) and which with the **present continuous** (PC)?

usually *PS*   at the moment [(a)]........
sometimes [(b)]........   today [(c)]........   never [(d)]........
always [(e)]........   (right) now [(f)]........   often [(g)]........

See page 145 for grammar reference and more practice.

SPEAKING & READING

1 💬 Work in pairs. Look at the symbols and discuss the questions.

- Do you know the names of these famous brands? What do they make?
- Are you wearing any brand names or designer labels today?
- Do you like brand names? Do you have any favourites?
- Can you buy fakes or copies of brand name goods in your town? Do a lot of people buy these goods?

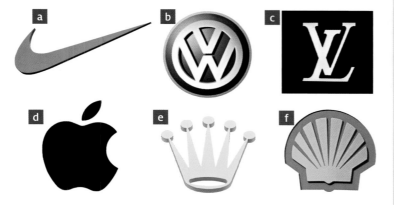

2 Read the article about fake brands and pirated goods. What is the purpose of the article?

1 to explain the legal problem
2 to give information about the situation
3 to give advice about what to buy

3 Read the article again and match the headings to sections a–d.

1 Fashion   3 Pirated goods
2 Imitation brands   4 Price

4 **a** Read the questions. Choose the best answer for each one or write your own.

(a) What do you think about fake goods?

1 They are good because the real thing is too expensive.
2 They are bad and create more crime.
3 Some fake goods are OK and can be fun!
4 _____

(b) Do you ever buy fake or pirated goods?

1 No, never.
2 Yes, sometimes, because they're cheap.
3 Yes, all the time. I don't like giving money to the big brand name companies.
4 _____

b 💬 Work in small groups. Compare your answers. Where they are different, explain your choice.

Fake...
and we love it!

Brand names are all around us – in the papers, on TV, on our computer screens – but we don't all have the money to buy them. So, what are we doing instead? Buying fakes!

What kind of fakes are people buying?

(a)_____: CDs, DVDs, etc. People make copies and then sell them in large quantities.

Fake goods: bags and watches which look real but are just good copies. Prada and Rolex are famous examples.

(b)_____: a logo or a label which is similar to a famous brand. 'Nire' could be 'Nike', for example.

Why are fakes so popular?

(c)_____: the real thing can be very expensive. A fake is usually good value for money. But not always. Fake watches can be very expensive, too. Remember, when they break there's no guarantee!

Easy to find: in most countries, fakes are very easy to find. You can get them on every street corner, and everybody buys them.

(d)_____: brands are important to a lot of people. Their favourite stars wear them. They want to wear them and they like other people to see them.

GEORGI·AMONI

VOCABULARY: Colours & clothes

1 a Look at the image above. How many colours can you find?

b Work in pairs. Try and find something in the classroom for each colour.

a white table, a red dictionary, a blue...

2 a How many colours can you see in the photo?

b Look at the photo again and find examples of the words in the box. Use a dictionary to help you. Which words can't you see?

> jeans T-shirt shirt trainers belt watch boots
> jacket sunglasses skirt shoes dress trousers

> **NOTICE** *JEANS*
>
> We can say *He's wearing jeans* or *a pair of jeans*, but NOT ~~*a jeans*~~.
> And *My jeans/sunglasses/clothes are* new NOT ~~*is new*~~.
> We can use colours as adjectives. Remember adjectives always come before a noun:
> *a red shirt, blue jeans.*

3 Work in pairs. Answer the questions using the words in 2b and the colours in 1.

1 What's the boy wearing?
2 What's the girl wearing?
3 What are you wearing?

4 Work in pairs. Write a short description of someone in your class. Describe what he/she is wearing. Read your sentence to the class. Can they guess who it is?

He's wearing blue jeans with a black belt, a white T-shirt and a pair of Nike trainers. Who is he?

5 a 💬 Work in small groups. Discuss the questions.

● What do you usually wear to go to work or school? At the weekend? At a party?
● What are your favourite clothes?
● Do you like shopping for clothes? Why/Why not?

b Tell a partner which people in your group

1 like wearing casual clothes.
2 like wearing formal clothes.
3 aren't really interested in clothes.
4 love following fashion.

SPEAKING & LISTENING

1 💬 Work in pairs. Look at the photos and answer the questions.

1 What kind of clothes is each person wearing?
2 Match the 'look' to the fashion.

emo   skater   punk   hippy

2 Look at the photos again. Which look, or looks, do you associate with

1 flowers?
2 unusual hairstyles?
3 dark clothes?
4 baggy shorts or trousers?
5 tattoos and piercings?
6 boys and girls looking the same?

3 🔊 6.4 Listen to the four people talking about their clothes. Match them to the photos.

4 a Read the sentences. Match them to the speakers.

1 It depends on the day, on the weather, on what I'm doing and where I'm going.
2 We listen to music, we go online, we meet in cafés and malls.
3 I meet up with friends there. Sometimes we listen to music.
4 I've got a tattoo of a flower, here, on my hand.
5 I work in a supermarket.
6 The hair's important, too.
7 I love my boots.
8 I love this kind of look. I think it's really happy.

b Listen again and check.

5 a 💬 Work in pairs. Discuss the questions.

● What kind of fashions do young people in your town follow?
● What kind of clothes do they wear?
● Where do they meet?
● What do they do there?
● Do you, or anyone you know, follow any of these fashions or have a particular look?

b Compare your answers with the rest of the class.

PRONUNCIATION: /ɜː/

1 🔊 6.5 Listen to the sentence.

/ɜː/   /ɜː/   /ɜː/

The girl is wearing a purple skirt.

2 a Underline all the /ɜː/ sounds in the sentences.

1 I always wear a shirt for work.
2 I like wearing short skirts in summer.
3 I love the world of fashion.

b 🔊 6.6 Listen and check. Then listen and repeat.

TUNE IN

1 💬 Work in pairs. Look at the pictures and answer the questions.

- Are the people buying something or are they just looking?
- What do you think the people are saying? Write two or three sentences for each picture.

a In a department store

b In a boutique

c At a craft market

2 🔊 6.7 Listen to five short conversations. Where are they taking place?

3 Listen again and match each conversation to one of the actions below.

a asking for directions
b trying something on
c just looking

FOCUS ON LANGUAGE

4 a Complete the sentences from the conversations in 2.

1 I .... just looking.
2 Where .... the changing rooms, please?
3 I .... looking for the children's department.
4 .... I try one on?
5 .... you have any in a smaller size?
6 How much .... it?
7 I .... looking for a pair of trainers.
8 .... I try them on?
9 .... I pay by card?

> **NOTICE**
>
> We say *I'm just looking* in shops to say we don't need help.

b Which conversation does each sentence come from?

5 💬 Check your answers in transcript 6.7 on page 164. Then practise reading the conversations with a partner.

6 💬 Look at the pictures in 1 again and try to act out one conversation for each picture.

❝ Intonation: *yes/no* questions ❞

🔊 6.8 Listen to the requests. Do the speakers' voices go up ↗ or down ↘?

Can I try them on?   Do you have any in a smaller size?
Can I pay by card?

Listen again and repeat.

Now practise saying these requests.

Can I help you?   Is there a toy department in the store?
Do you have them in other colours?

OVER TO YOU

7 💬 Work in pairs. Act out the following situations.

1
Student A: you are in a large department store. You can't find the perfume department.
Student B: you are a busy shop assistant in a large department store.

2
Student A: you work in a small boutique. You are very friendly and always try to help your customers.
Student B: you like the look of the boutique. You want to try something on, but you don't want to buy anything.

3
Student A: you are at a craft market. You want to buy a present for a friend. You see some T-shirts you like. You don't have a lot of money to spend.
Student B: you have a small stall in the market. You sell T-shirts that you print by hand.

8 💬 Think of a new shopping situation. Prepare a short conversation. Then act it out to the class.

TUNE IN

1 💬 Work in small groups. Discuss the questions.

- Do you usually take photos on your phone or with a camera?
- What kind of photos do you take? Of people, of places or of unusual things that are happening around you?
- Do you share photos with other people?
- How? Do you post them on a blog or send them by email or MMS?

2 🔊 6.9 Listen to two friends, Solmaz and Dario, talking about one of the photos. Answer the questions.

1. Which photo are they talking about?
2. Where is Dario?
3. What is he doing?

PREPARE FOR TASK

3 Dario emails the photo to a friend. Complete the description.

> Hi! Here are some of my photos from our holiday in ⁽¹⁾............... . This one shows the floating ⁽²⁾............... . It's a really ⁽³⁾............ place! On the right, there's a boat selling ⁽⁴⁾............... . ⁽⁵⁾............... to it, in the middle, there's a woman selling food for lunch. ⁽⁶⁾............ her, there are some bananas. On the ⁽⁷⁾............ side, on the shore, there are more stalls selling hats and CDs – you can't see them very well. We had a great time, but we didn't ⁽⁸⁾............... anything.

4 Look at another photo from Dario's trip. Write a short description to add to Dario's email.

This is one of a street market. There are lots of people. They're ....

....

....

....

5 💬 Think of two photos of you with your friends or family that you particularly like. Describe them to your partner. Tell him/her

- where you are
- who you're with
- what you're doing.

TASK

6 Write an email to a friend describing the photos you told your partner about in **5**.

REPORT BACK

7 **a** Work in pairs. Read your partner's email. Write three questions you want to ask about the photos. Give them to your partner.

b 💬 Answer your partner's questions.

➡ Go to Review B, Unit 6, p. 70 **67**

VOCABULARY
Rooms & spaces

1 Work in pairs. Write the names of ten rooms or places in a home. How many do you have in your home?

2 💬 Discuss the questions.
1 Where do you usually eat?
2 Where do you usually watch TV?
3 Where do you usually study or read?
4 Where do you spend most time? Why?

3 🔊 R6 Listen to Marco from page 41 answering the questions. Make a note of his answers.

Furniture & fittings

4 Write the names of two pieces of furniture for each description.
1 something you sit on *a chair, an armchair*
2 something you use in the kitchen
3 something you sleep on
4 something you put on the wall

5 Write definitions for three more pieces of furniture. Read the definitions to the class. Can they guess which piece of furniture it is?

Urban places

6 💬 Work in pairs. Look at the words in the box and answer the questions.

> park   bus stop   train station   local shop
> bar   café   sports centre   swimming pool
> cinema   theatre   museum   art gallery
> shopping centre   supermarket   news-stand
> police station   market

1 How many of the places in the box are
  a five minutes from your English school?
  b more than half an hour from your home?
2 Which do you visit most frequently? Why?

GRAMMAR
There is/There are

1 **a** Work in pairs. Rewrite the sentences below using *There is/There are*.
1 The street has two nice cafés.
2 It doesn't have a bank.
3 It doesn't have trees or plants.
4 The nearest café has Wi-Fi.

b Are the sentences true for the street outside your English school?

2 💬 Ask your partner questions about his/her neighbourhood. Use *Is there/Are there?* Ask about the things in the box.

> shops   places to eat   places to do sports
> public transport   things to do in the evening

Prepositions of place

3 Work in pairs. Look at the picture. Find the things in the box. Write sentences describing where they are. Use all the prepositions in the box at least once.

> a news-stand   a bus stop   a taxi rank   a hotel
> a burger bar   a park   a clock   a balcony   a dog
>
> in   on   above   under   next to   in front of   opposite
> near   between   behind   on the right/left

4 💬 Look at a similar picture on page 159. Find six differences.

FUNCTIONAL LANGUAGE
Giving directions

1 💬 Work in pairs. Student A, tell your partner the best way to get to your house or flat from the English school. Student B, draw a map of the directions as you listen.

2 Explain the map to your partner.

■ LOOKING BACK

- Think of five things you can say about your home.
- Think of five things you can say about your neighbourhood.
- Is there anything you want to look at again?
- Think of a way to practise this language at home or in class.

Vocabulary

Sports & pastimes

1 Work in pairs. Can you think of

1 five sports you play with a ball?
2 four sports you play in a team?
3 three sports you can play indoors?
4 two pastimes that need a pencil?
5 one sport you're very good at?

2 Look at the verbs and the lists of activities. In each list one activity does not go with the verb. Which one is it?

Play: dominoes chess judo tennis golf
Do: sudoku Pilates gymnastics crosswords cards
Go: swimming cycling basketball climbing jogging

3 💬 Work in pairs. Look at the lists of activities in 2 again. Answer the questions.

Which do you do
1 almost every day?
2 at the weekend?
3 on holiday?
4 never?

Parts of the body

4 🔊R7 Listen to the recording. Touch the parts of the body you hear.

5 Listen again and write them down.

Grammar

Imperatives

1 Work in pairs. Write instructions for your partner using the words in Vocabulary 5 and the verbs in the box.

> breathe clap close dance lie open
> put stand stop stretch wink whistle

2 Listen to your partner and follow the instructions.

Can/Can't (ability)

3 Write down the verbs for two things you can do

1 well. *play tennis*
2 very well.
3 quite well.

4 Make questions using the verbs in 3 and *can*.

Can you play tennis?

5 💬 Work in pairs. Ask and answer your questions in 4. Use *very well*, *quite well* and *not at all* in your answers.

Can you play tennis? Yes, I can, quite well./No, I can't, not at all!

Can/Can't (permission/possibility)

6 Work in pairs. Write a list of five things you can't do

1 in your classroom. *You can't smoke.*
2 in your town. *You can't ski – there's no snow.*

-ly adverbs

7 **a** Work in pairs. Write descriptions of the pictures. Use -ly adverbs.

b 🔊R8 Listen and compare your answers. Are they the same?

8 💬 Work in pairs. Answer the questions.

- Do you prefer eating quickly or slowly?
- Do you prefer playing music loudly or quietly?
- Do you ever sing happily in the shower?
- Do you always think carefully before you make a decision?

Functional language

On the phone

1 💬 Work in pairs. Student A, turn to page 159. Student B, turn to page 161.

2 💬 Change roles and repeat the conversation.

◼ Looking back

- Which section of this unit has been the most useful? Why?
- Write down five useful phrases from this unit and when you might use them.
- Tell a partner five things you can do in English after doing this unit.

VOCABULARY
Shops & amenities

1 💬 Work in pairs. Think of ten shops near your English school and answer the questions.
1 What kind of shops are they?
2 What do they sell?
3 Do you ever go there?

2 💬 Change partners and discuss the questions.
1 Do you have a favourite
   a clothes shop?   b music store?   c bar?
2 Where is it?
3 When do you go there?
4 Who do you go with?
5 What do you usually buy there?

Colours

3 a 💬 Work in pairs. Name the seven colours of the rainbow in the order they appear. Can you think of three more colours? Which colours do you prefer
1 to wear?   3 for a car, motorbike or scooter?
2 on the walls in your house?

b Compare your answers with the class. What are the most popular colours in the class?

Clothes

4 a You are going to a friend's house for the weekend. Make a list of the clothes you want to take with you.

b Compare your list with a partner. Do you have the same things on your list?

5 a Look at the words in the box. Which clothes and accessories do you associate
1 with men?   2 with women?   3 with both?

> shirt tie skirt jacket make-up
> long hair jewellery baggy jeans
> tattoos baggy shorts

b Think of two more things for each group, 1–3.

GRAMMAR
Present continuous

1 Write three sentences describing 1) what you are doing at the moment and 2) what you are not doing.
I'm writing... I'm not eating...

2 a Make questions from your sentences in 1.
Are you writing? Are you eating?

b 💬 Work with a partner. Ask and answer the questions.

Present continuous & simple

3 💬 Choose the correct option. Then ask and answer the questions with a partner.
1 *Do you study / Are you studying* for exams at the moment?
2 What *do you usually do / are you usually doing* at the weekend?
3 *Do you read / Are you reading* the newspaper every day?
4 What sports *do you do / are you doing*?
5 What *do you think / are you thinking* about now?

FUNCTIONAL LANGUAGE
Shopping

1 a Match the questions to the answers.
1 Can I help you?
2 Where are the changing rooms?
3 Can I try these on?
4 I'm looking for a shirt.

a What colour?
b Over there, next to the shoes.
c Yes, of course!
d No, thanks, I'm just looking.

b 🔊 R9 Listen and check.

2 💬 Work in pairs. Continue two of the four conversations.

▮ LOOKING BACK

- Which section of this unit was most useful for you?
- Write down five useful phrases from this unit.
- Tell a partner five things you can say to describe the people around you and what they're doing.

READING & SPEAKING

1 Work in pairs. Read the article and do the test.

Do you have a good visual memory?

Find a friend and try this simple test.

Turn to page 159 and look at the photo for exactly one minute. Then follow the steps below.

• Draw a very simple copy of the photo. Include as many details as you can.

• Compare your picture with a partner. Add new details, or make changes if necessary.

• Work in pairs and answer these questions.

1 How many people are sitting at the tables in the café?

2 How many people are walking out of the café?

3 What colour are the sunshades?

4 Remember one person in particular. What is that person doing?

2 a Look at the photo on page 159 again and check your answers.

b 💬 Do you and your partner have a good visual memory? Compare your answers in 1 with the class.

LISTENING

3 a 🔊 R10 Listen to three students talking about learning new words. Answer the questions.

1 What language is each student learning?
2 Who talks about a) the number ten, b) familiar sounds, c) word cards?

b 💬 Do you do any of these things when you learn new vocabulary? What else do you do?

VOCABULARY

4 a Look back at the new vocabulary in units 4–6. Choose ten words or phrases you want to remember.

b 💬 Work in pairs. Tell a partner why you chose these words or phrases.

5 Follow the instructions.

1 Write the words or phrases on a piece of paper.
2 Repeat each one ten times, quietly, then turn the paper over. Can you remember them all?
3 Try this again before you go to bed, and again in the morning. Does it make any difference?

▪ QUICK CHECK

Complete the checklist below.

Can you...	Yes, I can.	Yes, more or less.	I need to look again.
1 talk about your home and neighbourhood?	☐	☐	☐
2 give directions and explain where things are?	☐	☐	☐
3 talk about what you can and can't do?	☐	☐	☐
4 give and follow instructions?	☐	☐	☐
5 leave a message on the phone?	☐	☐	☐
6 talk about what's happening now?	☐	☐	☐
7 talk about people's appearance?	☐	☐	☐
8 get your message across when shopping?	☐	☐	☐

💬 Compare your answers with a partner.

• What else do you know now after studying units 4–6?
• Do you need to look again at any of the sections?
• Do you need any extra help from your teacher?

7 GOING PLACES

1 **a** Work in pairs. Match the photos to the places and seasons.

1 in a city, in the country, in the mountains, on the beach
2 spring, summer, autumn, winter

b 💬 What do you notice about the photos? Which place do you like most? Why?

2 🔊 7.1 Listen to four people describing the places. Which place is each person talking about?

KEY VOCABULARY

The weather

A Match the words in **bold** to the weather symbols. Use a dictionary to help you.

1 It's **raining**. [b]
2 It's **cold**. ☐
3 It's **snowing**. ☐
4 It's **windy** and **cloudy**. ☐ ☐
5 It's **sunny** and **warm**. ☐ ☐
6 It's **hot**, really hot. ☐

NOTICE TALKING ABOUT THE WEATHER

When we talk about the weather we use *it + be*:
It's cold. It's raining. It's cloudy.

B Look at the words in **bold** in transcript 7.2 on page 164. Use them to complete the thermometer.

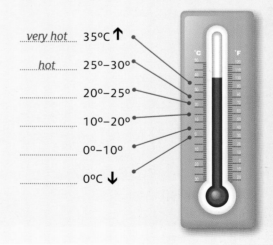

very hot 35°C ↑
hot 25°–30°
.... 20°–25°
.... 10°–20°
.... 0°–10°
.... 0°C ↓

3 Complete A in the KEY VOCABULARY PANEL ▪ .

4 💬 Discuss the questions with a partner.
- Where do you prefer to go on holiday: the city, the country, the mountains or the beach?
- Does it depend on the weather? Or the season?

In spring I like going to the mountains – it's usually warm and sunny, and the mountains are full of flowers.

5 🔊 7.2 Listen to a weather forecast for South America. Write the correct weather symbol(s), a–h, from A next to each town on the map above.

6 Work in pairs to complete B in the KEY VOCABULARY PANEL ▪ .

7 a Find four more adjectives in transcript 7.2 on page 164 to describe the weather. Can you use them to describe the climate in your home town?

b 💬 Work in pairs or small groups. Discuss the questions.
- What's the weather like where you live at the moment?
- Do you like this kind of weather? Why/Why not?

NOTICE WEATHER ADJECTIVES

Some weather adjectives come from nouns:
rain → rainy *cloud → cloudy*
wind → windy *snow → snowy*

When a noun has one syllable and ends in consonant–vowel–consonant, we double the final consonant:
sun → sunny *fog → foggy*

When a noun ends in -e, we replace the -e with -y:
ice → icy

Paradise Lost

1 You're looking at Dreamland beach in Bali. My favourite holiday destination. Or at least it **was** when I **was** first there in 1985. There **were** mostly local people and fishermen. There **weren't** many visitors. It **was** a great place to chill out and relax. It **was** good to have a meal in the local restaurants (*warungs*). It **was** perfect for swimming and surfing. And it **was** cheap! And as for the beach... what can I say? **Was** this paradise? Yes, it **was**! Or at least it **was** my idea of paradise. It **was** perfect, a long stretch of turquoise water and empty white sand.

2 I **was** there on holiday again in the 1990s. There **were** more foreign tourists, but that **wasn't** a problem. It **was** never crowded. It **was** still a great place for a quiet, relaxing holiday.

3 Twenty-five years later and Bali is very different. I'm standing here at the top of my favourite beach. And it just doesn't look the same. They're finishing the last hotel at Dreamland. I can't believe my eyes. The *warungs* aren't there anymore. Now there's a big, busy road, and an expensive 18-hole golf course. There are lots of new hotels, luxury villas and condominiums. Today there are many tourists and it's dirty and noisy. Everything is commercial and modern. It's not a dream land anymore! Back in 1985, Dreamland **was** a good name, but now it isn't dreamland – it's just a nightmare.

READING

1 💬 Look at the photos. They show a beach resort in Bali. Which photo do you like the most? Why?

2 Read the blog about Dreamland. Match the captions to the four photos.
1 Building Dreamland
2 Dreamland as it was
3 Dreamland in the 1990s
4 Dreamland today

3 What is the blog saying? Tick the correct sentence.
1 Dreamland is wonderful now.
2 The island of Bali is not very different now.
3 Not all the changes to Dreamland are bad.
4 Commercial interests change beautiful places.

4 Underline the positive words in paragraphs 1 and 2, and the negative words in paragraph 3.

5 💬 Do you agree that all the changes to Dreamland are negative? Can you think of a positive side to the changes?

GRAMMAR

1 Work in pairs. Look at the verbs in **bold** in paragraphs 1 and 2 of the blog. Complete 1–7 in the GRAMMAR PANEL ▪ with the verbs.

2 **a** Look at the two photos of Benidorm in Spain today and 60 years ago. Complete the sentences with the correct form (present or past) of the verb *to be*.

1 Before, there .... any big hotels.
2 Today, there .... lots of hotels.
3 Then, there .... many tourists.
4 Now, there .... lots of people.
5 The beach .... quiet in the past.
6 The beach .... quiet now.
7 Now, the view .... very pretty.
8 Then, the landscape .... really beautiful.

b Work in pairs. Think of three more sentences.

3 💬 Work in small groups. Think of a place you know well which was very different in the past. Tell your group about it. What was it like in the past? What things are different now?

PAST SIMPLE: *TO BE*

+
I (1) .... there on holiday.
You/We/They were very happy there.
He/She/It (2) .... perfect.

–
I wasn't there on business.
You/We/They (3) .... at work.
He/She/It (4) .... a problem.

?
Was I happy in Dreamland?
Were you happy in Dreamland?
(5) .... it paradise?

Yes/No
Yes, I was./No, I wasn't.
Yes, you/we/they were./No, you/we/they weren't.
Yes, he/she/it (6) ..../No, he/she/it wasn't.

We often use *be* with *there*:
There (7) .... n't many tourists.

See page 146 for grammar reference and more practice.

LISTENING & SPEAKING

1 🔊 7.3 Listen to Adam describing a visit to Benidorm. Was it a good trip? Why/Why not? What does he think of the town?

2 **a** Read the sentences below. Who is speaking, Adam (A) or his friend Will (W)?

1 How was your trip?
2 It was great, thanks, really great.
3 It wasn't all bad.
4 It was lovely in the past.
5 It was very busy.
6 The hotel was nice. There was a great pool and a sea view.
7 It was hot and sunny.
8 We were on the beach every day!

b Listen again and check.

3 **a** 💬 Work in pairs. Think of a trip to a town or city. Tell your partner about the trip and the place. Start your description like this.

I want to tell you about a trip to...
I was there...
It was...

b As you listen, ask your partner questions about the trip.

Was it a good trip?
What was the weather like?

■ PRACTISE THE PAST SIMPLE: REGULAR & IRREGULAR VERBS
■ TALK ABOUT WHAT HAPPENED IN THE PAST

LISTENING

1 💬 Work in small groups. Look at the photos and discuss the questions.

- What are the people doing?
- What do you usually do when it rains?

2 🔊 7.4 Listen to Lola talking about a rainy day. Which photos go with her story?

3 **a** Work in pairs. Which of the verbs in the box does Lola not talk about?

> eating pizza   going to the cinema   having coffee
> having a shower   playing cards   playing volleyball
> sitting on the bus   swimming   waiting   walking

b Listen again and check.

GRAMMAR

1 **a** Work in pairs. Read the extracts from transcript 7.4. Put them in the correct order.

a We missed the bus.
b We didn't want to wait for a bus in the rain.
c It started to rain.
d We decided to go home.
e We walked... all the way home.
f We went out for a pizza.
g We had a coffee.
h We played a couple of games of cards.
i Did you call a taxi? No, we didn't.

b Check your answers in transcript 7.4 on page 164.

2 Underline all the verbs in the sentences in 1a and complete 1–9 in the GRAMMAR PANEL ■■.

3 **a** Complete the dialogue using the verbs in brackets in the past simple.

> A What [1] *did you do* (you/do) at the weekend?
> B We [2] .... (want) to get away, so we went to the country.
> A Where [3] .... (you/go)?
> B To the mountains. We [4] .... (stay) in a campsite.
> A Nice. [5] What .... (you/do)?
> B We [6] .... (go) walking in the mountains, we [7] .... (have) a barbecue. It [8] .... (rain) a bit on Sunday. What about you?
> A Nothing special. I [9] .... (work) on Saturday. I [10] .... (need) to finish that report. On Sunday I [11] .... (stay) in and [12] .... (relax). I [13] .... (watch) some television, I [14] .... (do) some cooking – you know, the usual.
> B That's boring!
> A No, you're wrong. That's what rainy Sundays are for!

b 🔊 7.5 Listen and check. Whose weekend do you prefer? Why?

4 💬 Write questions in the past simple. Then ask and answer them with a partner.

1 What/do last weekend?
2 stay at home?
3 do anything interesting?
4 Who/see?
5 Where/go?
6 have a good time?

PAST SIMPLE: REGULAR & IRREGULAR VERBS

We use the past simple to talk about actions that happened in the past.

+

To form verbs in the past simple we add *-ed* to the infinitive:
miss – (1)_____ *, start –* (2)_____ *, walk –* (3)_____ *.*

–

We use *didn't* + infinitive for negative verbs:
We (4)_____ *want to wait.*

?

We use *did* + **subject** + **infinitive** for questions:
What (5)_____ *you do?*
(6)_____ *you call a taxi?*

Yes/No

We use *did/didn't* in short answers:
Yes, we did./No, we (7)_____ *.*

Some common irregular verbs

The verbs **have**, **do** and **go** have irregular past forms:
go – (8)*w_____ , do – did, have –* (9)*h_____ .*

See page 146 for grammar reference and more practice.

PRONUNCIATION: Past simple endings

1 a Write the past simple form of the verbs.

1 decide	_____	5 need	_____
2 play	_____	6 stay	_____
3 walk	_____	7 want	_____
4 watch	_____	8 work	_____

b 🔊 7.6 Listen to both forms of the verbs. Which verbs have an extra syllable in the past simple? Check your answers against the rule below.

> When the infinitive of a verb finishes in a /d/ or /t/ sound, we pronounce the past simple *-ed* ending as /ɪd/.

2 💬 Read the sentences. Work in pairs. Are any of them true for your last weekend?

1 I wanted to stay in.
2 I needed to do some work.
3 I watched a film on TV.
4 I played cards with my friends.
5 I decided to do some studying.
6 I walked around town for hours.

SPEAKING

1 a Work in pairs. Look at the photos. Write questions using *When did you last...?*
When did you last play cards?

b 💬 Ask and answer the questions. Were any of your answers the same?

When did you last play cards?
Last weekend. I played cards with my friends in a bar.

NOTICE *LAST*

We use *last* with **night**, **week**, **month**, **year**, etc. to form time expressions:
last night, last week, last month, last year.
You can also use *last* in questions:
When did you last...? = When was the last time you...?

2 a When did you last get caught in the rain? Read the questions and prepare to tell your story. Make notes about what you want to say. Use a dictionary to help you.

- Where were you?
- At home or away?
- When did it start raining?
- Did you get wet?
- Who were you with?
- What did you do?

b 💬 Work in small groups. Tell your stories.
One day I was...

VOCABULARY: Transport

1 Match the words in the box to the photos. Use a dictionary to help you.

> bus   plane   bike   boat   train   subway   car
> taxi   motorbike/scooter   tram   ferry

2 💬 Work in pairs. Discuss the questions.

- Which forms of transport exist in your home town? Which do you use? How often do you use them?
- Which of these forms of transport do you prefer for everyday life? For short distances? For long distances? Why?
- How many different forms of transport did you use last week? Where did you go?

LISTENING

1 🔊 7.7 Listen to four people, Bruno, Erykah, Carole and Alek, talking about changes to the transport they use every day. What two forms of transport does each person talk about?

2 Listen again. Match each speaker to the reason why he/she changed the form of transport.

1 There was no other alternative before.
2 They introduced a new service in his/her town.
3 His/Her job changed.
4 He/She didn't want to cause pollution.

NOTICE BY

We often use *by* + transport:
I go to school by bus.
I went to college by train.

3 a Work in pairs. Rewrite the sentences to make them true.

1 Bruno didn't hate flying before.
2 Erykah had a choice about how to get to school.
3 Carole didn't decide to change her form of transport.
4 Alek preferred the train because it was cheap.

b 💬 Check your answers in transcript 7.7 on pages 164–165. How does your daily journey compare?

My journey is short, like Carole's.

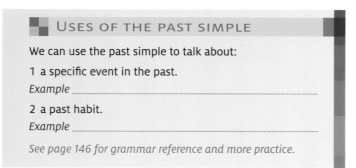

GRAMMAR

1 a Complete the extracts with a past simple verb.

BRUNO	I ⁽¹⁾w.............. to work by subway for years because I ⁽²⁾l.............. and ⁽³⁾w.............. in Rio.
ERYKAH	We ⁽⁴⁾w.............. to school, me and my friends. My life ⁽⁵⁾ch.............. overnight.
CAROLE	I ⁽⁶⁾w.............. to work by car. I talked to two friends who live near me and we ⁽⁷⁾d.............. to share a taxi.
ALEK	I always ⁽⁸⁾w.............. to college by train. Then I ⁽⁹⁾ch.............. my mind about it because the council introduced a new bike service.

b 🔊 7.8 Listen and check.

2 a Look at the sentences in 1a again. Which verbs are
1 talking about a past habit?
2 talking about a specific event in the past?

b Look at the GRAMMAR PANEL ■■ and complete the examples with sentences that are true for you.

3 💬 Work in pairs. Ask and answer the questions.
● How did you travel to school when you were younger?
● How did you get to class today? Do you always come by the same form of transport?

USES OF THE PAST SIMPLE

We can use the past simple to talk about:

1 a specific event in the past.
Example ....

2 a past habit.
Example ....

See page 146 for grammar reference and more practice.

READING & SPEAKING

1 a Read the messages. Match the forms of transport in VOCABULARY 1 to the messages.

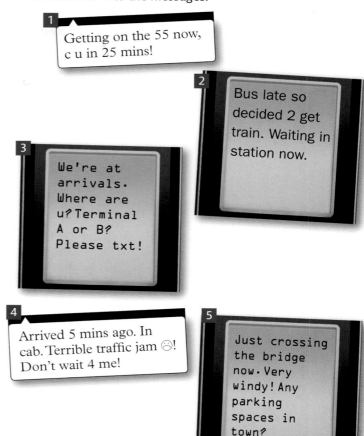

1
Getting on the 55 now, c u in 25 mins!

2
Bus late so decided 2 get train. Waiting in station now.

3
We're at arrivals. Where are u? Terminal A or B? Please txt!

4
Arrived 5 mins ago. In cab. Terrible traffic jam ☹! Don't wait 4 me!

5
Just crossing the bridge now. Very windy! Any parking spaces in town?

b 💬 Work in pairs. Answer the questions. Which person
● is waiting to travel?
● is travelling at the moment?
● is at his/her destination already?

2 a Find the text versions of the words in the box in the messages.

> you   see you   text   to   minutes   for

b What special text forms do you use in your language?

3 Work in pairs. Read the text messages again. Write them out as full sentences.

4 a 💬 Work in small groups. Choose the best form of transport for each situation. Explain why.
● It's raining. You want to go to the nearest supermarket.
● You and a group of friends want to go camping this weekend in the country.
● You need to go to the capital city of a neighbouring country for a business meeting.

b Compare your answers with the class.

TUNE IN

1 💬 Match the photos to the places in the box. What are the people doing in each photo?

> ferry terminal   taxi rank   train station
> tourist information   bus stop

2 a 🔊 7.9 Listen to five short conversations. Match them to the photos.

b Listen again and complete the sentences.

1 She wants to go to the ....
2 He wants to buy a train ....
3 He needs to go to terminal .... at the airport.
4 The .... takes an hour to get to the airport.
5 The next ferry is in .... minutes.

❝ One ❞

🔊 7.10 Listen to the two questions. Notice the stress on the word before *one*.

Is there another one?
When's the next one?

Listen again and repeat.

FOCUS ON LANGUAGE

3 Read the questions the passengers asked in the conversations. Who are they talking to? Use the people in the box.

> friend (F)   bus driver (BD)   taxi driver (TD)
> tourist information officer (I)   train station worker (TS)

1 How much is it? ....
2 We just missed the last ferry! When's the next one? ....
3 Hi! Can you take me to the airport, please? ....
4 Excuse me, are you going to the stadium? ....
5 Excuse me, how long does it take to get to the airport by train? ....
6 Excuse me, this ticket machine is out of order. Is there another one? ....

4 a Match the answers to the questions in 3.

a No, you need the number 2 bus.
b No, I'm afraid there isn't.
c Yeah, sure. Which terminal?
d That's £15.85, please.
e About 35 minutes. There's a train every half an hour.
f There's another one in 40 minutes.

b Check your answers in transcript 7.9 on page 165.

OVER TO YOU

5 💬 Look at the photos in 1 again. Act out the five situations.

TUNE IN

1 🗨 Look at the photos. Which places can you find in your town? Which can't you find? Which do you like to go to?

2 **a** 🗨 Work in groups. Think of two things to do, or two places to go, for a visitor to your town who likes

● sports
● art and museums
● music, dancing and cinema
● shopping
● eating good food
● visiting monuments and interesting buildings.

b Work in pairs. Did you do any of these things, or go to any of these places, during the last month? Tell your partner about it.

PREPARE FOR TASK

3 🔊 7.11 Listen to a tourist guide helping a visitor plan a day out in Lisbon. What kind of things does the visitor want to do? Complete the programme.

> *Morning*
> * _____ in the main square.
> * Visit the _____.
> * Take it easy in the _____ near the castle.
>
> *Afternoon*
> * _____ in the old town.
> * Visit the town hall and a _____ exhibition.
>
> *Evening*
> * Go to an open-air theatre in the _____.

4 **a** Complete the guide's suggestions with the expressions in the box.

> if it's sunny　I suggest　that takes　there's
> first of all　you can　why not

1 .... you can go to the main square.
2 .... you can sit outside.
3 Then .... visit the cathedral. .... about an hour and a half.
4 For lunch, ... you go to the old town.
5 .... visit the town hall? .... a photo exhibition on at the moment.

b 🔊 7.12 Listen and check.

5 Work in pairs. Write questions to ask two other students about what they like doing in their free time. Use the ideas in 2a to help you.

Do you like doing sports? What sports do you like?

6 🗨 Work with another pair. Ask your questions and make a note of the answers.

TASK

7 Work with your partner in 5. Plan a perfect day out in your town for the students you interviewed in 6. Write notes, using the programme in 3 to help you.

8 Work with your partners in 6. Explain the programme you planned. Are they happy with it?

REPORT BACK

9 🗨 Tell the class if you were happy with your programme. Why/Why not?

➡ Go to Review C, Unit 7, p. 102　➡ Go to Writing bank 4, p. 155　**81**

8 IN THE NEWS

1 💬 Look at the photos of the same place. Answer the questions with a partner.

- Where is the place?
- What's happening?
- Do you think this a good place to watch the news? Why/Why not?

2 Work in pairs to complete A, B and C in the KEY VOCABULARY PANEL ▣ .

3 a 🔊 8.1 Listen to three people answering the questions in A and B. Whose answers are most similar to yours?

b Listen again and complete the sentences.

1 Djamal doesn't find out about the news because he...
2 He thinks most news is...
3 Jeroen watches the news...
4 He doesn't like...
5 Amanda thinks reading the newspaper is...
6 But she thinks the news in newspapers is too...

■ KEY VOCABULARY

Talking about the news

Sources of news

A How do you find out about the news? Tick the answers in the list.

radio	☐	internet	☐
newspaper	☐	television	☐
mobile phone	☐	podcasts	☐
friends or people at work	☐		
other			

Types of news

B What kind of news are you interested in? Tick the answers in the list.

sports	☐	local news	☐
national news	☐	world news	☐
business	☐	celebrity gossip	☐
weather	☐	entertainment/culture	☐
other			

Verb collocations

C Complete the sentences using the verbs in the box. Sometimes more than one option is possible.

> listen to read watch

1 *I usually* .... the news *on TV every night at 11 p.m.*
2 *I sometimes* .... the business news *on the radio in my car.*
3 *I often* .... the local newspaper *in the bar when I'm having a coffee.*
4 *I generally* .... the news *on the internet.*
5 *I always* .... the sports news. *I love football!*

- 💬 Change the words in *italics* so that the sentences are true for you. Compare your sentences with a partner.

NOTICE *NEWS OR THE NEWS?*

News is uncountable and takes a singular verb:
The news is on TV.

We often use *the* when we talk about news in the media:
I didn't watch the news today.

We can also say *a piece of news* or *some news*:
I have some good news for you.

---

4 a 💬 Work in small groups. Number these facts about the news in order of agreement (1 = I totally disagree, 5 = I totally agree). Think of examples to support your answers.

- Bad news sells newspapers.
- Gossip and football distract people from real news.
- Nobody reads newspapers. Information is all online.
- The news is different depending on the channel you watch or the newspaper you buy.

b Compare your ideas with the class. Are your answers similar or different?

READING

1 💬 Work in pairs. Look at the images of blogs above and discuss the questions.

- What is a blog?
- What kind of news do you think these blogs talk about? Which blog would you like to read?
- Do you ever read blogs? If yes, what kind of blogs do you read? If no, why not?

2 a 💬 Work in pairs. Read the headline of the news story below and answer the questions.

1 What do you think the world's oldest blogger writes about?
2 Would you like to read her blog? Why/Why not?

b Read the article and check your answers.

3 a Read the questions. Can you remember the answers?

1 How old was María Amelia López when she died?
2 Where was she from?
3 When did she start blogging?
4 Why did she start?
5 What did she write about?
6 Why did she enjoy blogging?
7 Who was interested in her blog?
8 Why were they interested?

b Read the article again and check your answers. Why did so many people enjoy her blog?

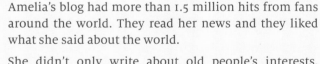

> **NOTICE** *WAS/WERE BORN*
> We usually use the past simple with *be born*:
> *When were you born? I was born in 1911.*
> **What do you say in your language?**

The world's oldest blogger

Before she died in May 2009, María Amelia López, at 97 years old, was the oldest blogger in the world.

This is her first message. She wrote it at the age of 95: 'My name is Amelia and I was born in Muxía, A Coruña, Spain, on 23 December, 1911. Today it's my birthday and my grandson gave me a blog.'

Just before she died, she sat down and wrote: 'When I'm on the internet, I forget about my illness. The distraction is good for you – being able to communicate with people. It's good for the brain, and makes you strong.'

Amelia's blog had more than 1.5 million hits from fans around the world. They read her news and they liked what she said about the world.

She didn't only write about old people's interests. Her blog spoke about everything, from politics and religion, to the power of the internet. She sent a positive message to many people of all ages. She thought life was for living and communicating!

During her life as a blogger, she made a lot of friends and met a lot of celebrities. The day she met the Spanish president, José Luis Rodríguez Zapatero, was an important day for her.

More than 500 readers left messages on her site after her family left a final note from Amelia to the world.

GRAMMAR

1 Work in pairs. Read the article again. <u>Underline</u> the past simple verbs. Complete 1–13 and a–d in the GRAMMAR PANEL ▪ .

2 **a** Complete the questions with the correct form of the verbs in the box.

| give   be born   make   meet   read   write |

1 When .... she .... ?
2 Why .... her grandson .... her a blog?
3 How long .... she .... her blog?
4 .... a lot of people .... her blog?
5 .... she .... a lot of friends?
6 Which famous politician .... she .... ?

b Answer the questions using full sentences.

3 Put the words in the correct order to make sentences in the past simple. Who is the celebrity?

1 born he 1958 was in Chicago in
2 in he 2009 died of 50 at the age
3 Elvis Presley's married he daughter in 1994
4 two children he from a second marriage had
5 his funeral on TV watched 31 million people

4 **a** Work in groups. Think of a celebrity. Write five sentences about his/her life.

b Read your sentences to the class. Can the other students guess who it is?

▪ **PAST SIMPLE: IRREGULAR VERBS & TIME EXPRESSIONS**

Irregular verbs

Some common verbs have an irregular form in the past simple:

go	*went*	meet (4)	....	sit (8)	....
give (1)	....	read (5)	....	speak (9)	....
have	*had*	say (6)	....	think (10)	....
leave (2)	....	send (7)	....	write (11)	....
make (3)	....				

In questions and negatives, we use the infinitive:
What did she (12) .... about?
She didn't only (13) .... about old people's interests.

Time expressions

We often use time expressions with the past simple:

| at   during   in   on |

(a) 2009   (c) .... the age of 95
(b) .... her life   (d) .... Tuesday

See page 147 for grammar reference and more practice.

PRONUNCIATION: Irregular past simple verbs

1 **a** Work in pairs. What are the infinitives of the verbs in the box?

| left   sat   gave   spoke   read   sent   met |
| said   wrote   made   went   had |

b ◀))) 8.2 Listen and check.

2 **a** Complete the table with the past simple of the verbs in 1a.

/əʊ/	/eɪ/	/e/	/æ/
spoke	gave	left	had

b ◀))) 8.3 Listen and check.

LISTENING & SPEAKING

1 ◀))) 8.4 Listen to three fans of Amelia's blog. What did they like about it?

2 Listen again. How many of the verbs in GRAMMAR 2a did you hear? Complete the sentences.

1 I .... Amelia's blog every day.
2 She .... great advice.
3 She .... some wonderful things about the past.
4 Her blog really .... my day.
5 It was wonderful that she .... the energy to do that.

3 💬 Work in small groups. Discuss the questions.
- Do you have a favourite blog or website?
- Why do you like it?
- How often do you visit it?

SPEAKING & LISTENING

1   Look at six photos related to three different news stories. Find the words in the box in the photos. Use a dictionary to help you.

> face masks   mud   live concert   soldiers   football fans
> celebrations   passengers   airport   music festival

2   Work in pairs. Discuss the questions.
- What is happening in each photo?
- Which photos go together? There are three pairs. Each pair shows a different story.
- What do you think the stories are about?

3   **a** 8.5 Listen to a short news bulletin. Check your answers in 2.

  b   Listen again and choose the best headline for each story.
  1   a   Argentinian soldiers fight new flu
      b   Flu pandemic in Argentina
  2   a   Rock festival in danger
      b   Singing in the rain
  3   a   Football heroes come home
      b   Fans celebrate league

VOCABULARY (1): Lexical sets

1   Work in pairs. Complete the stories with the words in the boxes.

> doctors   hospitals   pandemic   virus

Fears about the new flu (1)............ are increasing, particularly in inner-city areas. (2)............ suspect that 11 soldiers in the Argentinian army have the new (3)............ . (4)............ are on alert in major cities.

> bands   concerts   festival   tickets

The Rock in the Park (5)............ is in danger as storms hit Mar del Plata. The organisers cancelled last night's (6)............ and offered full refunds for (7)............ . They hope to make an announcement later today about tonight's show with big-name (8)............ Depeche Mode and The Killers.

2   Read the sports story in transcript 8.5 on page 165. Underline the words associated with football and winning. Then complete the text with the words.

> Lanús won the (1)............ last night for the first time in their history when they (2)............ Vélez Sarsfield, 2–0. José Sand (3)............ both (4)............ to give Lanús (5)............ . Celebrations continued for hours after the (6)............ .

SPEAKING & WRITING

1   **a**   Work in pairs. Think of recent news stories from your country. Make notes about what happened.

  b   Write a short summary of one of the stories. Use the words in VOCABULARY (1) 1 and 2 to help you.

2   **a**   Exchange stories with another pair. Write two or three questions asking for more information.

  b   Exchange questions and write replies.

VOCABULARY (2): Collocations

1 Work in pairs. Identify the noun in each list that you can't use with the verb. Which verb can you use it with?

1 **get:** the flu, a cold, the league
2 **go to:** a music festival, the news, a concert
3 **watch:** a prize, a football match, a film
4 **win:** a match, a show, a game of cards

2 a Complete the questions with the verbs in 1.

1 When did you last .... a film on television?
2 When did you last .... a cold?
3 When did your local football team last .... a match?
4 When did you last .... a concert?

b 💬 Ask and answer the questions. Ask more questions to get more information.

A: *When did you last get a cold?*
B: *About two weeks ago.*
A: *Was it bad? Did you go to the doctor?*

GRAMMAR

1 Choose the best subject for each sentence. Which story in SPEAKING & LISTENING 3a does each sentence come from?

1 Today, the *doctors / authorities* **decided to check** all passengers entering the country's main airports.
2 The *organisers / news reporters* **hope to make** an announcement later today about tonight's show.
3 The *club / team* **plans to organise** an official party.
4 The *club / fans* **want to welcome** the team home.
5 The *town / team* **would like to thank** their fans.

2 Look at the verbs in **bold** in the sentences in 1. Complete the list of verbs in the GRAMMAR PANEL ■ .

3 a Complete the sentences with the correct form of the verbs *get, go, see* or *stay*.

1 **I want** .... camping this weekend.
2 **I'd really like** .... a good film this evening.
3 **Next summer I plan** .... on holiday to an English speaking country.
4 **Last weekend I decided** .... at home and study.
5 **I hope** .... a job with the local TV station.

b Write sentences about you using the words and phrases in **bold**. Compare your sentences with a partner.

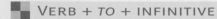

> ■ **VERB + *TO* + INFINITIVE**
>
> Some common verbs are always followed by *to* + **infinitive**.
> Here is a list: decide, ...
> *We want <u>to help</u> you.*
> *They planned <u>to escape</u>.*
>
> *See page 147 for grammar reference and more practice.*

LISTENING & SPEAKING

1 🔊 8.6 Listen to three young people explaining their hopes and plans for the future. Match them to the photos.

2 a 💬 Work in pairs. Talk about your hopes and plans for the future.

I plan to study abroad. I'd like to get a new job…

b Do you have similar hopes or plans? Explain the similarities or differences to the class.

READING

1 Read the headline and look at the photos. Put them in the order you think they happened.

2 Read the article and check your answers in **1**.

3 Read the article again and complete the sentences using the words in the box.

> building started filmed fine
> ropes top TV programme

1 Alain Robert didn't have any .... with him on the climb.
2 He climbed to the .... of the RBS tower before the police arrested him.
3 A TV company .... the climb for a ....
4 The police gave Robert a .... of 200 Australian dollars.
5 This was not the first time he climbed a tall ....
6 He was very young when he .... climbing buildings.

AUSTRALIAN POLICE ARREST FRENCH SPIDER-MAN ON SYDNEY SKYSCRAPER

SYDNEY police arrested Alain Robert, 44, also known as the Human Spider, as he climbed the 41-floor Royal Bank of Scotland (RBS) tower in Sydney. He didn't use any ropes or safety equipment and climbed in a strong wind.

A TV cameraman filmed his climb from a helicopter for a documentary programme. Hundreds of people stopped to look as he climbed the tower.

After he finished the climb, police officers took him to the police station, where Robert paid a fine of 200 Australian dollars. This was the Human Spider's eightieth 'free climb' (climbing without ropes), and his third in Sydney.

Robert first climbed a building at the age of 12 when he got locked out of his apartment and decided to climb up eight floors to an open window.

4 Read the tweets (Twitter messages) sent by eyewitnesses who watched the Human Spider as he climbed the tower. <u>Underline</u> information which is different from the information in the article.

twitter™

A helicopter is flying over him, it's the police, they're going to arrest him.

He's crazy, kids – do not imitate this!!!

He's climbing up there now, dressed as Spider-Man. It's incredible, the tower is 410 metres high at least!

I'm watching the Human Spider, but he's having trouble, I think he's going to fall... Oh no, he's falling!

5 💬 Work in pairs. Read the article and the tweets again. Which do you think is/are more interesting? Why?

GRAMMAR

1 Work in pairs. Put the events in order. (Not all the information appears in the newspaper article.)

1 He got to the top of the tower.
2 They took him to the police station.
3 They arrested him.
4 People stopped to watch him.
5 He started climbing the tower.
6 A helicopter arrived.
7 They found out the helicopter was from a TV company.
8 They asked for his ID.

2 8.7 Listen to an interview with one of the people watching the climb. Check your answers in 1.

3 Listen again. Complete the transcript with the sequencers in the box.

> finally   first   then (x2)   later   in the end

> We just didn't believe it! Was that a man on the RBS tower? Was it possible? More and more people stopped to watch. .... we saw a helicopter. It flew over the tower. We thought it was the police, but they started filming the man on the tower. .... I found out it was a TV company. We watched him as he climbed higher and higher. .... he got to the top. It was fantastic, we all cheered! When he came back down the police were there. .... they asked for his ID, ... they arrested him and took him away in a police car. I think, ... , they gave him a fine and let him go.

4 Complete 1–4 in the GRAMMAR PANEL ▪▪ .

5 **a** Work in pairs. Complete the text using some of the sequencers in 3.

> Yesterday was a long day. .... I had an interview in the morning, ... I went to work. In the evening I met some friends for a drink and .... we decided to go to a restaurant for something to eat. .... we went to a club and I missed my last train! .... I got home at 3 a.m. and .... I went to bed at about 4 a.m.

b 💬 Tell your partner what you did yesterday. Use as many sequencers as you can.

▪▪ SEQUENCERS

We use sequencers to show the order of events and actions in a story.
We use (1) .... to introduce the initial event or action in a series.
We use (2) .... to introduce the events or actions that follow.
We use (3) .... to explain that an event or action happened some time after the others.
We use *finally* or (4) .... to talk about the end of the story.

See page 147 for grammar reference and more practice.

LISTENING

1 8.8 Listen to a short radio report about Alain Robert. Which of the topics below does the reporter **not** talk about?

1 the beginning
2 the accidents
3 his family
4 the arrests
5 his future plans
6 the reasons why he climbs

2 **a** Listen again. Make notes about each topic. Which building in the photos does the reporter mention twice?

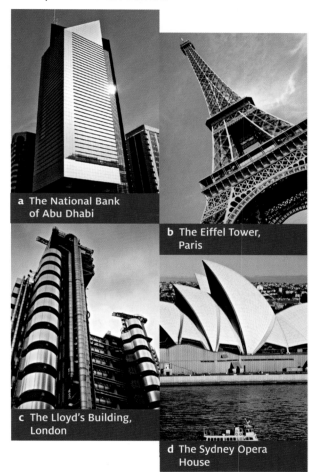

a The National Bank of Abu Dhabi

b The Eiffel Tower, Paris

c The Lloyd's Building, London

d The Sydney Opera House

b Work in pairs. Compare your notes. Check your answers in transcript 8.8 on page 165.

3 💬 Work in small groups. Retell the story of Alain Robert from memory. Then discuss the questions.

- Do you think Alain Robert is very brave or just crazy? Why?
- Are there any buildings near where you live that you think Alain would like to climb?

TUNE IN

1 💬 Work in pairs. Look at the photos. What's the news?

2 a 🔊 8.9 Listen and check your answers in **1**. Match the photos to the conversations.

b Listen again and complete the sentences.

1 José and Beth moved into their new house ....
2 Erika and Kristoff's baby was born ....
3 Adam lost his job ....
4 I passed my driving test ....
5 I can't come to your party ....

3 💬 Did you, or anyone you know, have similar news recently?

FOCUS ON LANGUAGE

4 a Match the responses to the news in **2b**.

a A girl? That's fantastic news!
b Did they? I didn't know it was ready.
c Oh, no! What a shame!
d That's awful! I'm really sorry to hear that.
e That's great news! Congratulations!

b Check your answers in transcript 8.9 on page 165.

5 a Match the responses in **4a** to the notes below.

> **Responding to news**
> 1 Use short questions: *Did you? Was it? Really?*
> 2 Use exclamations with *that's* + **adjective**: *That's good (news)!*
> 3 Use exclamations with *what* + *a/an* + **noun**: *What a pity! What a great idea!*

b Look at the responses in **4a** again. Which are used for
1 good news? 2 bad news?

66 Responding to news 99

🔊 8.10 Listen to the responses in **4a** again and mark the main stress in each. Notice how the speakers use exaggerated intonation to show pleasure and sympathy.

Listen again and repeat.

🔊 8.11 Listen to the three responses. Are the speakers really interested?
Oh, what a shame!
Was he?
Really? Well, that's good news!

Repeat the responses. Use the appropriate intonation.

6 🔊 8.12 Listen to the news and respond to it appropriately.

OVER TO YOU

7 Work in pairs. Complete the pieces of news. Make sure that some are good and some are bad.

1 They *lost / won* the .... last week.
2 My brother .... his final exam. He's really ....
3 My parents are hoping to ....
4 My boyfriend .... the job he really wanted.
5 Last night I decided not to ....
6 I'd really like to invite you to ....

8 💬 Change partners. Read your sentences to each other. Respond to the news. Use the language in **4a** and **5**. Use the appropriate intonation.

TUNE IN

1 💬 Look at the photo. What can you see? What do you think is happening, and where?

2 Read the article and check your answers in **1**. Choose the best headline for the article.

1 Monkeys interrupt official welcome party
2 Special guests at the mayor's buffet
3 Thai city celebrates annual monkey buffet

- -

Local news from around the world

More than 2,000 monkeys live in the Thai city of Lopburi. These wild monkeys live happily next to the human population of the city. In fact, the people of Lopburi love their monkey friends so much, they have a party for them at the Prang Sam Yot temple every year. The annual festival takes place on the last weekend in November. It includes a monkey 'tea party'. The people of the city prepare fruit, eggs and cucumbers in their honour. Last year the monkeys ate around 2,000 kilograms of food. The local people believe that giving food to the monkeys brings them good luck.

- -

3 **a** Work in pairs. Read the article again and <u>underline</u> the answers to the questions.

1 Where does the festival take place?
2 How often does it happen?
3 When exactly does it take place?
4 What happens? Why?

b 💬 Would you like to go and see this festival? Why/Why not?

PREPARE FOR TASK

4 💬 Work in pairs. You are going to read about two more unusual events. Look at the photos. What are the people doing? Why do you think they are doing it?

Summer redneck games

Cheese rolling

5 **a** Student A, turn to page 159. Student B, turn to page 161. Read about the events and answer the questions in **3a**.

b 💬 Tell your partner about the event. Does anything like this ever happen in your town or area?

> **NOTICE**
> *take place* = to happen
> *take part* = to participate

TASK

6 **a** Choose a local event that you think seems strange to an outsider. Think about the questions in **3a** and make notes about the event.

b Read the articles about the events in **2** and **5a** again. Make a note of useful language.

7 Write an article or news story about your local event.

REPORT BACK

8 Work in pairs. Read your partner's story. Together decide on a photo and a headline for the story.

9 💬 Share your stories with the class and decide on

1 the most unusual/interesting story.
2 the story/photo that tells most about your town.

➡ Go to Review C, Unit 8, p. 103 91

9 HUNGRY PLANET

1 Work in pairs. Look at the photo. What do you think it shows?

   1 the food a family of five people eat in one week

   2 an example of a healthy, balanced diet

   3 the food an average family wastes every month

2 💬 Check your answer on page 161. Are you surprised? Why/Why not? Do you think this is true in your country as well?

3 Look at the word box in the KEY VOCABULARY PANEL ▪. Which foods are in the photo?

4 Complete the exercise in the KEY VOCABULARY PANEL ▪.

5 💬 Work in small groups. Answer the questions.

- How many different foods from the word map did you eat yesterday? When did you eat them?
  I had rice and chicken for lunch.
- Did you eat or drink anything that isn't in the word map? Do you know how to say it in English? If not, look it up in a dictionary.
  I had 'cereales' for breakfast. I think that's cereal in English.

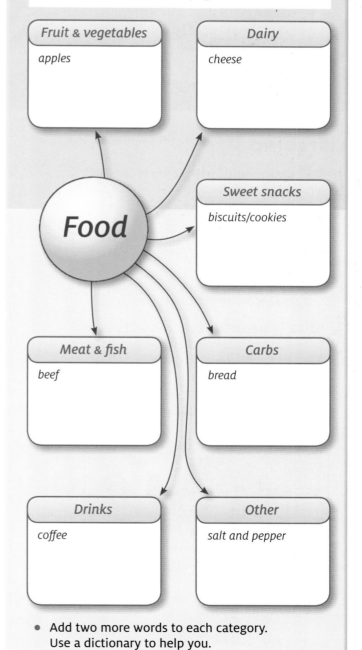

KEY VOCABULARY

Food & drink

Write the words in the correct category in the word map. Use a dictionary to help you. Some words can go in more than one category.

apples bananas beans beef
biscuits/cookies bread cakes carrots cheese
chicken chocolate coffee eggs fish
fruit juice ham lettuce milk olives onions
oranges pasta peas potatoes red meat
rice salt and pepper sausages sweets
tea tomatoes water yoghurt

Fruit & vegetables
apples

Dairy
cheese

Food

Sweet snacks
biscuits/cookies

Meat & fish
beef

Carbs
bread

Drinks
coffee

Other
salt and pepper

- Add two more words to each category. Use a dictionary to help you.

NOTICE *HAVE LUNCH/FOR LUNCH*

We do not usually use *the* with meals:
for lunch, for breakfast, have lunch, have breakfast
NOT *for ~~the lunch~~, have ~~the lunch~~.*

■ PRACTISE COUNTABLE & UNCOUNTABLE NOUNS
■ DISCUSS DIFFERENT BREAKFASTS

a Khao tom soup
b Doughnut and coffee
c Kahvaltı
d Papaya
e Huevos rancheros
f Muesli

LISTENING

1 💬 Work in pairs. Look at the photos and answer the questions.

1 Which foods look sweet and which look savoury?
2 What part of the world do you think the breakfasts come from? What makes you think that?

I think breakfast b is from the USA because Americans eat a lot of doughnuts.

2 🔊 9.1 Listen to a presenter on a TV show talking about breakfasts around the world. Number the photos in the order you hear them.

3 a Listen again and complete the table.

	Country	Key words	
1	*All over the world*	*a doughnut, a coffee*	
2			
3			
4			
5			
6			

b Work in pairs. Check your answers in 1. Is each breakfast sweet or savoury?

4 Complete the extracts. Listen again and check.

1 In Turkey, for example, breakfast consists of .... , ... and olives, with a cup of .... and maybe some .... and cucumber, or a boiled ....
2 A traditional Brazilian breakfast consists of different .... with fresh .... – papaya, pineapple or melon, for example.
3 Fruit is also very popular in Scandinavia – in Sweden or Norway people often have fruit with .... – usually muesli served with .... Another very healthy choice!
4 In Thailand people start the day with soup – soup with rice and some .... or ....

5 💬 Work in pairs. Which breakfast do you think is

1 the most filling?
2 the best for your health?
3 the most similar to a typical breakfast in your country?

NOTICE *A TOMATO/MILK*

Countable nouns – you can count them:
one tomato, two tomatoes.
Uncountable nouns – they have no plural, you can't count them: *milk* NOT ~~one milk~~, ~~two milks~~.

GRAMMAR

1 Work in pairs. Look at the food words in LISTENING 4.

   1 Which are countable?
   2 Which are uncountable?
   3 Which are used with *a* or *an*?
   4 Which are used with *some*?

2 Choose the correct option(s) to complete 1–5 in the GRAMMAR PANEL ▀ .

3 Look at the words in the box. Are they countable or uncountable in your language?

spaghetti	rice	toast	soup	coffee	
tea	meat	fish	fruit	food	wine

4 a Match the words in **3** to the expressions. Use a dictionary to help you. Some words can go with more than one expression.

a bowl of ....
a piece of ....
a slice of ....
a glass of ....
a cup of ....

b Think of one more item of food or drink for each expression.

5 a Complete the sentences with the correct option.

   1 I don't have a very healthy diet – I don't really like *fruit / fruits* very much.
   2 But I love dairy products – I always have *a / some* milk in the fridge at home.
   3 And I really like sweet foods, too, especially cakes and *a biscuits / biscuits*.
   4 I don't eat *egg / eggs* very often – I don't like the taste.
   5 I prefer to cook *a / some* pasta for a quick meal.

b Rewrite the sentences so that they are true for you.

▀ COUNTABLE & UNCOUNTABLE NOUNS

Countable nouns
a boiled egg, a cake or some biscuits
Countable nouns [(1)] *can / can't* be plural.
We use *a/an* with [(2)] *singular / plural* countable nouns.

Uncountable nouns
some toast with butter and jam
We [(3)] *can / can't* use *a/an* with uncountable nouns.
We [(4)] *can / can't* use numbers with uncountable nouns.

Some
some tomatoes and a boiled egg
some meat or fish
We can use *some* with [(5)] *uncountable nouns / singular countable nouns / plural countable nouns.*

See page 148 for grammar reference and more practice.

SPEAKING

1 Read the questionnaire and answer the questions.

1	What do you usually have for breakfast?
2	What did you have today?
3	Do you usually have breakfast
	a at home?
	b in a café on your way to work or class?
	c on the go (you buy something to take away)?
4	Do you have the same thing for breakfast at the weekend?

2 a 💬 Interview other students in your class. Make a note of their answers.

b Work in pairs. Compare your answers. Write four sentences about your results. Use the language below to help you.

Most people have/had...
Some people have/had...
Others have/had...
Nobody has/had...

3 💬 Share your results with the rest of the class. Do they agree?

SPEAKING & READING

1 💬 Work in pairs. Discuss the questions.

- Do you eat a lot of pasta in your family?
- What kind of pasta do you usually eat?
- When did you last eat it?
- What did you eat it with?

2 Read an article about pasta. Match the headings to the paragraphs. There are two extra headings.

a Different types of pasta
b Pasta: a world food
c Where to find a pasta restaurant
d How to cook perfect pasta
e Pasta in Italy

3 Read the article again and answer the questions.

1 How much pasta does the average Italian eat per year?
2 Why is pasta popular?
3 How many different types of pasta are there?
4 How can pasta be educational?
5 How does the writer like his/her pasta?
6 Does the writer think it's easy or difficult to make pasta?

4 a Work in pairs. Read the sentences. What does *it* refer to?

And **it** *is equally popular in a lot of other countries.* **It's** *tasty,* **it's** *filling and* **it's** *quick and easy to make.*

b Circle all the examples of *it* in the article. Which examples **don't** refer to pasta?

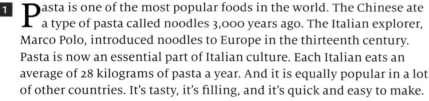

1 Pasta is one of the most popular foods in the world. The Chinese ate a type of pasta called noodles 3,000 years ago. The Italian explorer, Marco Polo, introduced noodles to Europe in the thirteenth century. Pasta is now an essential part of Italian culture. Each Italian eats an average of 28 kilograms of pasta a year. And it is equally popular in a lot of other countries. It's tasty, it's filling, and it's quick and easy to make.

2 Did you know that there are more than 350 different kinds of pasta shapes? You can buy pasta in almost any shape you can imagine. A lot of children even learn to write their first words with a plate of alphabet pasta! And you can serve it with all kinds of sauces: a spicy tomato sauce with a few olives, or a creamy sauce with cheese. Some people eat it with chocolate!

3 My favourite pasta sauce? It's very simple – olive oil, some black pepper and a little fresh Parmesan cheese, but not too much. And to make perfect pasta? Well, it depends on what kind of pasta you're cooking. It doesn't take much time at all – around seven or eight minutes is usually the ideal cooking time. Make sure that you have lots of water and that it is boiling when you add the pasta. Taste it before you serve it to make sure that it is *al dente* (still a little hard in the middle). You can't go wrong!

GRAMMAR

1 Work in pairs. Read the phrases, a–h. Which include

1 a countable noun?
2 an uncountable noun?

a How much pasta?
b How many different types of pasta?
c a lot of children
d a few olives
e a little fresh Parmesan cheese
f too much cheese
g some black pepper
h not much time

2 Complete 1–4 and a–d in the GRAMMAR PANEL ▪ .

3 a Work in pairs. Complete the questions with *much* or *many*.

1 How .... coffee do you drink every day? Do you think that's too .... coffee or is it OK?
2 How .... sweets, cakes or biscuits do you eat in a week? Do you think that's too .... ?
3 How .... fruit do you eat? And how .... vegetables?
4 How .... water do you drink? Or do you prefer to drink soft drinks?

b 💬 Ask and answer the questions.

4 💬 Write three more questions using *how much?* and *how many?* Ask and answer with the rest of the class.

SPEAKING

1 You are going to interview your classmates about their eating habits. Think of four or five questions to ask about

- things they like/don't like to eat or drink
- what time they eat
- where they eat and who they eat with
- snacks and eating between meals
- favourite foods.

Do you like...? Do you prefer... or...?
When/Where/Who do you usually...?
Do you ever...?

2 💬 Ask as many people as you can. Who has the most similar eating habits to you? Tell the rest of the class.

We both love spicy food. We both usually eat at home with our families. And we both love eating between meals.

QUANTIFIERS

Questions with *how much?* & *how many?*

how much?   how many?

Uncountable nouns

too much   a lot of

some   not much

1 part but not all ....
2 a large quantity ....
3 a small quantity ....
4 more than you need or want ....

Countable nouns

| too many | a lot of | some | a few/not many |

a ....   c ....

b ....   d ....

See page 148 for grammar reference and more practice.

■ TALK ABOUT DIFFERENT TYPES OF FOOD
■ DISCUSS ALTERNATIVES TO WASTING FOOD

LISTENING & READING

1 a Look at the advert. What is its message?

1 Buy only organic fruit.
2 Buy local fruit.
3 Don't waste food.

b Look at the image on page 159 and check your answer.

2 💬 Work in small groups. Discuss the questions.

1 Why do people throw food away?
2 What kind of food do people throw away most?

3 🔊 9.2 Listen to someone explaining the advert. Check your answers in 2.

4 a Listen again and complete the extracts.

1 It's sad but ....
2 That's .... million tonnes of food.
3 Fruit and vegetables are .... % of this.
4 The top five fruit and vegetables that go in the rubbish bin are .... , potatoes, ... , tomatoes and ....
5 We buy .... food.
6 Lots of people forget to put food in the .... in summer.
7 If you put fresh fruit and .... in the fridge, they stay fresh for longer.

b Check your answers in transcript 9.2 on pages 165–166.

5 💬 Work in pairs. Discuss the questions.

1 Do you think the facts you heard are true for your country, too? Why/Why not?
2 What can we do to waste less food? Think of at least three ideas.

6 a Compare your ideas in 5 to the ideas in the list.

1 Don't cook too much food – think about measurements, e.g. 120 grams of pasta per person.
2 Don't buy too much food – look at the sell-by dates on food and plan your shop.
3 Use leftovers (the food you leave on your plate at the end of a meal) for the next meal – use vegetables to make soups, or fruit to make juice.
4 Cook once, eat twice.

b Match the advice to the photos.

7 a Read the opinions and match them to the advice in 6a.

a	I don't like throwing food away. I try to measure food carefully and never cook more than I need.
b	I love inventing new ways of using leftovers. I use them to make a sauce, or put them in a sandwich.
c	When I cook I always make enough for two meals. That way I don't have to cook the next day!
d	I always buy more than I need. Going to the supermarket is a temptation. I try to make a list and keep to that!

b 💬 Do you do any of these things in your family?

SPEAKING

1 💬 Work in pairs. Match the photos to the food items. Do you usually eat each item or throw it away?

1 a piece of old pizza
2 a very ripe banana
3 leftover spaghetti
4 some dry bread
5 breakfast cereal past its sell-by date

2 💬 Think of some other food items and ask your partner's opinions.

PRONUNCIATION: /ʌ/, /ʊ/, /uː/

1 🔊 9.3 Listen to the sentence. Notice the pronunciation of the vowels in **bold**.

I love good food.

2 🔊 9.4 Listen and repeat the three words.

love /ʌ/   good /ʊ/   food /uː/

3 **a** Look at the words in the box. Match them to the vowel sounds in 2.

> choose   cook   fruit   look   much   put   soup   too

b 🔊 9.5 Listen and check.

4 **a** 🔊 9.6 Listen and complete the sentences with six of the words in 3a.

1 .... is good for you.
2 I love cold ....
3 I always .... fresh ....
4 People buy .... food.
5 .... fresh .... in the fridge.

b 💬 Rewrite the sentences so that they are true for you. Compare your sentences with a partner.

VOCABULARY: Talking about food

1 **a** Work in pairs. Add the food items in the box to the diagram. Some food can go in more than one category.

> ~~beans~~   burger   chips   fish   fruit   ice cream
> peas   pizza   ready meals   salad   sandwich
> vegetables

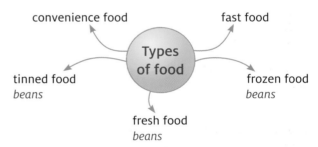

convenience food   fast food

Types of food

tinned food   frozen food
beans   *beans*

fresh food
beans

b Add one more word to each category. What type of food do you eat more of?

2 **a** Use vowels to complete the verbs in the diagram.

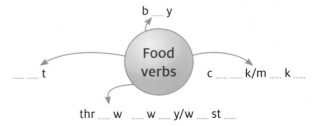

b ..... y

Food verbs

.... t   c .... k/m ..... k .....

thr ..... w ..... w ..... y/w ..... st .....

b Complete the questions with the verbs.

1 Do you ever .... takeaway food to eat at home? If yes, what kinds of food do you .... ?
2 Do you ever .... at your desk when you're working or studying? If yes, what do you usually .... ?
3 How often do you .... food at home? What kinds of food do you usually .... ?
4 If you have food on your plate at the end of a meal do you .... it .... or keep it for later?

3 💬 Work in small groups. Answer the questions.

TUNE IN

1 💬 Work in pairs. Read the menu and discuss the questions.

1 What kind of restaurant is it?
2 Are there any restaurants like this in your town?
3 Why are these restaurants so popular?

2 💬 What would you like to eat at this restaurant?

I think I'd like a starter and a main course.
I'd like a cheeseburger.

3 a 🔊 9.7 Listen to two friends, Owen and Sofia, ordering a meal from the menu. Complete the table with what they order.

	Owen	Sofia
Starter		
Main course		
Dessert		

b Was their order similar to yours?

FOCUS ON LANGUAGE

4 a Work in pairs. Mark the extracts Owen/ Sofia (OS) or waiter (W).

1 Can we have a table for two?
2 Are you ready to order?
3 Can I have the mozzarella and tomato salad, please?
4 Can I get you something to drink?
5 Some water for me, please.
6 Still or sparkling?
7 Would you like to see the dessert menu?
8 I'd like the brownie, please.
9 Can we have the bill, please?
10 Can I pay by card?

b 🔊 9.8 Listen and check.

> **❝ Intonation ❞**
>
> Listen again to the sentences in 4a. Do the speakers' voices go up ↗ or down ↘ ?
>
> Practise repeating the sentences using the correct intonation.

The Gourmet Burger Bar

Starters

Mozzarella and tomato salad
The finest mozzarella and beef tomatoes with fresh basil, pesto and extra virgin olive oil.

Chicken wings
Barbecued chicken wings served with homemade mayonnaise and green jalapeño peppers.

Burgers – Today's Specials

Habanero cheeseburger
100% organic beef, mozzarella cheese, hot and spicy sauce, salad and mayonnaise.

Veggie
Vegetarian burger, aubergine, goat's cheese and mixed-leaf salad.

Italian chicken
Organic chicken burger, avocado, pesto sauce and salad.

Desserts

Chocolate brownie and ice cream
Freshly baked brownie served with vanilla ice cream.

Fruit of the day
Fresh strawberries topped with a blend of honey and fresh yoghurt.

OVER TO YOU

5 💬 Work in groups of three. Student A, you are the waiter. Students B and C, you are the customers. Act out the scene.

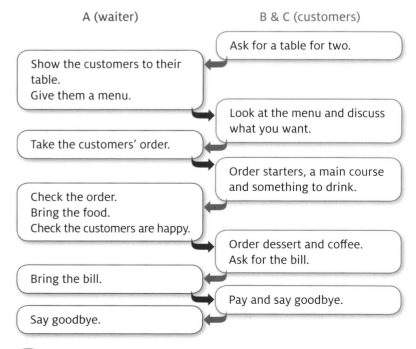

A (waiter) — B & C (customers)

- Ask for a table for two.
- Show the customers to their table. Give them a menu.
- Look at the menu and discuss what you want.
- Take the customers' order.
- Order starters, a main course and something to drink.
- Check the order. Bring the food. Check the customers are happy.
- Order dessert and coffee. Ask for the bill.
- Bring the bill.
- Pay and say goodbye.
- Say goodbye.

6 💬 Change roles. Turn to page 160 for a new restaurant and menu.

TUNE IN

1 💬 Look at the photos. How often do you eat like this?

2 **a** Read the sentences. Which are true for you?

- I eat out most days.
- I often eat out at weekends.
- I love eating out with friends.
- I only eat out on special occasions.
- I prefer to eat at home.

b 💬 Work in pairs. Compare your answers. Then discuss the questions.

1 When did you last eat out?
2 Where did you go?
3 Who did you go with?

PREPARE FOR TASK

3 🔊 9.9 Listen to Owen talking about his meal with another friend. Which of the adjectives in the box does he use? Is his general opinion positive or negative?

> busy   convenient   delicious   expensive   fast
> good   great   original   relaxed   slow

4 Listen again. Match the adjectives to the features.

1 the location (just round the corner)
2 you don't have to book
3 the atmosphere
4 the food
5 the menu
6 the burger
7 the service

5 Think about a bar, restaurant or café that you went to recently. Make notes about

- the place itself: pleasant/awful, old-fashioned/modern?
- the atmosphere: relaxed/formal?
- the food: boring/tasty, excellent/OK?
- the menu: varied, interesting, original?
- the staff: friendly/unfriendly?
- the service: fast/slow?
- the price: cheap/expensive?
- anything else: location, music, decor?

TASK

6 💬 Work in small groups. Talk about the restaurants you visited. Write your answers in the table below. Use the key.

7 💬 Work in pairs. Decide which place is best for

1 a business lunch or meeting.
2 a birthday party for a friend.
3 an evening out with your family.

REPORT BACK

8 💬 Discuss your decisions with the class.

Name of student	Name of restaurant	Location	Food	Atmosphere	Price
1					
2					
3					
4					

★★★★ out of this world   ★★★ very good   ★★ average   ★ don't go!

➡ Go to Review C, Unit 9, p. 104   ➡ Go to Writing bank 5, p. 156   **101**

VOCABULARY

The weather

1 a Complete the weather nouns with vowels.

s ..... n   f ..... g   ..... c .....
w ..... n d   s n ..... w   c l .... d

b Transform them into adjectives.

2 💬 Work in pairs. Discuss the questions.

1 What's the weather like now?
2 What was it like yesterday?
3 What's the weather usually like in your town in autumn, winter, spring and summer?
4 What do you do in extreme weather – when it's really hot, cold, rainy, etc.?

Transport

3 a Rank the forms of transport in order of preference (1–7) for use in your town.

> motorbike   car   bike   bus   train   subway   taxi

b 💬 Work in pairs. Discuss the questions.

1 Which form of transport do you usually use?
2 Which did you use today?
3 How was your journey? How long did it take?

4 🔊R11 Listen to Paul and Barbara discussing transport in Lyon. Mark the statements true (T) or false (F).

1 Paul says the new bike service is really cheap.
2 Barbara believes bikes and scooters are equally popular.
3 Paul says that people drive cars a lot because of the weather.
4 The price of petrol is expensive at the moment.

5 💬 What transport culture does your town/city have? Do people travel by car, scooter, bike or public transport? Why?

Public transport is slow here because the traffic is bad, but it's cheap.

GRAMMAR

Past simple

1 💬 Work in pairs. Think about the first time you did something. What did you do? When was it? Where were you? Who was with you? Did you like the experience?

The first time I went abroad: It was four years ago – I went to Greece with my family. It was our summer holiday. I had a great time!

2 a Write the past simple form of the verbs.

decide ....   do ....   go ....   travel ....
stop ....   have ....   wait ....   stay ....

b Write a paragraph about a recent trip. Try to use as many of the verbs as possible.

3 💬 Work in pairs. Ask your partner about his/her trip. Was it similar or different to yours?

FUNCTIONAL LANGUAGE

Using public transport

1 Write the words in the correct order.

1 next When bus is to city centre the the ?
2 you me take the to Can please train station ?
3 long How take get to to does the cathedral it ?
4 train this Does go the park to ?

2 a Read the questions again. Where are the people who are asking the questions? Who are they asking?

b 💬 Work in pairs. Continue the conversations.

■ LOOKING BACK

- Tell a partner what you did last weekend.
- Can you remember what the weather was like every day last week?
- Think of five things you did regularly when you were 10 years old. Compare your answers with a partner.

VOCABULARY
Talking about the news

1 💬 Work in pairs. Think of five different types of news, e.g. sports.

Which are you
1 always interested in?
2 sometimes interested in, it depends on the stories?
3 never interested in? Why?

2 💬 Discuss the questions.
1 What is the main story in the news today?
2 Did you know about this story before, or was it new to you?
3 How did you find out about it?
4 Would you like to know more about it?
5 How can you find out more?

Lexical sets

3 **a** Look at the groups of words. Which word in each group is not part of that lexical set?
1 doctor pandemic hospital ticket
2 concert alert festival band
3 goal virus victory score

b Work in pairs. Match the lexical sets in **a** to the types of news.
a entertainment   b health   c sports

4 💬 Think of three words to add to each lexical set. Then think of a story for each set. Take it in turns to tell your partner as much as you can about the stories.

Collocations

5 **a** Complete the questions.
1 Do you ever .... music festivals? Are there any big festivals in your area? When and where do they take place? Do you usually go? Why/Why not?
2 Did your country .... any medals in the last Olympics? Which sports is your country famous for? Do you play any of them?
3 What type of film do you usually .... ? What's your favourite film? Why?
4 Do you often .... colds? What do you usually do to help you feel better?

b 💬 Choose one of the groups of questions in **a**. Discuss them with a partner.

GRAMMAR
Past simple: irregular verbs

1 Write the verbs in the past simple.
1 I .... (write) about 20 text messages yesterday.
2 I .... (read) the news headlines on the internet this morning.
3 I .... (send) my friend an email for her birthday.
4 I .... (meet) my friends for a coffee.
5 I .... (speak) to my boss about a problem at work.
6 I .... (make) a mistake in my English homework.

2 💬 Are the sentences true for you? If not, write sentences with the same verbs that are true for you. Compare your answers with a partner.

Sequencers

3 **a** Look at the actions. Which did you do this morning?

> read the newspaper   have a coffee   get a bus
> listen to the radio   have a shower   call a friend
> go shopping   go to work   go to class

b 💬 What order did you do them in? Tell a partner. Use sequencers to explain the order.

4 💬 Were your mornings similar or very different?

FUNCTIONAL LANGUAGE
Responding to news

1 🔊R12 Listen to some people announcing some news. Choose the best response in the box to each piece of news.

> Did they? When?   Did she? I didn't know that!
> Oh, that's great news!   Oh no! What a shame!

2 💬 Work in pairs. Student A, turn to page 160. Student B, turn to page 161. Take it in turns to respond to your partner's news.

◼ LOOKING BACK
- What's the most memorable news story in this unit? Why?
- What good news and bad news did you have recently? Can you describe what the news was?
- How many irregular past simple verbs can you now use? How can you remember them?

VOCABULARY
Food & drink

1 a Work in pairs. Look at the food pyramid. How many foods can you name in two minutes?

b 💬 Discuss the questions.
- Which are your favourite foods?
- Are there any foods you don't like or can't eat?

2 a Match the words to the categories.

1 verbs	a	spicy, sweet, filling, _____
2 measuring food and drink	b	a bowl of, a slice of, a piece of, _____
3 types of food	c	eat, cook, waste, _____
4 adjectives to describe food	d	fast, fresh, tinned, _____

b Add one more word to each category. Then think of two more categories and four words for each one.

GRAMMAR
Countable & uncountable nouns

1 <u>Underline</u> the correct words to complete the descriptions.

Breakfast
I had (1)*a coffee / some coffees* and (2)*a slice / some slice* of toast with (3)*a / ø* butter and (4)*honey / honeys*.

Lunch
I had some (5)*salad / salads*, (6)*a / a bowl of* soup and some (7)*bread / breads*.

Evening meal
I had (8)*spaghetti / spaghettis* with (9)*a / some* seafood and a glass of (10)*wine / some wines*.

2 💬 Write descriptions of what you had to eat yesterday. Compare your descriptions with a partner.

Quantifiers

3 Complete the questions using *much* or *many*.

1 How _____ fruit did you eat yesterday?
2 How _____ different vegetables did you eat?
3 How _____ cups of coffee did you have?
4 How _____ water did you drink?

4 💬 Work in pairs. Ask and answer the questions in **3**. Who has the healthiest diet? You or your partner?

FUNCTIONAL LANGUAGE
Eating out

1 Order the phrases to form short dialogues.

1 a Certainly. Come with me.
  b Yes, can we have a table for two, please?
  c Are you waiting for a table?
2 a Yes, the buffet for me, please.
  b A house salad, please.
  c And for you, sir?
  d Are you ready to order?
3 a And some water, please.
  b Sparkling, please.
  c Can we have two beers, please?
  d Can I get you something to drink?
  e Still or sparkling?
4 a Yes, thanks. Can we have the bill, please?
  b Is everything OK?
  c Certainly. Just a moment.
5 a Can I pay by card?
  b Thank you.
  c OK, here you are.
  d I'm sorry, we only accept cash.

2 a 🔊 R13 Listen and check.

b 💬 Practise the dialogues in groups of three.

3 Use adjectives to complete the email.

> We went to that new restaurant I told you about yesterday. It was really _____ . It's very _____ , just two doors down from the office. The food is _____ . It's quite simple, but really fresh. And the staff are very _____ . We must go there together next time you're in town.
> P x

▪ LOOKING BACK

- Think of five questions you can ask about food and eating.
- Think of five things you can say about your eating habits.
- What other foods would you like to know the name of in English?
- Can you describe your favourite meal?

LISTENING

1 R14 Listen to Ruth talking about her language learning experiences. Answer the questions.

1 What two languages does she talk about?
2 Where did she learn the first one?
3 And the second one?
4 What did she enjoy most about learning the second language?

2 a Listen again. Match the statements to the two languages.

1 I can communicate in simple situations.
2 Reading really helps me to learn.
3 I passed all my exams.
4 We did a lot of speaking.
5 We did a lot of translating.
6 We played a lot of language games.

b Are any of the statements in 2a true about your language learning experiences? Compare your answers with a partner.

SPEAKING

3 a Work in pairs. Order the activities from 1 to 6 (1 = most important, 6 = least important).

☐ learning about grammar and pronunciation
☐ speaking with correction
☐ speaking with no correction
☐ listening to real conversations
☐ reading books or articles in English
☐ writing short texts and messages in English

b Compare your answers with the rest of the class.

4 a Think about five different kinds of activities you did in class in the last three units.

b Show your list to a partner and answer the questions. Compare your ideas with the rest of the class.

1 Which activity helped you most? Why?
2 Which activity did you enjoy most? Why?
3 What kind of activities would you like to do more of in the next three units?

QUICK CHECK

Complete the checklist below.

Can you…	Yes, I can.	Yes, more or less.	I need to look again.
1 talk about what happened in the past?	☐	☐	☐
2 talk about the weather?	☐	☐	☐
3 discuss forms of transport?	☐	☐	☐
4 talk about the news?	☐	☐	☐
5 respond to news?	☐	☐	☐
6 talk about food and your eating habits?	☐	☐	☐
7 order a meal in a restaurant?	☐	☐	☐
8 describe a meal?	☐	☐	☐

Compare your answers with a partner.

• What else do you know now after studying units 7–9?
• Do you need to look again at any of the sections?
• Do you need any extra help from your teacher?

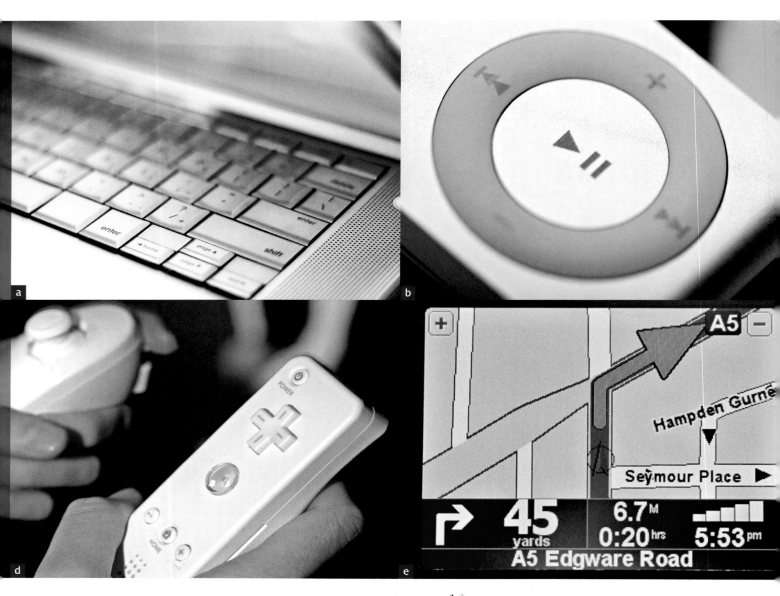

1 a Work in pairs to complete A in the KEY VOCABULARY PANEL ▓ .

   b 💬 Discuss the questions.
   ● Which gadgets do you have?
   ● Which do you use every day?
   ● Which is your favourite and least favourite? Why?

2 💬 Look again at the list of functions in A. Answer the questions.
   ● What did people use 30 years ago to do these things?
   ● Which of these 'old-fashioned' gadgets do you still use, if any?

3 a 🔊 10.1 Listen to two friends. Which of the gadgets are they talking about?

   b Listen again and complete B in the KEY VOCABULARY PANEL ▓ .

4 🔊 10.2 Look at the adjectives in B again and find seven pairs of opposites. Listen and check.

5 💬 Think of a gadget you have. Which of the adjectives in B can you use to describe it? Tell a partner about it.

I have an old digital camera. It's big and heavy. I'd like to buy a new one – something small and light.

KEY VOCABULARY

Technology

Gadgets

A Match the photos (a–f) to the gadgets.

> computer game digital camera satnav
> flatscreen TV laptop MP3 player

> **NOTICE**
>
> *gadget* = a small piece of equipment that does something useful or impressive

- Match the gadgets to the functions. Some gadgets have more than one function.

  1 You can use it to take photos.
  2 You can use it to store information.
  3 You can use it to listen to music.
  4 You can use it to get directions.
  5 You can use it to watch films and video clips.
  6 You can use it to play games.

Adjectives to describe gadgets

B 🔊 10.1 Tick the adjectives in the box that you hear.

> heavy new difficult small good
> light cheap quick bad old slow
> expensive big easy

Parts of a computer

C Label the computer with the words in the box.

> ~~screen~~ mouse keyboard webcam
> DVD drive speakers Wi-Fi memory stick

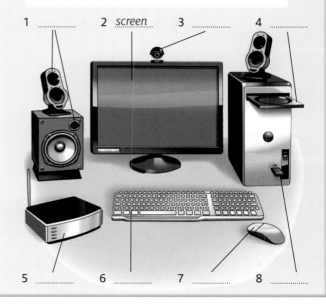

1 .... 2 *screen* 3 .... 4 ....

5 .... 6 .... 7 .... 8 ....

6 Work in pairs to complete C in the KEY VOCABULARY PANEL ▪.

7 a 💬 Discuss the questions with a partner.

- Do you use a computer?
- What kind of computer do you use (a PC, a laptop, a netbook)?
- What do you use it for?
- Does it have all the features in the picture in C?
- Are you happy with it, or would you like a new one? Why?

b Report back to the class.

Marek uses a computer at work and he has a laptop at home. He likes his laptop, it's new. But he wants a new computer at work. It's old and slow.

LISTENING & SPEAKING

1 a 💬 Work in pairs. Look at the photo and discuss the questions.

- What kind of gadget does it show?
- What can it do?

b 🔊 10.3 Listen and check.

2 Listen again and complete the description from an online magazine.

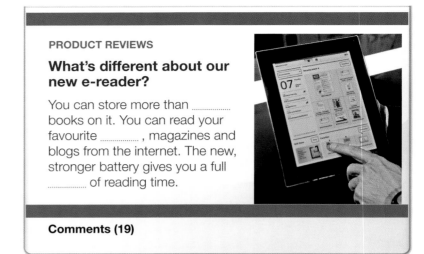

PRODUCT REVIEWS

What's different about our new e-reader?

You can store more than _____ books on it. You can read your favourite _____ , magazines and blogs from the internet. The new, stronger battery gives you a full _____ of reading time.

Comments (19)

3 💬 Work in pairs. Think of two advantages and two disadvantages of an e-reader. Compare your answers with the class. Would you like to buy an e-reader? Why/Why not?

Lucia

I have a screen at work, I look at it all day. I don't want another screen for reading. I'm **happier** reading a real book. I like to feel the pages, turn them over – it's **more relaxing**.

Paul

It's definitely **more expensive** than buying normal books. Just think, you can buy maybe 150–200 books for the price of one e-reader! And it's not only the money for the gadget: then you need to buy the e-books as well.

Kostis

Paul, imagine carrying 100 books with you everywhere you go! And remember, e-books are **cheaper** than paper books. I love my e-reader! And the new model is even **better** – it's **bigger**, the battery's **stronger**... I'm going to get one as soon as I can!

Kurt

I read the newspaper on my e-reader on the train every morning. It's definitely **better** than the conventional paper – **more comfortable**, **easier**... and it saves trees. This is the future, I think!

READING

1 Read the comments by four people. Does anybody make the same points as you in LISTENING & SPEAKING 3? What other advantages and disadvantages do the people talk about?

2 Read the comments again and answer the questions.

1 Which people are negative and which are positive about the e-reader?
2 Who owns an e-reader already? How do you know?
3 Who wants to buy a new one? How do you know?

3 Work in pairs. Mark the sentences true (T) or false (F).

1 Lucia likes reading e-books on her computer.
2 Paul says the e-reader is expensive.
3 Kostis prefers the old model.
4 Kurt is not very enthusiastic.

GRAMMAR

1 Work in pairs. Look at the words in **bold** in the comments on page 108. Complete 1–7 in the GRAMMAR PANEL ■ .

2 **a** Complete the sentences using the correct comparative form of the adjectives in brackets.

1 Reading a good book is .... *(relaxing)* than watching a TV programme.
2 Digital cameras are .... *(easy)* to use than conventional cameras.
3 Advances in technology make our lives .... *(safe)* and .... *(happy)*.

b 💬 Do you agree with the sentences? Why/Why not?

3 **a** Work in pairs. Look at the photos. Write sentences comparing the two models. Use the adjectives in the box.

big   cheap   expensive   fashionable   small

b 💬 Which one would you prefer to buy? Why?

4 💬 Work in pairs. Turn to page 160. Look at the pictures and follow the instructions. Compare your answers with the class.

■ COMPARATIVE ADJECTIVES

We use comparative adjectives to compare and contrast two things:
The e-reader is lighter than a book.

We use the preposition **than** with comparative adjectives:
The old model is heavier than the new one.

Forming comparative adjectives

One syllable: adjective + -er
fast → faster   cheap → (1) ....   strong → (2) ....

With some one-syllable adjectives the spelling changes:
big → (3) ....

Two syllables ending in -y: change -y to -i and add -er
easy → (4) ....   happy → (5) ....

Two syllables or more: *more* + adjective
expensive → more expensive   comfortable → (6) ....

Irregular adjectives
good → (7) ....   bad → worse

See page 149 for grammar reference and more practice.

SPEAKING

1 Work in pairs. Look at the gadgets below. Think of two adjectives to describe each gadget. Use a dictionary to help you.

2 **a** Complete the sentence comparing any two of the gadgets.
This gadget is .... than the other one.

b 💬 Read your sentence to the class. Can they guess which two gadgets you're talking about? Do they agree?

3 💬 Which gadget would you like to get as a birthday present? Why?

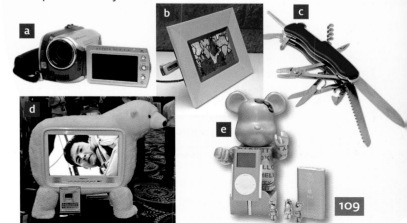

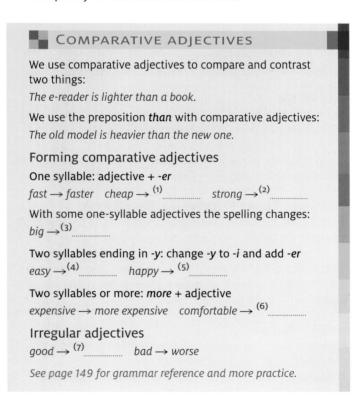

SPEAKING

1 a 💬 Work in pairs. Look at the photos. What are the people doing on their phones? Think of three other things you can do with your phone.

b Compare your list with the class. How many functions are there in total? Which do you use most? Why?

I send text messages, it's cheaper.

> ### NOTICE *MOBILE OR CELL?*
>
> *Mobile phone* is British English, *cell phone* is American English.
>
> We often say *mobile* or *cell* on its own, without *phone*:
>
> *Where's my mobile/cell?*

2 a 💬 Work in groups. You are going to take part in a survey on mobile phones. Turn to page 161.

b Report the group's answers to the class.

Dimitri's cell phone wakes him up in the morning with the alarm – it's the first thing he sees!

3 a 💬 Work in pairs. Are the items advantages or disadvantages of mobile phones?

- anti-social
- useful in emergencies
- cost
- you are never alone
- people know where you are
- public phones are terrible
- they can easily break

b Can you think of any other advantages or disadvantages? Share your ideas with the class.

READING

1 Work in pairs. Read the headline of the article below. What mobile phone functions do you think the article will talk about?

2 Read the article and check your answers in **1**. What is each person planning to do with his/her phone?

3 a Read the article again. Which person talks about

1 public information messages?   3 phone rental?
2 money transfer?

b Which programme do you think helps people most?

CELL PHONES FIGHTING POVERTY

Cell phones are changing the lives of millions of people around the world. They are giving them new job opportunities, improved medical conditions and the chance to make plans for the future. Here are a few true stories from people who are just receiving this technology.

Safaricom, Kenya
Samson lives in Nairobi and sends money home to his mother, who lives in the country. The bank system can be slow and very expensive. In the past he often lost money.
'Now I'm going to use my cell phone to send money to my mother. She can text me when the money arrives. It's quicker, safer and easier. Isn't that great?'

Grameen Village Phone Programme, Bangladesh
Hasina bought a phone from the Grameen programme for $110. She pays $2.50 a week to the programme. She rents the phone to people in her village for a small fee.
'I get about $25 a month from the phone. I'm not going to spend all the money. I'm saving it. I'm going to open a small grocery store with the money – I want to give my family some kind of future.'

FrontlineSMS, Malawi
Karen is a volunteer nurse. She works with HIV patients. The nurses have big problems contacting peope who live in remote villages.
'We're going to use the new phones to send text messages to patients with information about medicine and health care. We're going to distribute about 200 cell phones to remote villages. It's great news for rural Malawi.'

GRAMMAR

1 Work in pairs. Read the article again. Match the two halves of the sentences.

1 Samson is going to
2 Hasina isn't going to
3 The nurses are going to
4 The villagers are going to

a distribute 200 phones to remote villages.
b spend all the money she makes.
c send money to his mother.
d share the phones.

2 Underline all the examples of *going to* in the article and 1. Choose the correct option to complete 1–7 in the GRAMMAR PANEL ▇ .

3 Complete the sentences with the correct form of *going to*.

1 It .... be difficult to start with.
2 We .... teach two or three people in each village how to use the phone.
3 We .... limit the use of the phones to medical uses.
4 One man .... call his daughter.

4 a ◀))) 10.4 Listen to Karen talking about the project in Malawi and check your answers in 3.

b Listen again. Why are they going to do the things in 3?

5 a Write questions using *going to*.

1 you/stay in tonight?
2 you/do any shopping after class?
3 What/you/do next weekend?
4 What/you/do next summer?

b 💬 Work in pairs. Ask and answer the questions.

6 💬 Change pairs. Tell your new partner about your previous partner's plans.

GOING TO

We use *be + going to + infinitive* to talk about future plans.

+	I (1)*'m / 're / 's* going to send money to my mother.
	Hasina (2)*'m / 're / 's* going to open a grocery store.
–	You (3)*'m not / aren't / isn't* going to get a new phone.
?	(4)*Am / Are / Is* they going to distribute new phones?
	(5)*Am / Are / Is* she going to spend all the money?
Yes/No	Yes, they (6)*am / are / is*.
	No, she (7)*'m not / aren't / isn't*.

See page 149 for grammar reference and more practice.

PRONUNCIATION: /gənə/

1 ◀))) 10.5 Listen to the exchange. Notice the pronunciation of *going to*.

/gənə/
A What are you going to do?
/gənə/
B I'm going to wait and see.

2 a ◀))) 10.6 Listen to four questions. Match them to the answers.

a Youssef and Kelly.
b In the bar.
c Yes, I am.
d I don't know. Go for something to eat, maybe?

b Listen again and repeat the questions.

3 💬 Work in pairs. Talk about your plans for the evening.

VOCABULARY: Communication

1 Look at the pictures. What's the person doing in each?

2 a Work in pairs. Write the verbs on the correct line. Some verbs can go on both lines.

> answer call back email call
> text reply ring phone

contact: *call,* _____

respond: *answer,* _____

b Which verbs do you use

1 for talking on the phone?
2 for communicating by text or email?

3 💬 Work in pairs. Discuss which form of communication in **1** you think is best for the situations.

- You want to wish a friend happy birthday.
- You know you're going to be late getting home.
- You want to discuss a project with a colleague.
- You need to contact your parents overseas.
- You need to organise a meeting with a large group of people.

4 a 💬 Work in small groups. Think of three or four other ways we use to communicate with people.

b Match the adjectives in the box to the forms of communication in **1**. Then answer the questions.

> fast slow cheap expensive personal
> impersonal easy complicated

- Which do you use regularly?
- Which do you never use? Why?

LISTENING

1 Work in pairs. Match the photos to the captions.

> In memoriam
>
> It's No Pants Day!
>
> NY pillow fight
>
> A silent rave

2 a 💬 Look at the photos again and answer the questions.

1 Where are the people and what are they doing?
2 What do the photos have in common?
3 Which is different? Why?

b 🔊 10.7 Listen to a TV interview about the events in the photos and check your answers.

3 a Listen again. Mark the statements true (T) or false (F). If false, correct them.

1 Flash mobs meet in private.
2 These meetings last a short time.
3 People find out about them from the news.
4 The silent rave happened in New York.
5 The Espanyol fans organised the event by phone and text message.
6 Frederic doesn't have a favourite flash mob.

b 💬 Would you like to take part in a flash mob event? Why/Why not?

GRAMMAR

1 ◀))) 10.8 Listen to a conversation between two people and answer the questions.

1 What kind of event are they planning?
2 What time is it going to take place?
3 Where are they going to meet?

2 **a** Work in pairs. Look at the extracts and circle the correct answer.

| JON | Hi! Did you get the message? |
| CORINA | Yes, but I deleted (1)*it / them* by mistake. |

| CORINA | Did you text Tomas? I know (2)*he / him* 's really interested. |
| JON | No, I don't have his number. Can you call (3)*he / him*? |

| CORINA | Sure. What about Dan and Carlos? (4)*They / Them* definitely want to come, too. And Sue. (5)*She / Her* loved the last one! |
| JON | Oh no, I forgot about (6)*she / her*. |

| CORINA | What time are (7)*we / us* going to meet? How many of (8)*we / us* are going to be there? |

| JON | Bring your pillow, remember! And pass the message on! |
| CORINA | No problem. Let (9)*I / me* know if there's a change of plan! |

b Listen again and check your answers.

3 Work in pairs. Read the GRAMMAR PANEL ■. Are your answers in 2 subject pronouns or object pronouns? Complete 1–6 in the GRAMMAR PANEL ■.

4 **a** Complete the voicemail messages with a subject or object pronoun.

1 Hi! It's Tracey. Nothing urgent, but can you call .... when you get a minute? Bye!
2 Where are you? It's Adriana and João. Let .... know where you are. We're worried.
3 Hello. This is a message for Stefano. I spoke to the lawyers. Can you meet .... tomorrow at ten? Thanks. Let .... know asap! Bye!
4 Hi. This is Paul. Julie's still waiting for the book. Can you send .... to .... soon? Thanks! Bye!

b ◀))) 10.9 Listen and check.

■ PERSONAL PRONOUNS

We use personal pronouns instead of the names of people and things.
Subject pronouns come before the verb:
***I**'m going to call Tomas.*
Object pronouns come after the verb:
*I'm going to call **him**.*
We also use object pronouns after prepositions:
*Tomas is going to come with **us**.*

Subject	Object
I	(1) ....
you	you
he	(2) ....
(3)	her
it	(4) ....
we	(5) ....
(6)	them

See page 149 for grammar reference and more practice.

SPEAKING

1 💬 Work in groups to organise a flash mob in your town. Use the prompts to help you.

● My flash mob is going to be... (*fun/a protest/ something else*).
● It's going to take place in... (*place*) at... (*time*).
● I'm going to tell people via... (*text message, blog, etc.*).
● We're going to do... (*activity*) during the flash mob.
● It's going to last... (*minutes/hours*).

2 💬 Compare your ideas with the class. Are any of the ideas similar? Which do you think is the best event? Why?

British phone users want simpler phones

New phones are more difficult to use and have too many applications that a lot of us are not interested in. Many users are only interested in texting and making calls. Functions like taking photos and listening to music are popular, but not essential. Most of us are more interested in good sound quality, good coverage and, most importantly, checking the time!

However, there's the other extreme – the minority that loves these new applications. Did you know that now you can get a device that allows you to identify birdsong, another that tunes a musical instrument and even one that repels mosquitoes (the phone produces a noise that scares them away)! Can you believe it?

TUNE IN

1 Read a short article about British mobile phone users. Tick the functions mentioned.

1 making a phone call
2 sending a text message
3 receiving email
4 taking photos
5 shopping
6 listening to music
7 checking the time

2 Read the article again and answer the questions.

1 What other functions or features does the article talk about?
2 Which are the most important for British phone users?
3 Do you think mobile phone users in your country think the same? Why/Why not?

3 a 🔊 10.10 Listen to three short conversations. What functions or features do the people talk about?

b Listen again. What does each person want to do with the phone?

FOCUS ON LANGUAGE

4 a Match the functions to the instructions.

1 making a call
2 sending a photo
3 checking the time

a Click here – see where it says 'more'?
b Click on 'menu'.
c Press that button on the side.
d Press the button with the green phone.
e Select 'camera'.
f Select 'send'.
g Key in the number.

b Listen to 10.10 again and check. Which instructions are introduced using

1 just?
2 now?
3 then?

5 💬 Read transcript 10.10 on page 166. Are the instructions the same for your phone? Show your partner how to do the three functions in 4 on your phone.

> **❝ Checking understanding ❞**
>
> 1 *See?*   2 *Yeah, that's it!*   3 *Now I get it!*
>
> Which person is
> a saying that they now understand the instruction?
> b checking that the other person understands?
> c confirming that the other person is following the instructions correctly?
>
> 🔊 10.11 Listen. Does the speaker's voice go up ➚ or down ➘ ?
>
> Listen again and repeat.

OVER TO YOU

6 Work in pairs. Think of another useful gadget. Write instructions to explain one of its main functions.

7 Read your instructions to the class. Can they guess what the gadget is?

Internet forums can answer any question!

Do you know the saying, 'two heads are better than one'? Well, imagine how good 100 heads, or 1,000 heads or 100,000 heads can be! This is the idea behind internet forums, where you can ask a question, any question, online and get answers from people all over the world. Some of the answers are good; some of them are not so good. But when there are millions of people ready to answer your questions, sooner or later the answer will be very, very good – if not perfect! We tried it out to see. We posted this simple question and then waited for the answers.

I'm planning a trip to New York City. When is the best time to visit the city? Thanks.

Here are the answers.

1) October. Autumn colours are beautiful in Central Park and it's low season, so it will be cheaper to get a room.
☆☆☆☆☆ Rate the answer.

2) Christmas vacation, wonderful time for all your presents and it might snow! So romantic!
☆☆☆☆☆ Rate the answer.

3) August is the best month – all the New Yorkers go away then and you can have the city to yourself.
☆☆☆☆☆ Rate the answer.

As I said, not all good, but one was exactly what I wanted to know! Guess which one it was.

TUNE IN

1 Work in pairs. Look at the photos and discuss the questions.

- Where are the people?
- What questions do you think they want to ask?
- Who do you think is going to give the answer?
- Do you know someone who can give you the best answer to these questions?
  Which is the best computer to buy?
  Can you recommend a good restaurant?

2 Read the article about internet forums. How can they help you get the right answer to your questions?

NOTICE ANY

You can use *any* with a singular noun in affirmative sentences to show that there is no limit to the possibilities:
any question = all possible questions

3 Read the answers again and rate them

- not so good.　　　　　　　　★☆☆☆☆
- good.　　　　　　　　　　　★★★☆☆
- perfect – just what I needed to know.　★★★★★

PREPARE FOR TASK

4 **a** Work in pairs. Put the words in the correct order to make questions.

1 visit to best When town/city your is time the ?
2 the is make What way best new to friends ?
3 fast How I get really fit can ?

b Write answers to the questions. Compare your answers with the rest of the class. Who gave the best answer?

TASK

5 **a** Work in pairs. Write your own forum question. Share it with the class.

　b Write an answer to the forum questions from the other pairs in the class.

6 Read all the answers to your question. Rate the answers using the star system in 3.

REPORT BACK

7 Present and explain your ratings to the class.

➡ Go to Review D, Unit 10, p. 136

11 A WORKING LIFE

1 💬 Work in pairs. Look at the photos. Do you think they are from

1 an article about the current job situation?
2 a website for a job agency?
3 a poster selling university courses?

2 Work in pairs to complete A and B in the KEY VOCABULARY PANEL ▮ .

3 🔊))11.1 Listen to Caleb, Bel and Krista talking about their jobs. Which job does each one do?

4 a Match the questions, 1–4, to answers a–d. Who gives each answer, Caleb, Bel or Krista?

1 Where do you work?
2 Do you like your job?
3 What do you like about it?
4 Why do you hate it?

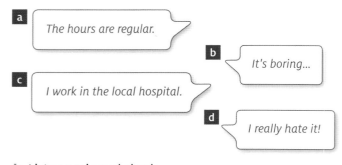

a *The hours are regular.*

b *It's boring...*

c *I work in the local hospital.*

d *I really hate it!*

b Listen again and check.

Work & jobs

Occupations

A Match the photos to 12 of the jobs in the box.

> hairdresser chef soldier dentist teacher
> lawyer banker computer specialist nurse
> builder factory worker doctor architect
> police officer waiter company director
> accountant journalist sports instructor
> office worker

● 💬 Discuss the questions. In which jobs do you
- work long hours?
- work regular hours?
- do hard physical work?
- work with money?
- travel a lot?
- make important decisions?
- help people?

> **NOTICE** *JOB & WORK*
>
> *Job* is countable. We say: *He has a great job!*
> *Work* is uncountable. We say: *It's hard work.*
> How do you say *job* and *work* in your language?

Adjectives to describe jobs

B Look at the adjectives to describe jobs. Match the adjectives to the jobs in **A**.

> active badly paid boring creative
> dangerous interesting responsible
> satisfying stressful well paid

● 💬 Which job did you want to do as a child? Would you still like to do this job? Why/Why not?

5 a 💬 Work in pairs. Ask and answer the quiz questions. What do you think the perfect job for your partner is?

What is your ideal job? Do our quick quiz and find out!

1 Do you prefer to work a) in a team? b) alone?

2 Are you happier working a) in an office? b) outside? c) from home?

3 Do you like a) giving orders? b) following orders?

4 Do you prefer to a) make things? b) sell things?

5 Do you like being a) active? b) creative? c) responsible for other people?

6 What's most important to you? a) money b) free time c) job satisfaction

b Report back to the class.

READING

1 💬 Work in pairs. Read the job satisfaction survey. Which three things do you think are the most important?

The job satisfaction survey

What's most important for you?

- ☐ friendly colleagues
- ☐ good pay
- ☐ a relaxed working atmosphere
- ☐ flexible hours
- ☐ a good boss
- ☐ being creative
- ☐ making a difference to people's lives
- ☐ good holidays

2 Look at the headline and the photo in the article below. Why do you think hairdressers are the happiest profession?

3 Read the article and check your answer in **2**. Which three things in the survey in **1** are most important to hairdressers?

4 Mark the sentences true (T) or false (F).
1 Hairdressers don't work at the weekend.
2 Hairdressers are generally well paid.
3 Hairdressing is a creative job.
4 Being happy and friendly is part of the job.
5 Salons are often relaxed and friendly places.
6 Hairdressers usually wear formal clothes.

5 💬 Work in pairs. Discuss the questions.
- Is your hairdresser a happy person?
- Would you like to be a hairdresser? Why/Why not?

If you want to be happy in your job, be a hairdresser! A recent survey showed that hairdressers are the happiest profession in a list of over eighty different jobs.

But why? Is it the money? No. Hairdressing is certainly not one of the best-paid professions around. But hairdressers are a lot happier than doctors, lawyers or bankers, who are all better paid. So money isn't the answer. And it isn't the hours either. Hairdressers often have to work long hours, and weekends are their busiest time.

So, what is the answer?

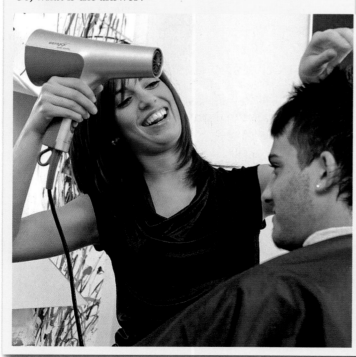

Hairdressers:
the *happiest* profession

'I love my job because I make people happy quickly,' said one hairdresser. 'I love the creative side of the job – that's the most important thing for me,' said another. 'A good hairdresser chats with the customers, and smiles and jokes. It's a very important part of the job,' said the manager of one salon.

So it seems that a creative job with friendly workmates and a relaxed working atmosphere is much more important than the long hours and the low pay.

'I don't need to get up early in the morning, wear a suit and tie, or sit in front of a computer all day. The customers I work with are my best friends. When I'm in the salon, I feel like I'm at home! And you ask me why I'm happy?'

So, if you're unhappy in your job, or looking for a change of career, you know what to do! Become a hairdresser!

GRAMMAR

1 a Mark the sentences true (T) or false (F).

1 Hairdressers and their customers are usually **best** friends.
2 A friendly smile is the **most important** thing for a good hairdresser.
3 Hairdressers are the **richest** profession.
4 Saturday is one of their **busiest** days.

b Complete 1–4 in the GRAMMAR PANEL ■ with the words in **bold**.

2 a Work in pairs. Write the superlative form of the adjectives in brackets.

1 Who has the .... (*creative*) job, an actor, a teacher or an architect?
2 Who has the .... (*easy*) job, a nurse, a builder or a soldier?
3 Which do you think is the .... (*interesting*) job, reporter, chef or film director?
4 Which is the .... (*old*) job, doctor, lawyer, soldier or teacher?

b 💬 Ask and answer the questions.

3 💬 Write two more similar questions. Ask and answer with the rest of the class.

■ SUPERLATIVE ADJECTIVES

We use superlative adjectives to compare or contrast something with all the other items in a group:
Hairdressers are the happiest profession. (= Hairdressers are happier than all the other professions.)

Forming superlative adjectives

One syllable: adjective + -*est*
old → *oldest*   *rich* → (1) ....

Two syllables ending in -*y*: change -*y* to -*i* and add -*est*
happy → *happiest*   *busy* → (2) ....

Two syllables or more: *most* + adjective
important → (3) ....

Irregular adjectives

good → (4) ....   *bad* → *worst*

We often use *the* or possessive adjectives (*my*, *your*, *his*) with superlative adjectives:
*It's **the** best job.*   *She's **my** best friend.*

See page 150 for grammar reference and more practice.

SPEAKING & LISTENING

1 💬 Work in pairs. Look at the photo. This person is a member of the second happiest profession. Discuss the questions.

- What does she do?
- What is she doing in the photo?
- Why do you think she enjoys her job?

2 a 💬 Which do you think are the other top five happiest and unhappiest occupations?

b 🔊 11.2 Listen to the news report and compare your answers.

3 a 💬 Look at the jobs in the box. Which are

1 the five worst-paid jobs in the UK?
2 the five best-paid jobs?
3 the five most stressful jobs?

> air traffic controllers   bankers   best-selling writers
> call centre workers   celebrities   cleaners
> fast-food restaurant staff   footballers   hairdressers
> inner-city teachers   junior doctors   lawyers
> miners   police officers   school cooks

b Turn to page 161 to check your answers. Were you surprised by any of the answers? Do you think the answers are different for your country?

LISTENING & SPEAKING

1   a 💬 Work in pairs. Look at the job advertisement. Discuss the questions.

- What does a caretaker usually do?
- What do you think an island caretaker does?
- Why do you think this is 'the best job ever'?

Vacancy
Island Caretaker
- six-month contract
- AUD$150,000
- live on a tropical island

The best job ever

b 🔊))) 11.3 Listen to two people discussing the job and check your answers.

2   a Listen again. Tick the things they talk about.

salary	☐	qualifications	☐
other benefits	☐	hours	☐
contract	☐	responsibilities	☐
training	☐		

b 💬 Compare your answers with a partner. Can you remember what the people said about each item?

3 💬 Do you agree that this is 'the best job ever'? Why/Why not?

It looks beautiful, but I think living on an island is very boring... or very lonely!

GRAMMAR

1 Complete the sentences with the correct option.

The winning candidate
1 *will / won't* need to pay for a place to live.
2 *will / won't* earn a good salary.
3 *will / won't* work a lot of hours.
4 *will / won't* use the internet.
5 *will / won't* have a long contract.

2 Read transcript 11.3 on pages 166–167. <u>Underline</u> examples of *will*, *won't* and *'ll*. Complete 1–7 in the GRAMMAR PANEL ■.

3   a Complete the job description with *will* or *won't*.

Position Vacant
Professional ice cream taster

○ **The ideal candidate**

(1) _____ need any formal qualifications.

(2) _____ have experience in the job.

(3) _____ have any food allergies.

○ **As part of the job he or she**

(4) _____ taste over 100 ice creams a day.

(5) _____ help create new flavours.

(6) _____ discuss recipes or ingredients with anyone outside the company.

b 💬 Work in pairs. Compare your answers. Which do you think is the best job, the island caretaker or the ice cream taster? Why?

4   a Work in pairs. Think of another 'dream job'. Write a short job description. Include the information in the box.

> job title   location   salary   abilities
> qualifications   duties and responsibilities

b 💬 Compare your job with the rest of the class. Which do you think is the best job? Why?

■	**WILL/WON'T**

We use **will/won't** + **infinitive** to talk about what we know and think about the future:
The winning candidate will receive a salary of $150,000. It'll be a fun job.

The contracted form of **will** + **not** is (1) _____ :
Glenn won't get the job. He can't swim.

The contraction of **will** is (2) _____ .

We use **'ll** after names and pronouns:
Tom will win. → *Tom* (3) _____ *win.*
He will enjoy the job. → *He* (4) _____ *enjoy the job.*

+	You (5) _____ receive a good salary.
–	He (6) _____ receive a good salary.
?	(7) _____ he receive a good salary?

See page 150 for grammar reference and more practice.

PRONUNCIATION: *will, 'll, won't*

1 🔊 11.4 Listen to a short interview with a professional whale-watcher. Would you like to do his job? Why/Why not?

2 **a** Complete the dialogue with *will, 'll* or *won't*.

   A So, tell me about your new job.

   B Well, I .... start until next year. First I .... fly to Oslo to do a three-week training course, and then I .... travel to the north, where I .... be on my own for four months.

   A You mean you .... see anybody for four months!

   B No, I .... But I .... have a satellite connection to talk to my family and my colleagues at base camp.

   A .... your family go over to Norway, too?

   B Yes, they .... For a short visit in the spring.

  b Listen again and check.

3 **a** Work in pairs. Notice when the full form of *will* is used. Match the examples to the rules.

   We use the full form of ***will***

   1 in questions   a *But I will have a satellite connection.*
   2 in short answers   b *Will your family go over, too?*
   3 for emphasis   c *Yes, they will.*

  b 🔊 11.5 Listen and repeat.

4 🗨 Work in pairs. Practise repeating the interview.

SPEAKING

1 🗨 Work in pairs. Look at the photos and answer the questions.

- What are the jobs?
- Do you agree that they are all 'dream jobs'?
- Which do you think is the hardest job? Why?
- What, in your opinion, is the best job in the world? Why?

SPEAKING & VOCABULARY: Work conditions

1 💬 Answer the questions. Use a dictionary to help you.

Do you know anyone who
- works a four-day week?
- works from home?
- works for himself/herself?
- runs a business?
- has a part-time job?
- has a temporary contract?
- has a permanent position?
- is unemployed?

2 💬 Work in pairs. Ask and answer the questions in 1. Use the questions in the box to find out more information.

> Where does he/she work?
> What does he/she do?
> Who does he/she work for?
> Does he/she like his/her job?
> Would he/she like to change jobs?
> What kind of job is he/she looking for?

READING

1 💬 Work in pairs. Read the first paragraph of the article. Which three predictions do you think will be in the article?

2 Read predictions 1–10. Are any of them the same as your suggestions in 1?

3 Read the predictions again. Which do you think
- are already true? • will soon be true? • will possibly be true at some time in the future?

Top Ten Predictions: The World of Work

We live in a world where everything changes very quickly. The world of work is no exception. We asked ten experts to give us their predictions about the biggest changes we can expect in the world of work over the next ten years.

1 All office workers will work a four-day week.
2 Working conditions and salaries will get worse.
3 More and more people will work from home.
4 Companies will only offer part-time and temporary contracts.
5 People won't retire until they are 75 or 80 years old.
6 Computer skills will be essential for all jobs.
7 Candidates for top jobs will need to speak at least two or three languages.
8 Many young people will need to travel to another country to find a job.
9 A university education won't guarantee a good job.
10 Finding a stable, permanent position won't be easy.

What do you think?

Post your comments below (56 comments)

4 💬 Read the comments. Which prediction(s) are they referring to? Do you agree with the comments? Why/Why not?

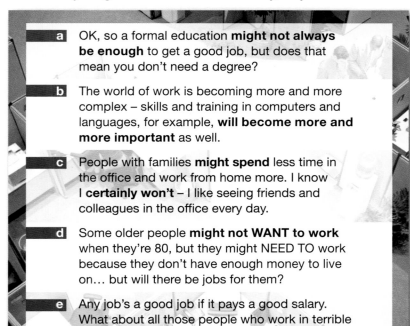

a OK, so a formal education **might not always be enough** to get a good job, but does that mean you don't need a degree?

b The world of work is becoming more and more complex – skills and training in computers and languages, for example, **will become more and more important** as well.

c People with families **might spend** less time in the office and work from home more. I know I **certainly won't** – I like seeing friends and colleagues in the office every day.

d Some older people **might not WANT to work** when they're 80, but they might NEED TO work because they don't have enough money to live on… but will there be jobs for them?

e Any job's a good job if it pays a good salary. What about all those people who work in terrible conditions for very little money? Will the future be brighter for them?

WILL & MIGHT

We can use both *will* and *might* to make predictions about the future:
The future will be brighter.
The future might not be bright.

We use (1)............ to say that we are sure something will happen.

We use (2)............ to say that we think something is possible, but we're not sure it will happen.

When we want to ask other people what their opinion is about the future we usually use
(3) .... :
(4) .... *there be jobs for them?*
(5) .... *the future be brighter for them?*

Might

+	You might get a good job.
–	There might not be enough jobs.

See page 150 for grammar reference and more practice.

GRAMMAR

1 Work in pairs. Look at the phrases in **bold** in the comments above. Do the writers think

1 this will definitely happen?
2 it's possible, but they're not sure?

> **NOTICE** DEFINITELY + WILL/WON'T
> We often use *definitely* with *will/won't* to stress that we are certain of what we're saying:
> *I'll definitely study English again next year.*
> *I definitely won't stay up late tonight.*

2 Underline the other examples of *will* and *might*. Complete 1–5 in the GRAMMAR PANEL ■.

3 Complete the predictions using *will/won't* or *might/might not*.

1 It .... rain tomorrow.
2 I .... go to bed early tonight.
3 I .... have a lot of work to do tomorrow.
4 I .... do some English homework this evening.
5 I .... have a (new) job next year.

4 a 💬 Work in small groups. Write three more predictions about the future of work. Use *will* or *might*.

b Share your predictions with the class. Which predictions do you think

1 will definitely come true?
2 might never come true?

SPEAKING

1 💬 Work in pairs. Look at the photo. What is the woman doing? What do you think she can see?

2 💬 Work in pairs. Discuss the questions.

● Is fortune-telling popular in your country?
● If yes, what kind of fortune-telling (cards, horoscopes) and where (on TV, in newspapers and magazines, on the streets)?
● Do people take it seriously or is it just for fun? If not, why not?

3 a 💬 Work in pairs.

Student A: you are a fortune-teller. Tell your partner's fortune. Turn to page 161.
Student B: prepare questions to ask the fortune-teller. Turn to page 159.

b Exchange roles.

4 💬 Tell the class what the fortune-teller predicted for you. Were you happy with the predictions? Why/Why not?

TUNE IN

1 **a** Work in pairs. Match the verbs to the objects. Use a dictionary to help you.

1 load/unload	a the dishes
2 set/clear	b the dishwasher
3 take out	c the table
4 wash/dry	d the rubbish/recycling

b Look at the pictures. Which household task does each image show?

2 **a** 💬 Which of the tasks do you have to do

1 every day?
2 every two or three days?
3 never – somebody else does it for me!

b Ask and answer with a partner. What other tasks do you do in the house? Who does more housework, you or your partner?

How often do you have to wash the dishes?
Never. We have a dishwasher!

3 🔊 11.6 Listen to four short conversations. What household tasks are the people talking about?

4 Listen again. Match the conversations to the people who are talking.

a a mother and son
b a married couple
c a father and daughter
d a host and guest

FOCUS ON LANGUAGE

5 **a** Read the sentences. Are they requests (R) or offers (O)?

1 **Will you** clear the table first, please?
2 **Let me** wash the dishes.
3 **I'll** load the dishwasher then.
4 **Can you** come and set the table?

b Look at the phrases in **bold**. Which are

a asking someone to do something?
b offering to do something?

6 Put the words in the correct order to make requests or offers.

1 you with help Let that me bag
2 me do Will you a favour ?
3 please the door open Can for me you ?
4 you that I'll for do

❝ Asking & offering ❞

🔊 11.7 Listen to the requests and offers in **6**. Underline the main stress.

Let me help you with that bag.

Listen again and repeat.

Notice that the verb in all these sentences is in the **infinitive**.

7 Work in pairs. Write a request or an offer for each of the situations. Use the language in 5 and 6.

1 You see someone carrying a lot of heavy books.
2 You want to leave the room. Your hands are full. The door is closed.
3 Your friend is having problems with an exercise.
4 You need some help with your computer.
5 Your friend is going to get a coffee from the coffee machine. You'd like one, too.

OVER TO YOU

8 💬 Work in pairs. Act out the situations in 7. Respond to the requests or offers.

9 💬 When was the last time you offered someone help? What help did he/she need?

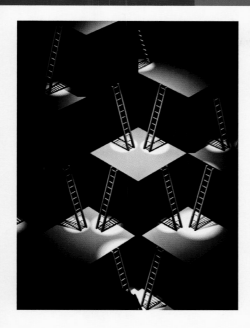

Upskilling for a new world of work

We live in a changing world. Jobs are changing, and the skills and qualifications you need to do the jobs are changing, too.

NOTICE

upskill = to learn or teach new skills. The word *up* gives the idea of progress and success: *Upskilling helps you get a better job and a better chance in life.*

Using a computer, driving a car, having a school or university education, all these basic skills and qualifications are still important, but they're not enough.

There are so many new jobs and so many new ways of working. There are so many new markets and so many new products. You need to make sure you're learning the right skills for this new and changing world. You need to **upskill**.

Upskilling is equally important for people with or without a job. If you have a job, new skills will help you keep your job; if you don't have a job, **upskilling** will help you find one.

The most important thing is to know what these skills are – and how to get them. We can help you. We can tell you what you need to do and how best to do it. We can make sure your skills are the ones you need in tomorrow's world of work.

Click here now and open up a new world of work.

Upskilling: training for a new world.

TUNE IN

1 🗨 Look at the image. What can you see? What do you think is the connection between the image and the world of work?

2 Read the article and check your answers in 1.

3 Read the article again. Is it
   1 giving useful information?
   2 asking important questions?
   3 advertising a training agency?

PREPARE FOR TASK

4 a 🗨 Work in groups. Read the skills and qualifications in the box and answer the questions.
   - Which skills and qualifications can someone teach you?
   - Which can you teach yourself?
   - Which come naturally or with time?

   speaking one or more foreign languages
   computer skills   familiarity with the internet
   familiarity with other cultures and countries
   knowledge of a specialist technical area
   a university degree   a vocational qualification
   experience in your field   flexibility
   creativity   people skills

   b Which three skills or qualifications do you think are the most important in today's job market? Why?

TASK

5 🗨 Work in pairs. Discuss the questions.
   - Which of the skills or qualifications will be important for you in a possible future job? Why?
   - Which of these skills and qualifications do you already have? Which would you like to get?
   - What's the best and quickest way to get these skills and qualifications? How long do you think it will take?

6 Write a personal action plan for upskilling over the next two years. Decide which skills you want to focus on and how you plan to develop them. Write short notes.
   - *improve computer skills*
   - *look for evening/weekend course*

REPORT BACK

7 🗨 Present your action plans to the class. Whose plan sounds
   1 the most realistic?
   2 the most ambitious?

12 LISTMANIA!

1 💬 Work in pairs. Look at the photos showing people's dreams and ambitions. Can you guess what they are? Check your answers in A in the KEY VOCABULARY PANEL ■.

2 💬 Work in pairs. Answer the questions.
   1 How many of the ambitions would you like to do/have you done?
   2 Can you think of any other ambitions to add to the list?

3 Complete this sentence so that it is true for you.
   My greatest ambition is to…

4 💬 Find out what your classmates' dreams and ambitions are. Which is the most common ambition? Which is the strangest?

5 Work in pairs to complete B in the KEY VOCABULARY PANEL ■.

c

f

6 🔊 12.1 Listen to Mared talking about what she did yesterday.

1 Which of the common collocations does she use?

2 Which of the ambitions on the list has she achieved?

7 💬 Work in pairs. Tell each other what you did yesterday. Use as many of the collocations as you can.

◼ KEY VOCABULARY

Dreams & ambitions

A Match the photos to six of the ambitions below.

Top ten lifetime ambitions

1 do a parachute jump

2 write a best-seller

3 run a marathon

4 have a big family

5 build your own dream home

6 go on a round-the-world trip

7 be your own boss

8 make a fortune

9 direct a film

10 speak at least three languages

NOTICE *own*

We often use *own* with a possessive adjective:
*I want to be **my own** boss.*
Don't use *own* with *a* or *the*: He built ~~a/the own dream home~~.
How do you say *own* in your language?

REVIEW: Common verbs & collocations

B Complete the lists of nouns in the circles. Some nouns go in more than one circle. Use a dictionary to help you.

~~dinner~~   a shower   a living   an exercise   lunch   the bus
a list   a message   a phone call   a rest   a (great) job
notes   the housework   a holiday   some work   children
a good time   a taxi   the shopping   a mistake
some cooking   money

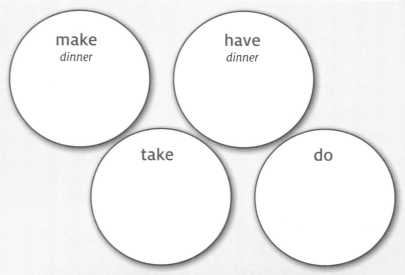

make
dinner

have
dinner

take

do

• Which of these common collocations would be different in your language?

In Spanish, we don't say 'have dinner' or 'have lunch', we have a special verb for those.

SPEAKING

1 💬 Work in small groups. Discuss the questions.

- When did you last write a list?
- What kind of list was it (a shopping list, a list of things to do, a list of presents to buy, etc.)?
- What was on the list?

2 🔊 12.2 Listen to someone answering the questions in 1. What kind of list is the person talking about?

READING & SPEAKING

1 Look at the book covers. Match them to the book review extracts.

1. 'This is *the* ultimate shopping list!'
2. 'More of a travel guide than a list – but then, everything's a list these days!'
3. 'The only problem is, will there ever be time to listen to them all?'
4. 'No surprises on this short list, but lots of good examples for living a long and happy life.'

2 In which of the books do these items appear?

1. the Great Wall of China
2. give more than you take
3. the first Radiohead LP
4. the finest diamond ring

3 💬 Think of three more items for the lists in each book. Which book (if any) would you like to read? Why?

4 Read another list. What do you think is the missing verb?

5 **a** Read the list again. Which of the activities

a. include animals?
b. can only happen in a specific place?
c. include a long journey?
d. include a form of transport?
e. can be dangerous?

b 💬 Which of the items on the list

- would you like to do?
- would you not like to do? Why not?

6 💬 Rewrite the list with your personal top ten. Compare your list with the class.

Book covers: **a** *101 things to buy before you die* (Maggie Davis, Charlotte Williamson) · **b** WISCONSIN Public TV — DR. JOHN IZZO hosts *the five secrets you must discover before you die* (Based upon the original television program and book, The Five Secrets You Must Discover Before You Die) · **c** *1001 ALBUMS YOU MUST HEAR BEFORE YOU DIE* (PREFACE BY MICHAEL LYDON, FOUNDING EDITOR OF ROLLING STONE; GENERAL EDITOR ROBERT DIMERY) · **d** ON AND OFF THE BEATEN TRACK — #1 BESTSELLER — *1,000 PLACES TO SEE BEFORE YOU DIE* — A TRAVELER'S LIFE LIST by PATRICIA SCHULTZ

Top Ten Things to _____ Before You Die

1. Go whale-watching
2. Ride a camel to the pyramids
3. Fly over a volcano
4. Drive a Formula One car
5. See the Northern Lights
6. Go skydiving
7. Explore Antarctica
8. Take the Trans-Siberian railway
9. Swim with dolphins
10. Ride a horse along a beach

Listening

1 a 🔊 12.3 Listen to three people, Hanna, Renata and Stephen, talking about the list in READING & SPEAKING 4. Which activities do they talk about?

b 💬 Work in pairs. Compare your answers. Do you think Hanna, Renata and Stephen like the list? Why/Why not?

2 a Listen again. Complete the extracts.

HANNA	I .... these lists.
RENATA	I think they're ....
HANNA	Life isn't a ....
STEPHEN	Some people think that life is just about ....
HANNA	I'd love to go ....
STEPHEN	I'd love to see ....

b 💬 Do you agree with what they say?

Grammar

1 Mark the sentences Hanna (H), Renata (R) or Stephen (S).

1 **Has he ever been** to Antarctica? Yes, **he has**.
2 They **haven't been** whale-watching, but they'd love to go.
3 **Have you ever seen** the Northern Lights? No, **I haven't**, but **I've seen** the midnight sun.
4 She**'s visited** Finland.
5 They**'ve travelled** a lot.

2 Work in pairs. Look at the words in **bold** in 1. Complete 1–10 in the GRAMMAR PANEL ▪️ .

3 a <u>Underline</u> the past participles in the questions.

Have you ever...
1 written a novel, a poem or a song?
2 worked in a bar?
3 won a prize?
4 travelled to another continent?
5 flown in a helicopter?
6 spoken in public?
7 lived in another country?
8 taught something to someone?
9 run a marathon?

b Which past participles are regular and which are irregular? What is the infinitive of the irregular past participles?

4 💬 Work in pairs. Ask and answer the questions in 3a.

🔲 PRESENT PERFECT: *HAVE YOU EVER...?*

We use the present perfect to talk about past experiences:
Have you ever been to Antarctica?
No, *I haven't*, but *I've been* to Argentina.

We form the present perfect with ***have/has*** + past participle.

+	I/You/We/They (1) .... been to Antarctica. He/She/It **'s** been to Antarctica.
–	I/You/We/They (2) .... seen whales. He/She/It **hasn't** seen whales.
?	(3) .... you ever been to Argentina? (4) .... she ever been to Argentina?
Yes/No	Yes, I have./No, I (5) .... Yes, she (6) ..../No, she **hasn't**.

Past participles

We form the past participle of regular verbs by adding *-ed* to the infinitive of the verb:
travel → (7) .... , *visit* → (8) ....

Some verbs are irregular:
see → (9) .... , *go* → *gone/* (10) ....

See page 151 for grammar reference and more practice.

Speaking

1 a Work in pairs. Write a new list on one of the topics.

Top five most...
● exciting things I've seen
● difficult sports I've played
● terrible places I've visited
● boring things I've done
● interesting people I've met

b Write questions for the five points on your list using *Have you ever...?*

I've been to a World Cup final.
Have you ever seen an important football match live?

2 💬 Ask and answer questions with the rest of the class. Has anybody else done all the things on your list?

READING & VOCABULARY: Describing places

1 a Read the phrases in the box. Which would you normally use to describe

1 the city?   2 the country?   3 either the city or the country?

Use a dictionary to help you.

> relaxed atmosphere   state-of-the-art airport   beautiful trees   cosmopolitan culture
> top-quality hotels   fresh air   wonderful lakes

b 💬 Which phrases can you use to describe where you live?

2 💬 Work in pairs. Look at the photos of two different cities. Discuss the questions.

1 What can you see in the two photos?   3 Which of the phrases in **1** can you use in your descriptions?
2 What do the cities have in common?   4 Do you know where these cities might be?

City 1

City 2

3 A style magazine recently voted these the top two cities in the world to live in. Read the texts.
Complete the sentences with the correct option.

City 1	City 2
Zurich is our number one choice. It has a transport system that is the best in the world. And because this is Switzerland, the trains are always on time! Now the city is expanding its tram system and state-of-the-art airport. It is also a world leader in protecting the climate. There is fresh air here, wonderful lakes and green hills all around.	Last year's winner is now number two, but Copenhagen is a city we still love. There is interesting architecture, very little crime and a relaxed atmosphere in a perfect location. It's great to bike your way around the city's cycle paths. The city is clean and green, and a fantastic place to live in. Like so many cities in Scandinavia, it has a very cosmopolitan culture.

1 The most important thing for the magazine when it chose these cities was
   a cultural life.   b the environment.   c tourist attractions.
2 Other aspects the magazine thinks are important include
   a transport.   b climate.   c the cost of living.
3 The two cities are similar because
   a they are modern and sophisticated.   b they have a great natural setting.   c they have many business possibilities.

4 a What things are important when choosing a town/city to live in? Put the items in the box in order of
importance to make your 'top ten'.

> job opportunities   location   climate   cultural life   safety   size   shopping   environment
> people   food   transport service/connections   atmosphere   schools and universities

b 💬 Work in pairs. Compare your lists. If you disagree with each other, defend your choice.

The most important thing is job opportunities. A beautiful, green, clean city is great – if you have a job.

5 💬 Think about your home town/city. Is it a possible candidate for one of the top ten towns/cities? Why/Why not?

LISTENING

1 🔊 12.4 Listen to two travel writers, Gus and Maria, talking about the two cities.

  1 Which city are they each talking about?
  2 Are they generally positive or negative?
  3 Which person has visited the city already?

2 Listen again and answer the questions.

  1 What does Gus like about the city?
  2 What does he like about the people?
  3 When did Maria go to Zurich?
  4 What doesn't she like about the city?
  5 What type of city does she prefer?

3 💬 Work in pairs. Make a list of the top five cities you would like to visit. Compare your lists. Are your tastes the same?

My number one city is Rio. I've always wanted to see Copacabana beach.

GRAMMAR

1 a Work in pairs. Read the extracts and answer the questions.

> I **went** to Zurich a few years ago, but I didn't like it much. I didn't have a very good time there.

> I**'ve been** to other cities in Europe which I like more… Berlin, for example.

  1 Do we know when Maria went to Zurich?
  2 Do we know when she went to Berlin?

b Choose the correct option to complete 1–5 in the GRAMMAR PANEL ▪▪.

2 a Read the present perfect questions. Match them to the past simple follow-up questions.

  1 Have you ever won a prize?
  2 Have you ever given a presentation?

  a Did you enjoy it?
  b What happened exactly?

  3 Have you ever met a famous person?
  4 Have you ever been in an accident?
  5 Have you ever worked in an office?
  6 Have you ever run a long-distance race?

  c What did you do there?
  d What was it about?
  e Who was it?
  f What did you win?

b 💬 Work in pairs. Ask and answer the questions. Ask two more follow-up questions.

PRONUNCIATION: Present perfect & past simple

1 a 🔊 12.5 Listen to six statements. <u>Underline</u> the verb you hear.

  1 lived / 've lived
  2 worked / 've worked
  3 studied / 's studied

  4 had / 've had
  5 read / 's read
  6 visited / 've visited

b Listen again and repeat.

▪ PRESENT PERFECT & PAST SIMPLE

We use the ⁽¹⁾*present perfect / past simple* to talk about our past experiences:
I've been to other cities in Europe.

We ⁽²⁾*give / don't give* a specific time in the past:
I've been to Rome last year.

We use the ⁽³⁾*present perfect / past simple* if we say when something happened:
I went to Zurich a few years ago.

We use the ⁽⁴⁾*present perfect / past simple* to ask an initial question about past experiences:
Have you ever been to Thailand?
Yes, I have.

We use the ⁽⁵⁾*present perfect / past simple* to ask for more information:
Did you have a good time there?
It was OK.

See page 151 for grammar reference and more practice.

SPEAKING & LISTENING

1 a 💬 Look at the photos from a video clip of a sporting event. Answer the questions.

  1 What kind of event do you think it is?   2 Which country do you think holds the most famous event?

b 🔊 12.6 Listen to the video clip commentary. Check your answers.

2 a Listen again and complete the statements.

  1 There are .... sports in a triathlon.
  2 The first .... - .... triathlon took place in Hawaii in 19............. .
  3 Finally the contestants have to run .... km.
  4 Women .... take part in the Ironman World Championship.

b 💬 Why do you think people take part in the Ironman World Championship? Would you like to?

3 💬 Read a blog entry about Klaus Sanderling who is preparing for the Ironman World Championship. Why does he think he's lucky?

4 a 💬 List five things you think Klaus needs to do before taking part in the triathlon.

b 🔊 12.7 Listen to an interview with Klaus talking about his preparations for the Ironman World Championship and check your answers.

HAWAII, HERE I GO!
Klaus Sanderling
13 February

Big news today! I'm the luckiest man alive! Today I found out that I will be in the starting line-up at Kailua-Kona in Hawaii in October. Yippee! Just 1,800 people have the chance to do this and thousands apply. Now the only problem is starting training!

5 Listen again and correct the statements.

  1 To enter the lottery, you need to do a full Ironman race somewhere in the world.
  2 He began as a cyclist.
  3 Running is his worst sport.
  4 On Fridays he usually rests.
  5 On Sundays he runs about 10 km.
  6 The weather will be cold when he does the triathlon.

GRAMMAR

1 Complete the sentences with the correct form of the verb in brackets.

1 I .... *(start)* with normal triathlons, like a lot of people, and I realised that I .... *(be)* quite good.
2 For the next six months I .... *(follow)* a very strict programme.
3 On Wednesdays I usually .... *(go)* for a short run, around 10 to 12 km.
4 Then, on Sundays I .... *(run)* a longer distance, about 20 km.
5 You .... *(can)* wear swimsuits made from certain material because they give you an advantage.
6 Right now I .... *(run)* with lots of clothes on to prepare myself for the heat.
7 In Hawaii the weather .... *(be)* hot.

2 a Check your answers in transcript 12.7 on page 167. Match the verbs in 1 to the verb forms, a–f, in the GRAMMAR PANEL ▪️.

b Match verb forms a–f to functions 1–6 in the GRAMMAR PANEL ▪️.

3 Read what Eli has to say about being a DJ. Why does she enjoy it?

I began deejaying when I was 14. I usually deejay twice a week. I didn't have a teacher, I taught myself. I've always loved dance music, that's how I started. When you're working, you can do what you like, there aren't any rules, but you can't take your eyes off the dance floor. You have to see what music the people like and what they're dancing to. Right now, I'm deejaying in two clubs. It's just a hobby for me, but I'm going to try and deejay in the future in different towns and cities. Whatever happens, I know I will always be a DJ.

4 a Read the text again. <u>Underline</u> the verb forms in the text and complete the questions.

1 When .... *(begin)*?
2 Why .... *(start)* it?
3 How often .... *(do)* it?
4 Who .... *(be)* your teacher or guide?
5 .... *(be)* there any rules to follow?
6 Where .... *(do)* it right now?
7 What .... you .... *(try)* and do in the future?
8 .... *(be)* a DJ in five years' time?

b 💬 Work in pairs. Check your answers. Take it in turns to role-play an interview with Eli.

▪️ REVIEW OF VERBS

We use the following verb forms
a the present simple
b the present continuous
c the past simple
d *going to*
e *will*
f *can*

to talk about
1 ability and permission.
2 what happened at a specific time in the past.
3 what we are doing now.
4 future plans.
5 what we know or think about the future.
6 things we do regularly.

See page 151 for grammar reference and more practice.

SPEAKING

1 💬 Think of an activity you can do well – a sport, a job, an interest, a hobby or something you're studying. Answer the questions in GRAMMAR 4a.

2 a 💬 Work in pairs. Ask and answer the questions. Write down the answers. Use the prompts to help you.

- X began... when...
- X started... because...
- X usually...
- X's teacher...
- X says you can/can't...
- Now X... every week/month.
- X's going to... in the future.
- X will always...

b Tell the rest of the class the information you find out about your partner.

3 💬 What kind of abilities do your classmates have? Are they similar or different to yours?

TUNE IN

1 💬 You want to go away for the weekend to a city you haven't been to before. How do you get information about where to go? Look at the photos for ideas.

2 Match the photos to the ideas.

1 look up the city online
2 take a friend's advice
3 read a guidebook about the city
4 read the travel section of the newspaper
5 go to a travel agent's

3 🔊 12.8 Listen to Roisin asking some friends, Monica, Petra and Lily, about where to go.

1 Which city or cities does each friend recommend?
2 What reasons does each give for her choice?
3 What city does Roisin decide on in the end?

4 Listen again and correct the statements.

1 Monica's been to Antwerp.
2 Antwerp is similar to Amsterdam now.
3 Roisin and Mark went to Paris five years ago.
4 Roisin's been to Copenhagen a few times.
5 Lily's never lived in Bologna.
6 The weather's good there all year round.

❝ Let me see/Let me think ❞

🔊 12.9 Listen to the extract from one of the conversations.

I wanted something a bit different.

Oh, I see. Let me think... Copenhagen?

Does the speaker's voice go up ➚ or down ➘?
Which word do we stress? Where are the pauses?

How do you say *let me see/let me think* in your language?

FOCUS ON LANGUAGE

5 a Match the responses, a–c, to Roisin's questions, 1–3.

1 Where do you recommend?
2 Have you been there?
3 I've never been there. What's it like?

a Yes, of course! I lived there, don't you remember?
b Beautiful nature, the people are great... a fantastic place!
c Well, I've never been, but everyone says Antwerp's great.

b 🔊 12.10 Listen and check.

NOTICE *WHAT'S IT LIKE?*

We use *What's it like?* to ask for a description of something. We can use the same question about people, too:

What's she/he like?

How do you say *What's it/she/he like?* in your language?

OVER TO YOU

6 💬 Work in pairs. Ask for information about a place to go for the weekend.

Student A: ask the questions in 5a.
Student B: recommend a place that you know.

7 💬 Take turns to recommend something else to your partner – a restaurant, a book, a film, a website, etc.

Top five tips for learning a language

1 First of all, make sure you always arrive at class on time.

2 Remember to do all your homework, especially the grammar exercises. Ask for extra homework if there's something you need more practice in. Remember, practice makes perfect!

3 Keep a vocabulary notebook. Write down any new words you learn in class. Carry it with you. Study it when you're on the bus or in a queue at the bank, or when you're having a coffee at work.

4 Make sure you understand everything in class. Make notes and study them as soon as you get home.

5 Last, but not least, keep a diary. Write about what you did in class, what you learned and what you had problems with. At the end of the course you'll be surprised to see how much you've learned!

TUNE IN

1 Look at the photos. What do they say about learning a language? What is more important for you, studying the grammar or speaking the language? Why?

2 a Read the tips for making the most of your language lessons. Which person, a or b, do you think wrote them?

b Work in pairs. Compare your answers. Do you think they are good tips? Why/Why not?

3 Work in pairs. The person who wrote the tips in **2a** is looking for a new language course. Which of the items do you think is more important for him/her?

- technology in the classroom
- a good atmosphere in class
- a good coursebook, with clear grammar and practical everyday English
- interesting topics to talk about
- plenty of opportunities to speak

4 Read the list in **3** again. Which of these things do you think helped you most on this course? Why? What else helped you to learn?

PREPARE FOR TASK

5 a Work in small groups. Write a list of things you can do when you finish your course to help you keep improving your English.

Watch films in English, organise a language exchange, do an online course...

b Which are the five most motivating ways to study outside the classroom?

6 a Read the tips in **2a** again and find

1 the phrase used to introduce the first point.
2 the phrase used to introduce the last point.
3 a well-known saying about learning.
4 at least five imperative verbs.

b What do you notice about the style of writing?

TASK

7 Work in the same groups as in **5**. Write a tip sheet called 'Five things to improve your English outside class'. Use your notes in **5** and the language in **6a**.

REPORT BACK

8 a Share your tip sheet with the class. Answer the questions in your group.

1 Do other groups have similar tips?
2 Which new tip or tips do you like best? Why?
3 Which tips do you think you will follow when you finish the course?

b Share your ideas with the class.

➡ Go to Review D, Unit 12, p. 138 **135**

VOCABULARY
Technology

1 💬 Work in pairs. Think of ten gadgets. Answer the questions.

Which
1 can't you live without?
2 do you really hate?
Why?

Communication

2 Look at the groups of verbs. Which verb in each group is not part of that lexical set? Why is it different?

1 call answer phone ring
2 email write call text
3 respond answer phone reply

3 **a** Choose a verb in **2** to complete the sentences.

1 I usually .... because it's quicker than calling and it's cheaper.
2 Sometimes people don't .... my emails and I think it's because they don't get them.
3 Nobody .... anymore and that's a shame. I love receiving letters.
4 I hate the telephone. If it .... all the time it can make me very nervous.

b 💬 Are these sentences true for you? Discuss your answers with a partner.

Adjectives

4 **a** Read the advice. Complete the sentences with a suitable adjective.

1 It's better to buy a s............... computer, like a laptop. It's more convenient than a desktop.
2 You don't need to buy an e............... computer. There are cheap ones that are equally good.
3 The most important thing about a laptop is the weight. It's best to get a l............... one.

b 💬 Do you think this is good advice? Think of more advice about buying computers.

5 Write three sentences of advice to someone who wants to buy one of the items in the box.

a car   a bike   a music player   a TV

GRAMMAR
Comparative adjectives

1 **a** Work in pairs. Write sentences comparing the pairs of things.

1 two rival football teams
2 two nearby towns/cities
3 two gadgets

b 💬 Compare your sentences with other students.

2 Think of technology now and in the past. Write a short paragraph on the role that technology plays in your life.

Before I didn't have a computer, now I can't live without one. It's easier to keep in touch with everybody now through email and cheaper to call as well...

Going to

3 **a** Look at the activities in the box. Tick the ones that you are going to do today or tomorrow.

read the newspaper   have a coffee   get a bus
listen to the radio   have a shower   call a friend
go shopping   go to work   go to class

b 💬 Compare your answers with a partner. What else are you going to do?

FUNCTIONAL LANGUAGE
Giving instructions

1 🔊 R15 Look at the photo. Listen to some instructions. What is the gadget and how does it work?

2 💬 Practise explaining the gadget to a partner.

◼ LOOKING BACK

- What did you discover in this unit about technology?
- Think of six different forms of communication and six different situations in which they would be appropriate.
- Think of three things you can say about your plans for the next few days.

VOCABULARY

Work & jobs

1 Work in pairs. Think of a job that matches all three adjectives.

1 well paid stressful interesting
2 satisfying creative badly paid
3 physical responsible dangerous

2 💬 Think of five close friends or family members who work. Write down the names of the jobs they do. Explain the list to a partner.

Doctor – my uncle's a doctor. He works at the hospital. He loves his job.

3 **a** Work in pairs. Match the expressions to their opposites.

1 work in an office   a work part-time
2 work long hours   b work alone
3 work in a team   c do a desk job
4 do hard physical work   d follow orders
5 make important decisions   e work outside

b 💬 Think of jobs where you have to do each of the things in the two lists. Which job(s) would you never do? Why?

Work conditions

4 💬 Work in two groups. Look at the work situations below.

Group A: discuss the advantages of each one.
Group B: discuss the disadvantages of each one.

- a four-day week
- a part-time job
- running your own business
- working from home

5 **a** 💬 Work in pairs with one student from group A and one student from group B. Compare your ideas.

b Discuss the questions.

- Which of the four situations would you prefer to work in?
- Why?

GRAMMAR

Superlative adjectives

1 Make sentences to compare the jobs in the photos. Use the correct form of the words in the box.

| good boring easy exciting stressful bad difficult well paid |

I think think the DJ is the best job!
I think the air steward is the most boring.

Will & might

2 **a** Complete the sentences using *will/won't*.

> On my next birthday I .... be (add your age)
> .... I .... have a big party. I ....
> get a lot of presents. I .... take a few days'
> holiday. I'm sure I .... have a great time.

b When can you replace *will/won't* with *might/might not*? Which is the best answer for you? Compare your answers with a partner.

FUNCTIONAL LANGUAGE

Offers & requests

1 **a** Work in pairs. Complete the requests and offers using one word.

1 .... me help you with that. It looks really heavy.
2 .... you give me another one of those? They're really delicious.
3 .... you hold this for me, please? My hands are full.
4 Don't worry. I .... get some when I go out.
5 Will you do me a favour, ... ? Can you get the keys from my pocket? Thanks.

b 🔊R16 💬 Listen and check. What exactly do you think is happening in situations 1–5 in 1a? What do you think the other person says in response? Act out the situations with a partner.

■ LOOKING BACK

- What's the most useful thing you've learned in this unit? Why is it useful?
- Which exercise was a) the most interesting? b) the easiest? Why?
- Think of three jobs that you would like to do in the future. Explain the reasons for your choices.

VOCABULARY
Common verbs & collocations

1 Work in pairs. Choose the best word in the box to complete each of the sentences.

> bus   shower   job   notes   shopping   rest

1 Whose turn is it to do the .... ? Come on, I cooked.
2 I didn't make .... during the lecture and now I can't remember anything.
3 If you have a short .... every couple of hours, it can help you work better.
4 I need to have a .... in the morning or I can't wake up!
5 You did a very good .... with that project, it got 10 out of 10.
6 If I take the .... in the morning, I get to work at a good time.

2 a Write the correct form of *do* or *make* to complete the sentences.

1 I .... some volunteer work in my year off.
2 I'd like to .... a lot of money before I die.
3 I like .... lists, it's a good way to organise my life.
4 I hate .... phone calls, I prefer to speak to someone face to face.
5 I .... a lot of sports at school, but not now.
6 I never .... the housework or the cooking at home, I'm very lazy.

b 💬 Work in pairs. Tell your partner if the sentences are true for you.

I wouldn't like to make a lot of money, but a good living is OK!

Describing places

3 Which of the nouns in the box can you see in the photos on page 130?

> lakes   architecture   hotels   airport   hills
> transport   trees   mountains   shops

4 Think of any positive adjectives which can combine with the nouns in 3.

5 💬 Work in pairs. Use the phrases in 4 to describe a place you know well.

GRAMMAR
Present perfect & past simple

1 Write the words in the correct order.

1 to Italy ever Have you been ?
2 office you Have worked an ever in ?
3 met famous you a ever person Have ?
4 read Have ever English book a you in ?
5 Have done really ever exciting you something ?
6 flown the you Have across ever Atlantic ?

2 💬 Ask and answer the questions in pairs. When the answer is *yes*, give more information.

Yes, I have. I went to Sicily two years ago.

Review of verbs

3 a Complete the questions with the correct form of the verbs.

1 When .... (begin) to study English?
2 How often .... (have) English classes?
3 Who .... (be) your first English teacher?
4 What .... (can) do well in English?
5 What .... (find) difficult about it?
6 What .... (want) to improve?
7 Where .... (study) English next year?
8 .... ever .... (visit) an English-speaking country?

b 💬 Work in pairs. Ask your partner the questions and report back to the rest of the class.

FUNCTIONAL LANGUAGE
Finding out & recommending

1 a Match the questions to the answers.

1 What's Ibiza like?
2 Can you recommend a hotel for us there?
3 Have you ever been to the Balearic Islands?

a Yes, they're beautiful. I've been lots of times.
b You'll find it very busy in the summer. June or September are good months to go.
c Try the Marina Suites hotel in Ibiza Town. You'll love it!

b 🔊 R17 Put the questions and answers in the correct order. Listen and check your answers.

2 💬 Work in pairs. Practise recommending places to go on holiday with your partner.

■ LOOKING BACK

- Which section of this unit do you think is the most memorable?
- Think of five useful phrases from this unit you can use tomorrow.
- Think of five things you can say to describe your experiences and achievements.

READING

1 a Read the students' answers to their teacher's homework question. Which students talk about

    1 a past experience?   2 future plans?   3 English at work?

Do you use English outside the classroom?
Homework task, 9 July

Javi says ✕

My company does a lot of business with companies in Central Europe. We always communicate in English. Sometimes it's really difficult.

Montse says ✕

I use English a lot online. It's really easy to make friends – from all over the world! We chat about stuff and send photos and videos.

Marisa says ✕

There are a lot of tourists and visitors in my town in the summer. I sometimes speak to them on the street. They ask me for directions.

Lin says ✕

Last year I went to Poland on holiday. It was great. I spoke a lot of English!

Guido says ✕

I don't really use English much outside the classroom ☹ – I hope to start a language exchange with someone who wants to learn Italian.

Elena says ✕

I've never been to an English-speaking country, but this year I'm going to visit my brother in Australia. I really need to improve my English before I go!

Jordi says ✕

I work in a bar. Sometimes people come in and ask for something in English. Sometimes we chat about where they come from and what they're doing in town.

b Read the answers again. Which students do you think use English most?

2 💬 Write your answer to the teacher's question. Compare with a partner. Which student is most similar to you?

SPEAKING

3 a Answer the questions for yourself.

1 Have you ever visited an English-speaking country?
2 Have you ever visited a country where you needed to communicate in English?
3 Have you ever met an English-speaking person in your home town?
4 Have you ever spoken English with a visitor to your town?
5 Have you ever used English to speak to friends online?

b 💬 Work in pairs. Compare your answers and discuss your experiences. Also discuss any questions you answered 'No' to.

Would you like to visit an English-speaking country? Which one?/Why not?
How can you find people to talk to in English in your town?

◼️ QUICK CHECK

Complete the checklist below.

Can you...	Yes, I can.	Yes, more or less.	I need to look again.
1 talk about future plans?	☐	☐	☐
2 make predictions?	☐	☐	☐
3 talk about past experiences?	☐	☐	☐
4 make offers and requests?	☐	☐	☐
5 compare jobs and work conditions?	☐	☐	☐
6 compare and discuss options?	☐	☐	☐
7 give instructions?	☐	☐	☐
8 make recommendations?	☐	☐	☐

💬 Compare your answers with a partner.

- What else do you know now after studying units 10–12?
- Do you need to look again at any of the sections?
- Do you need any extra help from your teacher?

1.1 PRESENT SIMPLE: TO BE

	Full form		Short form	
+	I am You/We/They are He/She/It is		I'm You/We/They're He/She/It's	French.
−	I am not You/We/They are not He/She/It is not		I'm not You/We/They aren't He/She/It isn't	Mexican.
Wh-?	Where	am are is	I you/we/they he/she/it	from?
Y/N?	Am Are Is		I you/we/they he/she/it	Spanish?
Y/N	Yes, I am. Yes, you/we/they are. Yes, he/she/it is.		No, I'm not. No, you/we/they aren't. No, he/she/it isn't.	

► 1.1

1.2 THIS, THAT, THESE, THOSE

Use *this* and *these* to talk about things that are near (here).

Use *that* and *those* to talk about things that are far (there).

Use *this* and *that* with singular nouns.

Use *these* and *those* with plural nouns.

	Here ▼	There ↗
Singular	This is my book.	That is your book.
Plural	These are my books.	Those are your books.

► 1.2

1.3 POSITION OF ADJECTIVES

Adjectives can come:

1 after the verb *to be*: *We're tired.*

2 before nouns: *It's a big bag.*

There is no plural form:

The bags are big. NOT *The bags are ~~bigs~~.*

► 1.3

1.4 POSSESSIVE ADJECTIVES

Use possessive adjectives before a noun:

It's my bag.

The adjective agrees with the person, not the object:

It's her bag. ♀

It's his bag. ♂

There is no plural form:

They're my bags. NOT *They're ~~mys~~ bags.*

I	my
you	your
he	his
she	her
we	our
they	their

► 1.4

1.1

a Write the contracted forms of the verbs in **bold** where possible.

*Hi. My name **is** Yukiko. I **am** Japanese. I **am not** from Tokyo. I **am** from Kyoto. This **is** Lee. He **is** a good friend. He **is not** Japanese. He **is** Korean. He **is** from Seoul. We **are** students at the same English school. We **are not** very good at English – but we like it!*

b Complete the questions using the correct form of the verb *to be*.

1 Where .... Lee from?

2 .... Lee and Yukiko friends?

3 .... you Japanese?

4 Where .... you from?

c Answer the questions in b. Use full sentences.

1.2

Complete the captions using *this, that, these* or *those*.

1 .... is my mobile phone.

2 Are .... your keys?

3 .... are my new sunglasses.

4 Hey! ....'s my iPod!

1.3

Correct one mistake in each sentence.

1 That is a bag big.

2 Your sunglasses are very smalls.

3 We're really hungrys!

4 This is my friend good, Yuri.

1.4

Choose the correct possessive adjective.

This is me and these are [1]*my / our* friends. We play in the same football team. This is [2]*your / our* coach. [3]*Your / Her* name's Jenny. She's great! This is [4]*his / her* boyfriend, Tom. And this is [5]*your / their* house. It's very near the park where we play football.

2.1 PRESENT SIMPLE: *HAVE*

We use *have* to talk about families and possessions.

+	I/You/We/They He/She/It	have has		three sisters.
–	I/You/We/They He/She/It	don't doesn't	have have	any sisters.
Wh-?	How many cousins	do does	I/you/we/they he/she/it	have?
Y/N?	Do Does	I/you/we/they he/she/it	have	any sisters?
Y/N	Yes, I/you/we/they do. Yes, he/she/it does.		No, I/you/we/they don't. No, he/she/it doesn't.	

Some people also use *have got*. This is more common in British English:

I've got three sisters.
Have you got any cousins?   Yes, I have.
She's got two brothers.
Has she got any sisters?   No, she hasn't.

NOTE: *'s* can be three things:

1 the contracted form of *is*: *He's my brother.*

2 the contracted form of *has* in *has got*: *He's got two children.*

3 the possessive *'s*: see **2.2** below.

▶ 2.1

2.2 POSSESSIVE *'S*

We use name + *'s* to show possession:

Anna is Daniel's mother. (= the mother of Daniel)

Daniel is Julia's brother. (= the brother of Julia)

For names ending in *-s* you can add *'s*: *Gus's friend* OR *'*: *Gus' friend.*

For plural nouns that end in *-s* add *'*: *his parents' family.*

▶ 2.2

2.3 PRESENT SIMPLE: *I, YOU, WE, THEY*

We use the present simple to talk about facts – things that are generally true.

+	I/You/We/They	live		in Mexico.
–	I/You/We/They	don't	live	in Mexico.
Wh-?	Where	do	I/you/we/they	live?
Y/N?	Do	I/you/we/they	live	in Mexico?
Y/N	Yes, I/you/we/they do.		No, I/you/we/they don't.	

▶ 2.3

2.4 *WH-* QUESTION WORDS

We use *who, what, where, how many* and *how old* to ask questions.

Who?	a person	How many?	a number
What?	a thing or idea	How old?	age
Where?	a place		

When we use prepositions in questions they normally go at the end:

*Who do you live **with**?*

▶ 2.4

2.1

Complete the sentences with *have/has* or *don't have/doesn't have* to make them true.

1 We .... a computer at home.
2 My brother/sister .... a dog.
3 My parents .... two cars.
4 I .... a good relationship with my family.
5 My mother .... a job.

2.2

a Look at the photo. Complete the sentences with the correct names and *'s*.

1 Shada is .... sister.
2 Kamal is .... brother.
3 Yousef is .... husband.
4 Fatima is .... wife.

b Look at the photo again. Write *'s* or *'* in the correct place in the sentences.

1 Kamal is Yousef son.
2 His parents names are Fatima and Yousef.
3 Shada and Kamal are Fatima and Yousef children.
4 Fatima got two children.

c Which of the sentences in **b** is different? Why?

2.3

a Match 1–4 to a–d to make four sentences about the family in **2.2**.

1 The children love	a in Mumbai.
2 Fatima and Yousef speak	b their iPods.
3 The children don't share	c two languages.
4 The family live	d a room.

b Transform the sentences in **a** into questions. Answer them with short answers.

Do they love their iPods? Yes, they do.

2.4

Choose the correct question word to complete the sentences.

1 *What / Where / Who* is this place? It's in Dubai.
2 *What / Where / Who* is your surname? It's Sánchez.
3 *What / Where / Who* is this woman? She's an artist.
4 *How much / How old* is the building? It's 50 years old.
5 *How many / How much* people do you see in the photo? Ten.

3.1 FREQUENCY ADVERBS

We use frequency adverbs to say how frequently we do things.

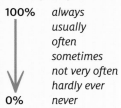

100%	*always*
	usually
	often
	sometimes
	not very often
	hardly ever
0%	*never*

Position of frequency adverbs

Frequency adverbs go before most verbs. But they go after the verb *be*:

I usually work/I don't usually work on Saturdays.
I'm usually/I'm not usually late for work.

Expressions with *once* & *every*

We say *every + day/week/month/year*.

We say *once + a day/a week/a month/a year*.

These expressions normally go at the end of a sentence:

I go shopping once a week. I get up late every day.

▶ 3.1

3.2 PRESENT SIMPLE: 3ʳᵈ PERSON SINGULAR

When we use the present simple with *he/she/it* in positive sentences, we add *-s* or *-es* to the verb. For questions and negatives, we use *does/doesn't* + infinitive:

What does he do all day? He sits on the sofa and plays video games.
He doesn't go to work.

+	He/She/It	comes	from Mexico.	
–	He/She/It	doesn't	come	from Mexico.
Wh-?	Where	does	he/she/it	come from?
Y/N?	Does	he/she/it	come	from Mexico?
Y/N	Yes, he/she/it does.		No, he/she/it doesn't.	

Spelling rules

With verbs that end in *-s*, *-sh*, *-ch* and *-x* we add *-es*:

He watches television.

With verbs that end in consonant + *y* we change the *-y* to *-i* and add *-es*:

She studies hard every night.

Some verbs are irregular:

have → has, do → does, go → goes

▶ 3.2

3.3 LIKE, LOVE, HATE + -ING

When we use a verb after *like*, *love* and *hate* in the present simple, we often use verb + *-ing*:

I love walking along the beach.

▶ 3.3

3.1

Night duty. Manchester General Hospital.

	Weeks 1–15	Weeks 16–31
Dr Johann Klein	✓	✓
Dr Mar Benítez		
Dr Ray Fuller	✓	

a Look at the schedule and complete the sentences with *always*, *sometimes* and *never*.

1 Dr Klein _____ works nights.
2 Dr Benítez _____ works nights.
3 Dr Fuller _____ works nights.

b Put the words in order to make sentences.

1 before / a / have / o'clock / usually / coffee / I / ten
2 the / ever / go / to / hardly / cinema / I
3 evening / I / television / the / always / in / watch
4 go / to / once / week / a / I / gym / the
5 bed / sometimes / very / I / to / late / go.
6 I / in / read / before / I / to / sleep / always / bed / go

c Rewrite the sentences so they are true for you.

3.2

a Complete the description of Karen with the correct form of the present simple.

Karen Wong is a teacher. She ⁽¹⁾ _____ *(come)* from Shanghai. She ⁽²⁾ _____ *(teach)* Chinese at a night school in Vancouver. She ⁽³⁾ _____ *(not have)* a typical routine because she ⁽⁴⁾ _____ *(study)* in the morning and ⁽⁵⁾ _____ *(work)* in the evening. She ⁽⁶⁾ _____ *(go)* to work by bus and ⁽⁷⁾ _____ *(arrive)* at about 7 o'clock. She ⁽⁸⁾ _____ *(finish)* at 10 o'clock at night. She ⁽⁹⁾ _____ *(not like)* life in Canada much because she really ⁽¹⁰⁾ _____ *(miss)* China and her family.

b Write four questions about Karen. Use *where*, *what*, *when* and *what time*.

3.3

Complete the sentences about what Justin and Patricia like and dislike.

1 Justin 👍 + walk with his 🐕

   Justin quite likes walking with his dog.

2 Patricia ❤ + shop

3 Justin 👎 + eat 🍕

4 Patricia 👍👍 + play ⚽

4.1 THERE IS/THERE ARE

Talking about one thing:

+	There's a big sofa.
–	There isn't a kitchen.
?	Is there a shower?
Y/N	Yes, there is./No, there isn't.

Talking about more than one thing:

+	There are some tables and chairs.
–	There aren't any lamps.
?	Are there any bookshelves?
Y/N	Yes, there are./No, there aren't.

We often use *a/an* with *There is/isn't* and *Is there?*

We often use *some* with *There are.*

We use *any* with *There aren't* and *Are there?*

When we talk about a group of people we use *There are/is*:
There are two of us./There's two of us. NOT ~~We are two~~.

▶ 4.1

4.2 PREPOSITIONS OF PLACE

We use prepositions of place before a noun to explain where a person or thing is situated:
*The window is **next to** the bed.*

1
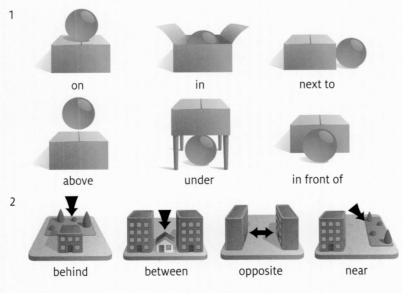

on   in   next to

above   under   in front of

2

behind   between   opposite   near

On & at

on the left   on the right   on the other side of the road   at the end of the road

▶ 4.2

4.1

a Look at the map of a beach resort. Correct the statements about it.

1 There are four car parks.
2 There isn't a swimming pool.
3 There are two banks.
4 There's a supermarket and two cinemas.
5 There's an art gallery.
6 There are a lot of hotels.

b These are true sentences about the map. Insert *some*, *any* or *a/an* where necessary.

1 There isn't airport.
2 There are beaches.
3 There's train station.
4 There aren't bars.

4.2

a Look around your classroom and answer the questions. Use a dictionary if necessary.

1 What's **in** your pockets now?
2 What's **on** the table?
3 Who or what's **in front of** you?
4 Who or what's **next to** you?
5 What's **above** your head?

b Look at the map again. Circle the best option, a or b.

1 a There's a bank next to the hotel.
  b There's a bank opposite the hotel.
2 a There's a cinema near the train station.
  b There's a swimming pool between the train station and the campsite.
3 a At the end of the main road there are some restaurants.
  b Near the main road there are some restaurants.
4 a Behind the train station there's a car park.
  b On the right of the bank there's a car park.

c Write five more sentences about where different places are on the map. Use *between*, *opposite*, *near*, *next to*, etc.

5.1 CAN/CAN'T

+	I/You/He/She/It/We/They		can	swim.
–	I/You/He/She/It/We/They		cannot/can't	swim.
?	Can	I/you/he/she/it/we/they		swim?
Y/N	Yes, No,	I/you/he/she/it/we/they		can. can't.

We use *can/can't* with the infinitive without *to*: *I can sing.*

We don't add *-s* for the third person singular: *He can ski.*

The contracted form of *cannot* is *can't*: *You can't use dollars here.*

We use *can/can't* + infinitive to talk about:

1. ability: *I can ski.* (= I know how to ski.)
2. permission and prohibition: *You can/can't smoke here.*
3. rules and regulations: *Three people can play.*
4. possibility: *You can ski in the mountains in winter.*

▶ 5.1

5.2 VERY WELL, QUITE WELL, NOT VERY WELL

very well = ✓✓✓   quite well = ✓✓   not very well = ✗

We often use *very well*, *quite well* and *not very well*:

1. in short answers with *can*:
   Can you ski? Yes, but not very well.
   Can Madeleine ski? Yes, very well.

2. with *can* + infinitive in full sentences:
   Marcia can read very well. Max can sing quite well. He can't talk very well.

We also use *(very) well* in questions:
Can Marcia read well? Can Max sing very well?

▶ 5.2

5.3 IMPERATIVES

The imperative form does not have a subject pronoun:
Touch your toes.

We form the negative with *don't*:
Don't stop!

We use the imperative:

1. to give instructions: *Touch your nose.*
2. to give orders: *Stop here! Show me your passport!*
3. to make an offer: *Have another drink!*
4. to make an invitation: *Come out with us tonight!*

Sometimes we use *just* + imperative for emphasis:
Just do it!

▶ 5.3

5.4 -LY ADVERBS

We use adverbs ending in *-ly* to describe a verb. They tell us **how** we do the action.

We form *-ly* adverbs by adding *-ly* to an adjective:
careful → carefully, slow → slowly

For adjectives that end in *-y*, change *-y* to *-ily*:
happy → happily

▶ 5.4

5.1

a Complete the sentences with *I*, or the name of someone you know well, so that they are true.

1. .... can play a musical instrument.
2. .... can't ski.
3. .... can only speak one language.
4. .... can play lots of different sports.
5. .... can't swim.
6. .... can't ride a bike.

b Look at the airport signs. Use the words in the box to write what they mean.

mobile   bus   liquids
luggage   car   information

6 = *You can ask for information here.*

5.2

Write full sentences or questions using the prompts.

1. Tom / ski / ✓✓✓
   Tom can ski very well.
2. Antonia / speak English / ✓ / ?
3. Jordi / swim / ✗
4. Feli / sing / ✓ / ?

5.3

a Connect the nouns and verbs. Then write the orders with an imperative.

Finish your drink.

1. finish — — — a toes
2. open   b shoes
3. take off — c drink
4. touch   d bag

b Think of a situation for each order in **a**.

5.4

Change the adjectives into adverbs. Then complete the orders with the correct adverb.

careful   quick   loud   quiet   slow

1. Drive ...., the road is quite dangerous.
2. Work ...., please – this is a library.
3. Finish your work ...., it's very late!
4. Hold it ...., it's very fragile.
5. Speak ...., he can't hear very well.

6.1 PRESENT CONTINUOUS

We use the present continuous tense to talk about what is happening **now**.

+	I'm You're/We're/They're He's/She's/It's	looking.
–	I'm not You/We/They aren't He/She/It isn't	looking.
?	Am I Are you/we/they Is he/she/it	looking?
Y/N	Yes, I am. Yes, we/you/they are. Yes, he/she/it is.	No, I'm not. No, we/you/they aren't. No, he/she/it isn't.

Spelling rules for *-ing* form

1 When a verb ends in consonant–vowel–consonant, double the final consonant and add *-ing*:
   shop → shopping

2 When a verb ends in *-e*, drop the *-e* and add *-ing*:
   dance → dancing

▶ 6.1

6.2 PRESENT CONTINUOUS & PRESENT SIMPLE

We use the present simple to talk about:

1 things that are generally true:
   I study Medicine.

2 habits and routines:
   He plays football on Saturdays.

We use the present continuous to talk about actions that are happening at the moment:
   I'm studying for my final exams right now.
   He's playing football in the park.

We use time expressions like *usually, sometimes, never, always* and *often* with the present simple.

We use time expressions like *at the moment, today* and *(right) now* with the present continuous.

▶ 6.2

6.1

a Complete the text with the correct forms of the present continuous.

> *The boss isn't here, so I can talk... Yes! ... No, we* (1)_____ *(not work) at the moment...*
> *Craig* (2)_____ *(read) the newspaper, Petra* (3)_____ *(write) on Facebook, Guido and Antonio* (4)_____ *(smoke) outside, Laura* (5)_____ *(listen) to her iPod and Rhona* (6)_____ *(not feel) well, she* (7)_____ *(sit) outside as well. Incredible, isn't it? What* (8)_____ *(you/do), Mary?* (9)_____ *(you/study)? Your exam is next week, you know...*

b Label the people in the illustration.

6.2

a <u>Underline</u> the correct form, present simple or present continuous, to complete the questions.

1 What *are you doing / do you do* at the moment?
2 What *are you usually wearing / do you usually wear* for work/college?
3 *Are you studying / Do you study* anything right now?
4 *Are you usually working / Do you usually work* every day or just on weekdays?
5 *Are you having / Do you have* a good day today?
6 *Are you always doing / Do you always do* your English grammar exercises?

b Write true answers to the questions.

7.1 PAST SIMPLE: *TO BE*

+	I/He/She/It was You/We/They were	very happy.	
–	I/He/She/It wasn't (was not) You/We/They weren't (were not)	very happy.	
?	Was I/he/she/it Were you/we/they	happy?	
Y/N	Yes, I/he/she/it was. Yes, you/we/they were.	No, I/he/she/it wasn't. No, you/we/they weren't.	

We often use *was/were* with *there*.

Use *was* to talk about single things:

Was there a swimming pool?

There wasn't a swimming pool, but there was a beach.

Use *were* to talk about more than one thing:

Were there a lot of tourists?

No, there weren't. There were local families and lots of children.

▶ 7.1

7.2 PAST SIMPLE: REGULAR & IRREGULAR VERBS

We use the past simple to talk about actions that happened in the past.

Most verbs have a regular past form. With regular verb forms in the past simple we add -ed to the infinitive.

We use *didn't* to form negative verbs and *did* to form questions.

+	I/You/We/They He/She/It	missed		the bus.	
–	I/You/We/They He/She/It	didn't	miss	the bus.	
?	Did	I/you/we/they he/she/it		miss	the bus?
Y/N	Yes, No,	I/you/we/they/he/she/it			did. didn't.

Spelling rules

1 When a verb ends in consonant–vowel–consonant, double the final consonant and add -ed: *stop → stopped*

2 When a verb ends in -e, drop the -e and add -ed: *dance → danced*

3 When a verb ends in consonant + y, change the -y to -i and add -ed: *try → tried*

4 When a verb ends in vowel + y, simply add -ed: *play → played*

Irregular verbs

Some verbs have an irregular past simple form in the affirmative. Here are some common irregular verbs:

do → did, go → went, have → had

▶ 7.2

7.3 USES OF THE PAST SIMPLE

We also use the past simple to talk about:

1 specific events in the past: *Yesterday I played football.*

2 habits and routines in the past: *I took the bus to school when I was younger.*
   (= I did this every day, not just on one specific occasion.)

▶ 7.3

7.1

a Choose the correct form of the verb. Then decide if the sentences are true or false.

1 There *was / were* a wall between East Berlin and West Berlin before 1989. T / F
2 Tokyo, Vienna and Sydney *was / were* all Olympic cities. T / F
3 Rio de Janeiro *was / were* once the capital of Brazil. T / F
4 The Vikings *was / were* from Scandinavia. T / F

b Order the words to make questions. Then answer the questions.

1 born / you / were / where ?
2 name / the / what / of / your / primary / school / was ?
3 you / at / home / last / night / were ?
4 with / your / family / you / were ?

7.2

Read about Leona's weekend. Six of the verbs in bold are incorrect. Find and correct the mistakes.

First I **goed** to the doctor's on Friday morning and everything was fine. After that I **tried** to get a haircut, but the hairdresser's was closed. That was bad luck. Then I **haved** my English class. It was great and I **talked** a lot in English. I think I'm improving. The class **finished** at ten, so I **went** for a drink with the other students. On Saturday I **played** tennis with my friend Luke. In the afternoon I **chated** with some friends on the internet. I **didn't want** to go out, so I **stayed** in and **watchd** TV. In the evening I **went** for dinner at the Capri with Gloria. Sunday was quiet. I **didn't did** anything until the evening, when I **had** a date at the theatre. After the show, I was really tired – what a weekend!

7.3

a Write three sentences about what you did yesterday.

1 ....
2 ....
3 ....

b Write three sentences about things you did every day when you were at primary school.

1 ....
2 ....
3 ....

8.1 PAST SIMPLE: IRREGULAR VERBS

Here are more common verbs that have an irregular form in the past simple:

give → gave	read → read /red/	speak → spoke
leave → left	say → said	think → thought
make → made	send → sent	write → wrote
meet → met	sit → sat	

Remember that in questions and negatives, we use *did/didn't* and the infinitive:

*What did she **write** about?*
NOT *What did she ~~wrote~~ about?*
*She didn't **speak** about our interests.*
NOT *She didn't ~~spoke~~ about our interests.*

Past simple: time expressions

Here are some common time expressions we use with the past simple:

- *in* + year: *in 1966*
- *at* + age: *at the age of 16*
- *during* + period of time: *during his career*
- *on* + day: *on his birthday, on the day he died*

▶ 8.1

8.2 VERB + *TO* + INFINITIVE

Here are some common verbs that are always followed by *to* + infinitive:

- decide: *We decided to go to the party.*
- hope: *She's hoping to go to university next year.*
- plan: *They're planning to buy a new house.*
- want: *I want to watch the football.*
- would like: *I'd like to see a film tonight.*

▶ 8.2

8.3 SEQUENCERS

We use sequencers to show the order of events and actions in a story. Here are some common sequencers and their uses:

- *first* or *at first*: to introduce the initial event or action in a series
- *then*: to introduce the events or actions that follow
- *later*: to explain that an event or action happened some time after the others
- *finally* or *in the end*: to talk about the end of the story

▶ 8.3

8.1

a Complete the sentences with one negative and one positive form of the verb in brackets.

1 Agatha Christie ___*didn't write*___ romances, she ___*wrote*___ crime novels. *(write)*
2 Hadrian _____ 'Veni, vidi, vici,' Caesar _____ it. *(say)*
3 Cromwell _____ America, Columbus _____ it. *(discover)*
4 People _____ emails in the past, they _____ letters. *(send)*
5 People _____ e-books in the past, they _____ paper books. *(read)*
6 People _____ a partner online in the past, they _____ in person. *(meet)*

b Choose the correct preposition to complete the sentences. Then change the sentences so they are true for you.

1 I started school *at / on* the age of seven.
2 I was born *in / on* 1992.
3 I went to Norway *at / during* the summer holidays.
4 I went to the cinema *at / on* my birthday.

8.2

Order the words to make sentences. Are these statements true about you?

When I was a kid…
1 hoped / famous / I / be / to / one day
2 make / a lot of money / planned / to / I

Now that I'm older…
3 happy / want / I / have / life / to / a
4 better / like / a / be / I'd / to / person

8.3

Complete the story using *finally*, *later*, *at first* and *then*.

I always wanted a large house and lots of money, so I married a rich man. _____ we were very happy. _____ my husband lost his job. _____ we lost the house, the car and all our money! But we still had each other. _____ I understood that money isn't everything!

9.1 COUNTABLE & UNCOUNTABLE NOUNS

Countable nouns can be singular or plural:

an egg/some eggs
a cake/some cakes

Uncountable nouns are always singular:

some toast with butter and jam

We can't use *a/an* or numbers with uncountable nouns:

~~*a butter*~~
~~*one butter*~~

A/An & some

	Singular	Plural
Countable nouns	a/an a banana an egg	some some tomatoes
Uncountable nouns	some some milk some rice	

1 Some nouns can be both countable (C) and uncountable (U), e.g. *coffee*:

C: *I had a coffee for breakfast.* (= a cup of coffee)

U: *Coffee is good for you.* (= coffee in general)

2 Some words are uncountable in English but countable in other languages, e.g. *toast*. We say:

some toast, a piece of toast, a slice of toast, NOT ~~*a toast*~~.

▶ 9.1

9.2 QUANTIFIERS

We use quantifiers to talk about quantity:

• *How much/many...?* = asking a question about quantity

• *too much/too many* = more than you need or want

• *a lot of/lots of* = a large quantity

• *some* = a part of something but not all

• *a little/a few, not much/not many* = a small quantity

Notice which ones we use with uncountable nouns and which with countable nouns:

Uncountable nouns	How much (butter)? too much/a little/not much (milk)
Countable nouns	How many (bananas)? too many/a few/not many (tomatoes)
Both uncountable & countable	a lot of/lots of/some (rice/biscuits)

▶ 9.2

9.1

Match the labels,1–6, to the photos, a–f. Then choose the best word to complete the labels.

1 *a /(some)* water ..d..   4 *a / some* rice ....
2 *a / an* apple ....   5 *a slice of / a* bread ....
3 *a / some* coffee ....   6 *some / an* onions ....

9.2

Complete the statements with the words in the boxes. Do you agree with what the people say? Why/Why not?

> a few   how much   lots of   much

(1) .... *salt and sugar do I eat? I don't use* (2) .... *salt. I think it's bad for you. The problem is I love sugary foods. Chocolate is my favourite. I eat* (3) .... *chocolate! I try to eat* (4) .... *fresh vegetables when I can.*

> a lot of   how much   many   much

(5) .... *fruit do you think I need to eat? I eat* (6) .... *bananas and apples, but I don't eat* (7) .... *exotic fruit. I don't like the taste of mango or papaya, not* (8) .... *people do.*

10.1 COMPARATIVE ADJECTIVES

We use comparative adjectives to compare two things and talk about the difference between them:

The e-reader is lighter than a book.

The form we use depends on the length of the adjective.

One syllable	Two syllables ending in -y	Two syllables or more
Add -er *fast → faster*	Change -y to -i and add -er *easy → easier*	Use *more* + adjective *expensive → more expensive*

We use *than* with comparative adjectives:

*It's bigger **than** mine.*

Spelling rules for one-syllable adjectives

1 When the adjective ends in -e add -r: *white → whiter*

2 When the adjective ends in consonant–vowel–consonant, double the last letter and add -er: *fat → fatter, big → bigger*

3 Some adjectives are irregular, e.g. *good → better, bad → worse*

▶ 10.1

10.2 *GOING TO*

We use *be* + *going to* + infinitive to talk about future plans.

+	I You/We/They He/She/It	'm going to 're going to 's going to	work hard.	
−	I You/We/They He/She/It	'm not going to aren't going to isn't going to	work hard.	
?	Am Are Is	I you/we/they he/she/it	going to	work hard?
Y/N	Yes, I am. Yes, you/we/they are. Yes, he/she/it is.		No, I'm not. No, you/we/they aren't. No, he/she/it isn't.	

▶ 10.2

10.3 PERSONAL PRONOUNS

We use personal pronouns instead of the names of people and things.

Subject pronouns tell us who, or what, the subject of the verb is. They usually come before the verb:

I'm going to call Tomas.

Object pronouns tell us who, or what, the object of the verb is. They come

1 after the verb: *I'm going to call **him**.*

2 after prepositions: *Tomas is going to come with **us**.*

Subject	Object		Subject	Object
I	me		we	us
you	you		you	you
he	him		they	them
she	her			
it	it			

▶ 10.3

10.1

a Choose the best form of the adjective in brackets to complete the sentences.

1 Dogs are .... (friendlier / more friendly) than cats.

2 Coffee is .... (more nice / nicer) than tea.

3 English is .... (easier / more easy) to learn than Chinese.

4 The flu is .... (badder / worse) than a cold.

5 The mountains are .... (more good / better) than the beach for a holiday.

6 Trains are .... (more expensive / expensiver) than planes.

b Do you agree with these statements? Change the ones you do not agree with.

c Look at the sentences in a again. Write a different sentence comparing the two things. Use a dictionary to help you.

Dogs are noisier than cats.

10.2

a Reorder the sentences to write questions using *going to*.

1 What / you / to / going / do / are / tomorrow ?
What are you going to do tomorrow?

2 going / you / are / do / to / When / some / studying ?

3 What / you / to / are / going / study ?

4 see / your / When / going / to / are / you / friends ?

5 you / watch / going / tonight / Are / to / TV ?

6 are / What / you / to / going / watch ?

b Write true answers to the questions. You can use positive and negative sentences.

10.3

Complete the sentences with subject or object pronouns.

1 This is Annie Leibovitz. I like .... a lot. ....'s a great photographer.

2 This is my watch. ....'s an old Rolex. My grandfather gave .... to .... when I was 10 years old.

3 My brother and I had this bike. .... rode it when .... were children. .... has a lot of happy memories for ....

11.1 SUPERLATIVE ADJECTIVES

We use superlative adjectives to compare people/things with all the other people/things in a group:

Hairdressers are the happiest profession. (= Hairdressers are happier than all the other professions.)

The form we use depends on the length of the adjective.

One syllable	Two syllables ending in -y	Two syllables or more
Add -est fast → fastest	Change -y to -i and add -est easy → easiest	Use most + adjective expensive → most expensive

We often use *the* or possessive adjectives (*my, your, his*) with superlative adjectives:

It's **the** best job. She's **my** best friend.

Spelling rules for one-syllable adjectives

1 When the adjective ends in -e add -st: *white → whitest*

2 When the adjective ends in consonant–vowel–consonant, double the last letter and add -est: *fat → fattest, big → biggest*

3 Some adjectives are irregular, e.g. *good → best, bad → worst*

▶ 11.1

11.2 WILL/WON'T

We use *will/won't* + infinitive to talk about what we know and think about the future:

I'll be 30 next birthday. (Future fact: I know this is true.)

It'll be a great party. (Prediction: I think this is true.)

+	I/You/He/She/It/We/They	'll (will)	win.
–	I/You/He/She/It/We/They	won't (will not)	win.
?	Will	I/you/he/she/it/we/they	win?
Y/N	Yes, No,	I/you/he/she/it/we/they	will. won't.

We use the contracted form of *will* (*'ll*) after names and pronouns:

I think Tom will win. → *I think Tom'll win.*
He will enjoy the job. → *He'll enjoy the job.*

▶ 11.2

11.3 WILL & MIGHT

We can use both *will* and *might* to make predictions about the future.

We use *will* to say that we are **sure** something will happen.
We use *might* to say that we think something is **possible**, but we're not sure:

He'll pass all his exams. (I'm sure this is true.)
He might pass all his exams. (This is a possibility, but I'm not 100% sure.)

When we want to ask other people what their opinion is about the future we usually use *will*:

Will there be jobs for them? What will they do?

+	I/You/He/She/It/We/They	might	win.
–	I/You/He/She/It/We/They	might not	win.

▶ 11.3

11.1

a Complete the questions with the superlative form of the adjective in brackets.

1 What's the _____ thing about learning English? *(easy)*
2 What's the _____ thing about learning English? *(difficult)*
3 What's the _____ bar you know? *(good)*
4 What's the _____ city you know? *(interesting)*
5 What's the _____ place in your town? *(busy)*
6 What's the _____ thing about travelling? *(bad)*
7 What's the _____ gadget that you have? *(new)*
8 Which company is the _____ employer in your region? *(big)*

b Answer the questions and explain your answers.

The easiest thing about learning English is the grammar. The grammar in my language is more complicated!

11.2

Write predictions using *will/won't* and the prompts.

1 by 2020 / there / be / food for everybody in Africa
2 my team / win / cup next season
3 the temperature of the planet / increase a lot over the next ten years
4 doctors / find / a cure for cancer in the next ten years
5 I / run a marathon next year

11.3

a Make predictions for the weather where you live using *will/won't* or *might/might not*. Use the vocabulary on page 73 to help you.

1 Tomorrow it _____ .
2 Next weekend it _____ .
3 On my birthday it _____ .
4 Next December it _____ .
5 Next July it _____ .

b Change the predictions for a town/city in another country.

12.1 Present perfect: *have you ever...?*

We use the present perfect to talk about past experiences:

Have you ever been to Argentina?   No, I haven't, but I've been to Chile.

We form the present perfect with *have/has* + past participle.

+	I/You/We/They He/She/It	've (have) 's (has)	been to Brazil.
–	I/You/We/They He/She/It	haven't (have not) hasn't (has not)	been to Brazil.
?	Have Has	I/you/we/they he/she/it	(ever) been to Brazil?
Y/N	Yes, I/you/we/they have. Yes, he/she/it has.	No, I/you/we/they haven't. No, he/she/it hasn't.	

Past participles

We form the past participle of regular verbs by adding *-ed* to the infinitive of the verb: *visit → visited*

The spelling rules of regular past participles are the same as the rules for regular past simple affirmative verbs. See page 146.

Some verbs are irregular: *meet → met, see → seen, win → won*

Been/Gone

Go has two past participles, *been* and *gone*. When we use the present perfect to talk about experience, we usually use *been*:

He's been to London. (= He went to London at some time in the past, but he's not there now.)

He's gone to London. (= He went to London at some time in the past and he's still there now.)

▶ 12.1

12.2 Present perfect & past simple

We use the present perfect when we don't give a specific time in the past:

*I've **been** to Rome.* (We don't say when.)

We use the past simple if we say when something happened:

*I went to Zurich **a few years ago**.*

We use the present perfect to ask an initial question about past experiences:

Have you (ever) been to Thailand? Yes, I have.

We use the past simple to ask for more information:

Did you have a good time there? It was OK.

▶ 12.2

12.3 Review of verbs

We use the present simple to talk about things we do regularly:
I go to English class twice a week.

We use the present continuous to talk about what we are doing now:
I'm watching the football.

We use the past simple to talk about what happened at a specific time in the past: *I went to bed late last night.*

We use *going to* to talk about future plans: *I'm going to start a business.*

We use *will* to talk about what we know or think about the future:
Jack will be 6 on Saturday.

We use *can* to talk about ability and permission: *Can you speak Japanese?*

▶ 12.3

12.1

a Order the letters to make irregular past participles. Then write the infinitive form of the verb.

1 neeb   *been – go*
2 tem   ....
3 konpes   ....
4 tenrwit   ....
5 nlwof   ....
6 nru   ....
7 neod   ....
8 tugaht   ....

b Reorder the words to make questions with the participles in a.

1 you / Have / a marathon / run / ever ?
2 father / Has / a letter / ever / your / written / to you ?
3 you / flown / Atlantic / the / Have / across / ever ?
4 to / spoken / Has / your / ever / mother / English / anyone ?
5 done / you / Have / any unusual sports / ever ?
6 taught / you / ever / Have / anything ?
7 met / a / you / ever / Have / person / famous ?
8 of / been / your / family / a / member / to / ever / Australia / Has ?

c Write true short answers to the questions.

1 *Yes, I have./No, I haven't.*

12.2

Choose three questions in 12.1b. Give more information about each one using the past simple.

5 Have you ever done any unusual sports?
Yes, I have. I played a sport called Jorkyball once. It's a kind of football. I played it when I was in Italy. I liked it. It was fun.

12.3

Look at the pictures. Write two or three sentences for each to talk about 1) the past, 2) the present, 3) the future. Make the sentences true for you.

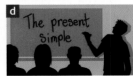

I had a dog when I was a kid, but I don't have one now. I'm not going to buy one because my flat is very small.

WRITING BANK

1 FILLING IN FORMS

a

Create a new account

First name: [_____]

Surname: [_____]

Login name: [_____] @freemail.com

Choose a password: [_____]
Minimum of 8 characters in length.

Re-enter password: [_____]

b

APPLICATION FOR ENTRY AND EXIT VISA

1 NAME AND SURNAME (please use block capitals)

2 GENDER (tick the correct box)
   Male [ ]   Female [ ]

3 MARITAL STATUS (delete as applicable)
   I'm married / single

4 DATE OF BIRTH (day/month/year)

5 PLACE OF BIRTH (town and country)

6 NATIONALITY

7 PASSPORT OR NATIONAL IDENTITY CARD NUMBER

8 OCCUPATION

9 PRESENT ADDRESS

10 TELEPHONE NUMBER

I declare that the statements made in this Application are true and correct.

Signature ....

Date ....

---

1 Look at the forms above. Which form is

1 to ask for a visa to visit a foreign country?
2 to open a new email account?

2 Look again. Which form(s) ask(s) for

1 your full name?
2 your email address?
3 your ID number?
4 your address?

3 **a** Which person, a or b, followed the instructions correctly?

> 1 **Please use block capitals.**
>   a *Samuel Pérez Rodríguez*
>   b *SAMUEL PÉREZ RODRÍGUEZ*
>
> 2 **Tick the correct box.**
>   a male [✓] female [ ]
>   b (male) [ ] female [ ]
>
> 3 **Delete as applicable.**
>   a I'm married / <u>single</u>
>   b I'm ~~married~~ / single

b How do you say *tick* and *delete* in your language? What do forms in your country say?

4 Complete forms a and b above. Follow the instructions very carefully.

> **TIP**
> Always read all the instructions very carefully before you start to fill in a form. If it's important, ask a friend or a family member to check it for you.

2 A BLOG POST

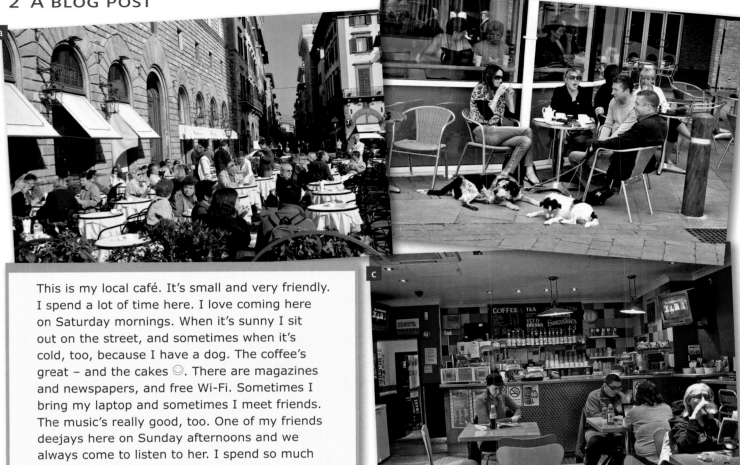

This is my local café. It's small and very friendly. I spend a lot of time here. I love coming here on Saturday mornings. When it's sunny I sit out on the street, and sometimes when it's cold, too, because I have a dog. The coffee's great – and the cakes ☺. There are magazines and newspapers, and free Wi-Fi. Sometimes I bring my laptop and sometimes I meet friends. The music's really good, too. One of my friends deejays here on Sunday afternoons and we always come to listen to her. I spend so much time here it's almost my second home!

1 a Read the blog post. Choose the best photo, a, b or c, to go with it.

b Write a title for the post.

2 Read the post again. Are the statements true (T) or false (F)?

1 The style of writing is very formal.
2 The writer uses the first person.
3 He/She is talking about a personal experience.
4 He/She does not expect a reply.

3 a Imagine you have a blog. You want to write a post about a favourite place. Complete the notes with the information you want to include.

The place _____
Where it is _____
When you go there _____
What you do there _____
Why you like it _____

b 💬 Compare your ideas with a partner.

4 Write your blog post in a similar style to the post in 1a. Use your answers in 2 as a guide.

5 Show your post to a partner. Ask him/her to give it a title.

> **TIP**
> Blog posts are usually short and interesting. They often describe a personal experience. They normally speak directly to the reader and use a friendly, relaxed style.

3 A SHORT NOTE

1 a Read the note below. <u>Underline</u> the important information.

> At Jake's Bar. Want to join us?
> Get #2 bus to High St. Jake's Bar
> on left, next to bank.

b What does the note do? Tick the correct options.

1 explain where the writer is ☐
2 explain how to get somewhere ☐
3 arrange a time to meet ☐
4 invite the writer's friend for a drink ☐
5 explain the bus routes ☐

2 Read a voicemail message with the same information as the note in 1a. <u>Underline</u> all the words that are not included in the note.

> We're at Jake's Bar. Do you want to join us? You can get the number 2 bus to the High Street. Jake's Bar is on the left, next to the bank.

3 a Read another voicemail message. Cross out all the unnecessary words.

> Hi, there! Pablo's at football practice. They're in the park, you know the one, next to the swimming pool. Do you think you can give him a lift home at about 8 o'clock? Thanks a lot! It's a big help!

b Write the message as a short note. Use as few words as possible.

4 a 💬 Work in pairs. You want to do something together as a class. Decide on what you want to do and where.

b Write a short note for the rest of the class. Explain

● what you want to do and where
● where the place is
● how to get there.

5 Compare your note with the rest of the class. Decide which plan is best.

TIP

When you write a short note, you don't need to use full sentences. You just need to make sure you include the most important information.

4 AN EMAIL TO A FRIEND

To: Ulrike
From: Carola
Subject: Hi!

a Hi, Ulrike, thanks for your email! Did you finish your work on time? How was your weekend?

b We had a great time. John loved his birthday present. Thanks for the idea! He knew nothing about it – it was a big surprise. We just told him we wanted to take him out for a special meal – he was really surprised when we arrived at the kayaking centre!

c It was a fantastic day! We did a three-hour trip down the river – all the way to the beach. It's really beautiful there. And the weather was perfect – warm, sunny, no wind. When we got back we had a picnic under the trees. It was really quiet and peaceful – Toni and John went to sleep!

d We really have to do it again soon. Maybe next time you can come, too! How about some time next month? What do you think?

Speak soon,

Carola

1 Read Carola's email to a friend. Why did she write the email?

1 to invite Ulrike to a party
2 to thank Ulrike for her birthday present
3 to tell Ulrike about her weekend

2 Read the email again and answer the questions.

1 What was John's birthday present?
2 Who suggested the idea first?
3 Was it a good idea? Why/Why not?
4 Does Carola want to go again? How do you know?

3 Work in pairs. Look at the structure of the email. Which paragraph

1 describes what happened that day?
2 shows that Carola is answering an email from Ulrike?
3 invites Ulrike to reply?
4 tells us the main reason why Carola is writing to Ulrike?

4 **a** What phrases does Carola use to begin and end her email? What other phrases can you use?

b Look at the phrases in the box. Which go a) at the beginning, b) at the end of an email?

Great to hear from you!   Hope all's well with you.
Keep in touch!   How's it going?   Take care!   Bye for now.

5 Answer the questions about the email.

1 Are the sentences long or short?
2 What is the dash (–) used for? Can you use dashes like this in your language?
3 Which tense is used in the email? Where does this change?

6 Write an email to a friend describing something you did last week.

TIP

When you write an email to a friend, always start with a personal question or comment. Use paragraphs to separate the different sections. Use simple sentences in an informal style. Remember to finish the email with a friendly ending!

5 A REPLY TO A BLOG POST

1 Read the blog post. What help does the writer need?

Recently a friend asked me for some advice. She had some visitors for the weekend. She wanted to take them out to eat somewhere special – somewhere they could eat some really nice, typical local food. I suggested a restaurant next to the market in the centre of town. They serve fresh fish from the market there. It's one of my favourite places. My friend agreed – she loves it, too. But the problem was that one of her visitors was a strict vegetarian and the other didn't like fish!

We live in a seaside town, and most of the best restaurants serve fish. The ones that don't serve fish, serve meat! There aren't really any vegetarian restaurants. We looked in the phone book, we looked online... no luck! Does anybody out there have any ideas?

Tags food vegetarians local restaurants **comments** (3)

2 **a** Read the post again. What was the writer's suggestion? Why wasn't it a good suggestion?

b Read the comments and answer the questions.

1 Is Tan's suggestion a good one?
2 Why/Why not?
3 Why does Kelly write two replies?

Comments

Tan says How about this? The Banana Tree Café. A new Asian restaurant that opened two weeks ago. It serves fish, but it also specialises in vegetarian meals. The food's great, the prices are good, the atmosphere is very relaxed and it's open seven days a week.

Kelly says Thanks, we'll try it and let you know.

Kelly says Thank you so much, Tan! My friend tried it with her visitors. They loved it! It's now one of my favourite restaurants, too ☺

3 Read the blog post and comments again. <u>Underline</u> all the adjectives. What do they describe? Are they positive or negative?

4 **a** 💬 Work in pairs. Imagine that the blog writer lives in your town. Discuss which restaurants you can recommend and decide on the best one.

b Write a short reply to the blog post. Suggest a place to eat and say why you think it's a good option. Remember to use adjectives in your description.

5 Exchange replies with another pair. Write a comment back to them. Continue exchanging comments until you have nothing left to say.

TIP

When you add a comment or reply to a blog post, use simple language and keep the comment short and to the point. If you are the blog writer, remember to thank people for their comments.

6 A REPLY TO AN ONLINE ADVERT

1 Read the email. Which advert (a–d) is Ana answering? What are the other adverts about?

> **Subject:** Advert
>
> Hi,
>
> I saw your advert in Small Ads. I'd like to know where the next meeting is, please. And do I need to pay anything or is it free?
>
> Thank you,
>
> Ana

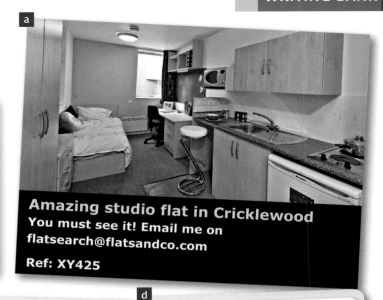

a

Amazing studio flat in Cricklewood
You must see it! Email me on
flatsearch@flatsandco.com

Ref: XY425

b

I'm driving from London to Rome at the beginning of August.

Anyone want to share the driving and the expenses?

Email me on *rosa89@gomail.net*

c

Want to practise your English?

Join us at the Language Exchange. We meet every Thursday evening at 8 p.m. for a drink and a chat. Email languageexchange@gomail.net to find out where the next meeting is.

See you there!

d

3 for 1 computer games

Do you have any games you don't play anymore? Why not bring them to us!

Three second-hand games get you one brand new game of your choice.

3for1@oldfornew.com

2 Read the email again and answer the questions.
1 Which descriptions match Ana's email best?
  a short and direct
  b formal and polite
  c friendly and polite
  d formal and distant

2 What does Ana's email **not** do? Tick the options.
  a give information about herself
  b ask for more information about the Language Exchange
  c arrange a time to meet
  d thank the person she's writing to
  e explain where she saw the advert

3 **a** Imagine you are interested in two of the other adverts. Write short, polite emails asking for more information.

b Show your emails to a partner. Can he/she guess which adverts you're answering?

4 **a** Read the reply to Ana's email. Does it answer all her questions?

> **Subject:** Meeting place
>
> Hi Ana,
>
> We're meeting at the Cactus Café on New Street, next to the old theatre. There's no fee to pay, but all members buy their own food and drink.
>
> Hope to see you on Thursday!
>
> Stefan

b Write similar replies to your partner's emails in 3a.

TIP

Remember to make your emails short, clear and to the point. They do not need to be formal. They should have a polite but friendly tone.

COMMUNICATION BANK

4.1 Grammar, page 41, Exercise 5

4.5 Writing task, page 47, Exercise 3

http://www.lagoazul.es

Swimming pool open from 8 a.m. to 8 p.m. – free to guests
Wi-Fi access in cabins – $10.50 a week
Free Wi-Fi in the bar and restaurant
Bikes   1 hour: $5   half a day: $20
Kayaks   1 hour: $5   half a day: $20
Horse riding on request – ask at reception

4.2 Grammar, page 43, Exercise 5

5.5 Speaking task, page 57, Exercise 7

Read the extra information about Nia and her family. <u>Underline</u> the important information. Compare your notes on the two interviews. Then decide who is the best childminder for her, and why.

Nia Thomas

We live in a big house in the country. It's 10 km to the nearest town. There's no public transport. A car or bike is essential. The childminder can use our car if necessary. The boys have bikes and they love cycling. There are lots of good places to cycle near the house. I don't want the boys to watch TV or play computer games during the day. In the morning the boys do two hours of schoolwork – reading, writing, Maths and Spanish. Jake has judo lessons twice a week and Josh plays the guitar. They need to practise every day. We have a swimming pool in the garden. The boys can swim, but need an adult with them at all times. We have three big dogs. They love playing with the boys. I do all the cooking and cleaning, but sometimes I need help with the shopping.

REVIEW B, page 68, Grammar, Exercise 4

REVIEW B, page 69, Functional language, Exercise 1

Student A

Act out a phone conversation. Call student B and ask to speak to Joy. You want to talk to her about a game of tennis. You want to change the time to 6.30 p.m.

11.3 Speaking, page 123, Exercise 3

Student B

Think of three questions to ask a fortune-teller about each of these topics:

love, life, health, holidays, work

REVIEW B, page 71, Reading & Speaking, Exercises 1–2

8.5 Writing task, page 91, Exercise 5

Student A

The summer redneck* games take place every year in July in East Dublin, Georgia, USA. The first games took place in 1996, the same year as the Olympics in Atlanta, Georgia. The games were a comic version of the official Olympics. They were a great success. Five thousand people came to the first games. There were lots of strange competitions, including diving into mud (see photo on page 91). The games still take place every year and thousands of people come to watch and compete.

* *redneck* = a working-class white person from the southern states of the USA

9.3 Listening & Reading, page 98, Exercise 1b

We throw away a THIRD of the food we buy...

... makes you CRY, doesn't it?

9.4 Functional language, page 100, Exercise 6

Students A and B, you are the customers. Student C, you are the waiter. Act out the scene using the menu below.

PIZZA PALACE

STARTERS

Asparagus
The finest asparagus with fresh Parmesan cheese and extra virgin olive oil.

Antipasto
A choice of cured Italian meats, served with baked ciabatta, rocket, rustica tomatoes and Parmesan cheese.

MAINS

Margherita
Mozzarella and tomato: pure and simple.

American
Nothing but a big helping of pepperoni for those who love their flavours strong and simple.

Four Seasons
Four pizzas in one: mushrooms, pepperoni, mozzarella, olives, anchovies and capers.

Pollo Siciliano
Chicken in a rich tomato sauce, served on a bed of rice.

DESSERTS

Tiramisu
Italian for 'pick me up': espresso coffee, cocoa, rich cream, mascarpone and Marsala sponge.

Fragole Fresche
Fresh strawberries topped with a blend of honey and fresh yoghurt.

REVIEW C, page 103, Functional language, Exercise 2

Student A

Tell student B your news. Take turns responding to each other's news.

I passed the exam. I got an A.

Dad bought a new car last week.

I left my bag on the train!

Helen wrote me an email last week. She's in Australia!

10.1 Grammar, page 109, Exercise 4

Look at the pairs of pictures and answer the questions.

1 What's the difference between the two items?
2 Which item do you prefer in each pair? Why?

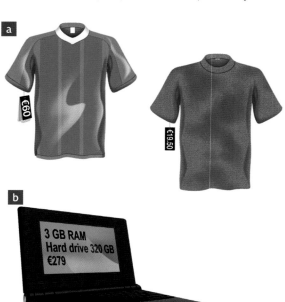
a

b

3 GB RAM
Hard drive 320 GB
€279

6 GB RAM
Hard drive 500 GB
€730

c

10.2 Speaking, page 110, Exercise 2

Read the survey questions. Answer them with *always*, *sometimes* or *never*. Who is the most dependent on their mobile phone in your group? Why?

You and your mobile

1 Do you send more than 15 texts a day?
2 Do you use your mobile like a radio in public places?
3 If you get a missed call, do you phone back immediately?
4 Do you make calls instead of texting, even if it's an expensive time or it's long distance?
5 Do you look at your mobile first thing when you wake up?
6 If you're at a concert, do you leave your phone on silent and take photos with it?
7 If you leave your mobile at home, do you go back home to get it?
8 Do you text or make calls when you're bored?
9 Do you get anxious if a person doesn't respond to your call or text at once?
10 Do you ever turn off your mobile? When?

11.1 Speaking & Listening, page 119, Exercise 3b

1 **The five worst-paid jobs in the UK (with salaries of less than £10,000 a year):**
call centre workers, cleaners, fast-food restaurant staff, hairdressers, school cooks

2 **The five best-paid jobs in the UK (with salaries of over £1,000,000 a year):**
bankers, best-selling writers, celebrities, footballers, lawyers

3 **The five most stressful jobs in the UK:**
air traffic controllers, inner-city teachers, junior doctors, miners, police officers

11.3 Speaking, page 123, Exercise 3

Student A

Think of three predictions that student B might want to hear about these topics:

love, life, health, holidays, work

Then answer student B's questions.

REVIEW B, page 69, Functional language, Exercise 1

Student B

Act out a phone conversation. Student A calls you and asks to speak to Joy. Explain that Joy isn't in, she's at a music lesson. Take a message.

8.5 Writing task, page 91, Exercise 5

Student B

In a small village in Gloucestershire*, south-west England, a strange event happens every year: a cheese-rolling competition. Last year thousands of people took part. The event is hundreds of years old. It takes place on the last Monday in May. The event consists of a number of races down a very steep hill. At the start of each race, a local celebrity rolls a cheese down the hill. The racers run after the cheese. The first person to reach the bottom of the hill is the winner. The winner gets... guess what... the cheese they ran after, of course!

* Gloucestershire is famous for its rich red cheese.

9.0 page 92, Exercise 2

The photo shows the food an average family wastes every month.

REVIEW C, page 103, Functional language, Exercise 2

Student B

Tell student A your news. Take turns responding to each other's news.

I failed my driving test – again! That's the fifth time!

My parents are buying a new house – with a swimming pool!

Sorry, I can't play tennis with you tomorrow.

The school is offering free English classes in the morning.

2.10, *p. 22, Ex 6*

H = Harry   S = Sara

H: Hi, I'm Hans.

S: Hi, I'm Sara.

H: What do you do, Sara? Do you work here?

S: No, I'm a student.

H: Oh? What do you study?

S: Medicine – I want to be a doctor.

H: So what university do you go to?

S: I'm at Central College.

H: And what year are you in?

S: The second year, I have four more years to go!

H: Well, good luck!

S: And you, Hans … What do you do?

H: I'm a reporter.

S: Oh? Who do you work for?

H: I work for a local newspaper.

S: And where do you work? At home?

H: Yes – and sometimes I go to the newspaper offices for meetings.

S: What do you write about?

H: Sports … and travel.

S: That sounds fun.

H: Yes, it is.

3.4, *p. 26, Ex 2*

Michelle

During the week I get up early, at about half past six. Then I have a shower and I get dressed. I always have a coffee before I leave the house. I get the bus to work. I work in a bank in the town centre. I start work at 8 a.m. At the weekend I usually get up early, too, at about seven / seven-thirty. I go for a run before breakfast. In the evenings, I usually stay in. I don't like going out. I watch DVDs with my boyfriend. On Sunday I go to church and then I clean the house. I hardly ever go out for a drink.

Veronica

I work in a restaurant in town. We often work late. Sometimes we close at one-thirty or two o'clock in the morning! I usually get up at about ten-thirty and I have a long breakfast. I don't do much in the morning. I sometimes watch DVDs or talk to a friend on the phone. I sometimes go to the gym, but not very often! I have lunch at about half past two and then I start work at four-fifteen. After work I go home, I have a shower and I go to bed. At the weekend, I always go out for a drink after work and we usually go clubbing. And I go shopping once a week!

3.6, *p. 29, Ex 3*

Well, it's true that I live at home and I'm 35. It's comfortable at home. But I'm not a slob, I do something to help in the house. In fact we all help! I go shopping at the supermarket every weekend, my brother Max cleans the house and my parents cook dinner. As for my hobbies, my mum doesn't know about them! I have lots of hobbies – I do sports. I usually play tennis on Saturday morning and I always play football on Thursdays. I go out every weekend, to the cinema or to a bar. And, of course, I watch television every night. It's great! But, it's true, I don't have many friends. I'm not lazy, I'm just very shy.

3.13, *p. 33, Ex 5*

I = interviewer   H = Hannah

I: Can I ask you a few questions?

H: Yes, of course.

I: Thank you. What's your favourite free-time activity?

H: Erm … I don't know … I really like spending time with friends … going out … you know, to the cinema, dancing…

I: How often do you go out with your friends?

H: We usually go out two or three times a week.

I: Do you like watching TV?

H: Yes, I do.

I: Do you watch TV every night?

H: Yes, more or less every night.

I: How much time do you spend watching TV every night?

H: I don't know … it depends … about two or three hours, I guess.

I: And what's your favourite programme?

H: Well … I love watching films.

I: OK, that's it. Thanks a lot.

H: You're welcome.

4.1, *p. 39, Ex 5*

This is the plan of my flat. There's only one floor. This is the entrance, here, see? Number 1. This is the hall – number 2 – and this is the bedroom on the right, number 3. Next to the bedroom is the bathroom, number 4. The living room is here, on the left – number 6. It's quite big and I have a study in the corner. The kitchen is next to the living room – number 5 – you can't enter it from the hall. And here's my favourite place in the flat – the balcony, number 7. I love sitting out here in the evening.

4.2, *p. 40, Ex 3*

H = Hugo   P = Patrick   L = Leonor

H: Hello, Patrick. Thanks for talking to me, I'm Hugo.

P: *Bonjour* … sorry, good morning … nice to meet you!

H: So tell me, Patrick, what's all this about?

P: Well, we're here to protest about the problems of homeless people. It's very expensive to buy or rent a flat here in Paris. Lots of people live on the streets. We're here to help them … to try and help them. It's a very serious problem. There are thousands and thousands of homeless people in France.

H: I see. One question, Patrick – are there protests in other cities in France?

P: Yes, in lots of other cities … Bordeaux, Marseilles, Lyon – all the big cities. It's a national protest, Hugo. It's a national problem.

H: Can you show me around the camp, Patrick?

P: Yes, sure, come with me. Look, here are all the tents. There are about three hundred, I think. There are lots of protesters here.

H: How many? Do you know?

P: I don't know exactly, maybe 400 … maybe 500. Look, there are tents here, along the river, and over there too, in the square. Come on, let's take a look in one of the tents. *Bonjour* Leo – this is Leonor.

H: Good morning, can you show us your tent?

L: Yes, of course! Come in! Well, this is our tent. There are two beds and there's a light … and that's it. It's a small tent. There are two of us in this tent – and our bags, that's all. The street is our living room – look, there's a table – and some chairs and lights!

H: Are there any bathrooms?

L: No, there aren't, but there are some toilets.

H: Is there a place where you can wash?

L: No, there isn't, but there are hostels for a shower – you pay 2 or 3 euros. It's OK if you're on the street for one or two nights … but it's really difficult when you're really homeless.

H: Thanks, Leonor.

L: *De rien – ciao!*

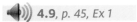

4.9, *p. 45, Ex 1*

1 A: Excuse me.
   B: Yes?
   A: Is there a post office near here?
   B: Yes, there's one over there. At the end of the road. See? Opposite the supermarket.
   A: Thanks.

2 A: Excuse me, can you help me?
   B: Yes, of course.
   A: Where's the nearest bus stop, please? Is there one near here?
   B: Yes, look ... it's over there, on the other side of the road. Next to the news-stand.
   A: Great – thanks!

3 A: Excuse me, is there a café near here?
   B: Yes, there is. It's over there, behind the park. Can you see it? It's got red chairs and tables.
   A: Oh, yes, thanks! I can see it now.

4 A: Excuse me, is there a car park near here?
   B: Hmm ... let me think. Ah, yes, there's one at the end of the road. It's on the left, opposite the cinema.
   A: Thanks a lot.
   B: You're welcome.

5 A: Excuse me, where's the police station?
   B: It's over there, on the right. See? Between the café and the cinema.
   A: OK, thanks!

5.6, *p. 54, Ex 3*

1 Her eyes ... eyes tell you a lot about a person.
2 I look down at his shoes! I don't like men with small feet.
3 Their teeth ... teeth are very important for me. You can't smile with bad teeth.
4 I know it's strange, but I notice people's arms.
5 Lips and a nice smile! That's so important!
6 I look at people's hair. Long hair is really attractive.
7 I can't help it, but I look at legs ... in a woman or a man!
8 I don't look at eyes ... I prefer ears and noses! I love little ears and big noses!

5.9, *p. 55, Ex 4*

1 Sit down and hold your feet.
2 Stand up straight and hold your left leg.
3 Lie on your back and hold your head up.
4 Stretch your arms carefully up over your head.
5 Lie on your front, put your hands on the floor and push your body up slowly.

5.11, *p. 56, Ex 2*

1 J = Jo   D = Dan

J: Hello? Is that Dan?
D: Yes, it's me. Hi, Jo, is Ted there?
J: Yes, but he's in the shower. Can I take a message?
D: Yes, can you tell him it's about football tonight? Can you ask him to call me when he's out of the shower?
J: Yes, sure. No problem.
D: Great! Thanks! Bye.
J: Bye.

2 D = Dan   T = Ted

D: Hi, Ted.
T: Hi! Is that you, Dan?
D: Yeah.
T: So, what time's football tonight?
D: 8 p.m. Can you give Steve and Ali a lift in your car?
T: Yes, sure. Do you want me to call them?
D: Yes, thanks. Then you can make plans for where and when to meet.
T: OK. See you later, then.
D: Yeah, see you later.

3 A = Ali   T = Ted

A: Hi, Ted
T: Hi, Ali. How are things?
A: Good.
T: Dan says you and Steve need a lift to football this evening.
A: Yeah, that's right.
T: I can meet you at the corner of your street at 7.30. How's that?
A: That's great, thanks!
T: Can you call Steve? I don't know his mobile number.
A: Yeah, sure, no problem.
T: OK. See you later.
A: See you.

6.4, *p. 65, Ex 3*

S = Sue

1 S: Hi, I'm Sue from Radio WBK...
   A: Hi!
   S: I'm doing a report on street fashion. Can I ask you some questions?
   A: Yes, sure.
   S: First of all, can you tell our listeners what you're wearing today?
   A: Yeah, erm ... I'm wearing a black and white shirt, a black T-shirt and black jeans.
   S: Are the kind of clothes you wear important to you?
   A: Yeah, definitely ... I mean, the clothes are an important part of the look.
   S: The look?
   A: Yeah, you know, the emo look ... the hair's important, too.
   S: The hair?
   A: Yeah, black hair, over one eye ... that's definitely the emo look!
   S: And what kind of things do you like doing with your friends?
   A: Erm ... we listen to music ... we go online, we meet in cafés and malls ... the usual thing.
   S: OK, thanks a lot. Bye.

2 S: Hi, I'm doing a programme on street fashion. Can you tell our listeners what you're wearing today?
   B: Sure ... I'm wearing jeans – baggy jeans – a T-shirt and black trainers – nothing special.
   S: Do you always dress like this?
   B: Erm ... not always, I wear jeans and a jacket when it's cold – it depends on the day, on the weather, on what I'm doing and where I'm going!
   S: And what do you do most days?
   B: I go to the skate park. I meet up with friends there. Sometimes we skate ... sometimes we listen to music...
   S: OK, thanks a lot!

3 S: Excuse me, I'm doing a report on street fashion – on what people are wearing – can I ask you a few questions?
   C: Yes ... of course.
   S: Can you quickly tell our listeners what you're wearing?
   C: Erm ... yeah ... well ... I'm wearing a black leather jacket and black jeans ... and big boots. I love my boots.
   S: Tell our listeners about your hair.
   C: Oh, yeah, I love my hair ... well, it's green and yellow and it stands up in these ... erm ... spikes ... I guess it's different.
   S: Do you always dress like this?
   C: No, I can't. I work in a supermarket. We wear a uniform. But I always dress like this – with

the hair and everything – in my free time.

4 S: Excuse me, I'm doing a report on street fashion – for the radio – can you tell our listeners something about the clothes you're wearing?
D: Yeah, sure ... I'm wearing a shirt with flowers and lots of colours – I love this kind of look. I think it's really happy...
S: Yes ... there are certainly lots of colours!
D: Yeah, and look ... I've got a tattoo of a flower, here, on my hand.
S: That's really pretty.
D: Thanks!
S: And thank you!

6.7, p. 66, Ex 2

1 A: Hello, can I help you?
B: No, thanks. I'm just looking.
A: OK ... let me know if you need anything. We've got some great new dresses ... and these boots are really nice ... everybody's buying them!
B: Er, no, thanks, I'm just looking, it's fine...
A: OK. No problem.
B: Yeah, well, goodbye.
A: OK. Have a nice day!

2 A: Excuse me?
B: Yes?
A: Where are the changing rooms, please?
B: They're over there, next to the men's trainers.
A: Thanks!

3 A: Excuse me?
B: Yes, can I help you?
A: Yes, please. I'm looking for the children's department.
B: It's over there, see, next to the escalators.
A: Thanks.

4 A: These rings are really beautiful. Can I try one on?
B: Yes, sure, help yourself. They're from Africa – the Ivory Coast.
A: Do you have any in a smaller size?
B: Yes, sure, just a minute ... here you are.
A: Yeah, that's great. How much is it?
B: Six euros.
A: OK, thanks. Here you are.
B: Thanks ... and here's your change. Have a nice day.

5 A: Erm, excuse me...
B: Just a second ... yes, how can I help you?
A: Erm, yeah ... I'm looking for a pair of trainers ... black trainers ... they're in the window...
B: These?
A: Yeah, those ones.
B: What size are you?
A: Thirty-eight.
B: OK. Just a minute ... Here you are.
A: Can I try them on?
B: Of course ... sit down here.
A: Thanks ... yeah, they're great. Can I pay by card?
B: Yes, of course you can. Can I see some ID?
A: Here you are...
B: Thanks ... sign here, please.
A: Thank you. Bye.

7.2, p. 73, Ex 5

Let's take a look at the weather today in the South America region. It's very hot, dry and sunny in Paraguay, with a maximum temperature of 35 degrees in the capital Asunción. It's a **cool**, wet day in São Paulo. It's raining, with a maximum temperature of 15 degrees centigrade. It's **warm** and sunny in Montevideo, with an expected high of 21 degrees. Meanwhile, it's a windy day in Buenos Aires with the maximum temperature a cool 12 degrees there. As for tourist spots, it's not a good day for the beach in south Brazil. It's raining in Florianópolis with a temperature of only 17 degrees. For those of you who are visiting the glaciers in El Calafate, it's snowing and the temperature is only just above **freezing** ... it's showing a very cold 1 degree centigrade at the moment – a very **cold** and icy day in this part of Patagonia. In the north of Argentina, on the border with Brazil, it's still warm. At Iguazu Falls there's a pleasant high of 23 degrees, but it's cloudy and humid.

7.4, p. 76, Ex 2

P = Patti L = Lola

P: How was the beach?
L: Oh, it was a total disaster!
P: Disaster? What do you mean?
L: Well, first of all, we arrived there and within, like, ten minutes it started to rain ... and I mean really rain!
P: Yeah, I remember. That was quite a storm at the weekend! So, what did you do?
L: Well, to start with, we waited in one of the beach cafés ... you know ... for the rain to stop, or something. We

had a coffee, we played a couple of games of cards ... but it didn't stop, it just rained ... and rained ... and rained. So in the end we decided to go home.
P: Yeah?
L: Yeah ... well, we walked to the road, to the bus stop, but just as we reached it ... there was the bus, far away in the distance! We were too late ... we missed the bus and there wasn't another one for two hours!
P: Oh, no!
L: Oh, yes! We didn't want to wait for the bus in the rain, so we walked...
P: What? All the way home?
L: Yes, all the way home...
P: Did you call a taxi?
L: No, we didn't. I wanted to ... but hey, it was too expensive ... we didn't have any money.
P: So what did you do when you finally got home?
L: We changed out of our wet clothes, had hot showers ... and then we went out for a pizza and a movie!
P: A much better idea in the rain!

7.7, p. 78, Ex 1

1 **Bruno**

I went to work by subway for years because I lived and worked in Rio. Now I work in São Paulo and Rio, so I go to work by plane. There's an air shuttle every half an hour and I can take any plane I like. I don't travel like this every day, of course. When I go to São Paulo, I normally stay for three or four nights, so it's easy enough. The plane trip is only one hour. I hated flying before, but now it's OK.

2 **Erykah**

Before, we walked to school, me and my friends – 3 km there and 3 back. We didn't have a choice, because the roads were not in good condition ... or there weren't any roads. Now the roads are better, and there's a school bus that picks us up from the main square in the village. My life changed overnight. It was hard going everywhere on foot...

3 **Carole**

I went to work by car, I admit it. A single person in a big family car! I like driving, but it's not very good for the environment. I realised one day that this was terrible, so I decided to make some changes. I talked to two friends who live near me and we decided to share a taxi together in the mornings. It costs more or less the same and we don't cause so much pollution. The problem is the taxi driver is not always very friendly.

4 Alek

I always went to college by train. It was quite comfortable and there weren't many delays. Then I changed my mind about it because the council introduced a new bike service. The idea is great, but there are always problems. The bikes are sometimes broken, or there aren't any when you want one … or there isn't any space to leave them. And on rainy days…! Well, it was expensive, but I preferred the train!

 **7.9**, *p. 80, Ex 2*

1   **A:** Excuse me, are you going to the stadium?
    B: No, you need the number 2 bus. The stop's over there, next to the petrol station.

2   **A:** Excuse me, this ticket machine is out of order. Is there another one?
    B: No, I'm afraid there isn't. You need to go to the ticket office.

3   **A:** Hi! Can you take me to the airport, please?
    B: Yeah, sure. Which terminal?
    A: Just a second … erm … Terminal 4, please…
    …Thanks, that's great. How much is it?
    B: That's £15.85, please.

4   **A:** Excuse me, how long does it take to get to the airport by train?
    B: About 35 minutes. There's a train every half an hour.
    A: And by bus?
    B: The bus takes about an hour. It leaves every hour on the hour, from the bus stop over there.
    A: Thanks!

5   **A:** Oh, no! We just missed the last ferry! When's the next one?
    B: I don't know. Let me check the timetable … There's another one in 40 minutes.
    A: Why don't we have a coffee while we wait?
    B: Yeah, look there's a bar over there.

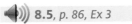 **8.5**, *p. 86, Ex 3*

Latest news on the hour every hour. It's nine o'clock and here are tonight's headlines for English speakers in Buenos Aires.

Fears about the new flu pandemic are increasing. Today, the authorities decided to check all passengers entering the country's main airports. Doctors suspect that 11 soldiers in the Argentinian army have the virus. Hospitals are on alert in major cities such as Cordoba, Mendoza and Rosario.

And now the latest from the Rock in the Park festival in Mar del Plata…

Disaster at this year's Rock in the Park as storms hit the coast of Mar del Plata. The country's biggest rock festival is in danger. Last night it rained non-stop and organisers cancelled Friday's concerts. They hope to make an announcement later today about tonight's show with big name bands Depeche Mode and The Killers. Meanwhile, the fans are learning to live with the mud!

Finally, sports news with Clara García…

Thanks, Tom. Yes, amazing but true! They did it … Lanús won the league last night for the first time in their history, when they beat Vélez Sarsfield, 2–0. José Sand scored both goals to give Lanús victory. Last night, parties continued for hours after the match but the club plan to organise an official party for next weekend.

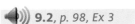 **8.8**, *p. 89, Ex 1*

Alain Robert is an incredible man – and an incredible climber. He started climbing as a young boy and he climbed his first building at the age of 12. One day he got home, looked in his pockets, but he didn't have his door key. He didn't want to wait for someone to come home, so he decided to climb up the outside of the building – all the way to the eighth floor. This was the beginning of a great passion.

As a young man he had two serious accidents. After the second accident, doctors said that his climbing career was over. But Alain didn't listen to them. He wanted to climb. At first he climbed mountains and then he started to climb towers and famous buildings.

First he climbed the Eiffel Tower in Paris and then the Opera House in Sydney. It is usually impossible to get permission to climb these buildings, so Alain usually starts his climbs in the early hours of the morning, using only his hands and some climbing shoes. And his climbs often end in his arrest! Chinese authorities arrested him in 2007, Brazilian police arrested

him in São Paulo in 2008 and British police arrested and fined him when he climbed the Lloyd's building in London in 2009. And so the story continues…

When reporters ask him why he does it, he says what all great climbers say: 'Because I can.' At first he climbed for fun, then he climbed to protest – to protest against his arrests – he really doesn't like authority! – and later to protest about climate change. Some of his climbs were also for money. In 2003 he climbed the Abu Dhabi Bank building to celebrate its opening. Then he climbed the Lloyds building in London in a Spider-Man costume to promote the *Spider-Man* movie. The media started to call him the Human Spider or the French Spiderman.

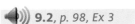 **8.9**, *p. 94, Ex 2*

1   **A:** José and Beth moved into their new house last week.
    B: Did they? I didn't know it was ready.
    A: Yeah, I went to see it at the weekend. It's lovely.

2   **A:** Erika and Kristoff's baby was born last night – at 10 p.m. It's a girl. She's gorgeous!
    B: A girl? That's fantastic news! Kristoff really wanted a girl! What's her name?

3   **A:** Did you hear about Adam? He lost his job.
    B: Oh, no! When did that happen?
    A: Two days ago. More than a hundred people lost their jobs. The company's in big trouble.
    B: That's awful! I'm really sorry to hear that.

4   **A:** I passed!
    B: You passed?
    A: Yes, I passed my driving test! Two hours ago!
    B: That's great news! Congratulations!

5   **A:** Sorry, but I can't come to your party this evening. I've got some work to do.
    B: Oh, no! What a shame! Can't you come later?
    A: Yeah, maybe. I can try, anyway.

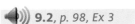 **9.2**, *p. 98, Ex 3*

It's sad but true. Every year we throw away one third of the food we buy. That's 6.7 million tonnes of food in the UK. Fruit and vegetables are 40 per cent of this. The top five fruit and vegetables that go in the rubbish bin are apples, potatoes, bananas, tomatoes and oranges.

But why do we waste so much food? The reason is simple. We buy too much food, we don't use it all and then we throw it away. For example, lots of people forget to put food in the fridge in summer. Obviously, if you put fresh fruit and vegetables in the fridge they stay fresh for longer and you don't need to throw them away.

🔊 10.7, *p. 112, Ex 2*

P = presenter   FH = Frederic Hedstrom

P: Welcome to *Buzzword*, the programme that looks at new words, what they mean and how we use them. In the studio today we have Frederic Hedstrom, who is going to talk about flash mobs. What does that mean exactly, Frederic?

FH: Well, a mob is a large group of people, right? And 'flash' suggests speed, something that happens suddenly, something that happens very quickly. Flash mobs are events where big crowds of people meet in a public place and do something together for maybe five minutes … and then that's it.

P: What's the connection with technology, then?

FH: Well, people know what's happening, and where and when to meet, because they get a text message on their cell phone – or perhaps an email. This means that these events happen very quickly, there's no need to plan in advance. People call, text or send an email and the flash mob takes place only a few hours or minutes later.

P: Yes, I think that's the exciting part of it, they're very spontaneous…

FH: Absolutely.

P: What kind of flash mobs do people organise?

FH: Well, a lot of them are just for fun. There is a very popular one – The Pillow Fight. It takes place all over the world. People get together and fight each other with pillows. That's it. It's silly but great fun!

P: How many people are we talking about here?

FH: More than 5,000 in the New York pillow fight. That's the biggest flash mob ever, bigger than London's silent disco.

P: Silent disco? What's that?

FH: A silent disco – or rave – is when a lot of people meet in a public

place, listen to music on their iPods and dance. It looks really strange. Everybody's dancing, but you can't hear any music! That's why it's called a silent disco – or rave!

P: It all seems very silly. Aren't there any serious flash mobs?

FH: Well, one famous event happened in 2009. Dani Jarque, a footballer and captain of the football club Espanyol in Barcelona, died suddenly at the age of 26. Fans of the club organised a meeting to pay their respects to him. Thousands of people phoned, or sent text messages, like a chain … and they all met in the same place to light candles and leave flowers.

P: Where did they meet?

FH: At gate 21 of Espanyol's stadium.

P: Why was that?

FH: Because Jarque's shirt number was always 21.

P: I see … Finally, what's your favourite flash mob, Frederic?

FH: Oh, something silly! There was a No Pants Day in New York. A lot of people got on the subway without their trousers … it was very funny … and it was a cold day, too!

🔊 10.10, *p. 114, Exs 3 & 4*

1 A: Oh, no!
   B: What's up?
   A: I don't have any battery!
   B: Use my phone if you want. Here.
   A: Thanks! What do I do?
   B: Key in the number and then press the button with the green phone.
   A: OK. Thanks!

2 A: Hey, is that a new phone?
   B: Yeah.
   A: It's the same as mine.
   B: Really? Hey, maybe you can help me. I want to send a photo, but I don't know how.
   A: It's easy! Look, click on 'menu' … here, see?
   B: Yes…
   A: Then select 'camera', here in the corner…
   B: No, I don't want to *take* a photo, I want to *send* one. Look, here's the photo … but I don't know how to send it.
   A: Let's see … oh, yes, click here – see where it says 'more'? Now select 'send'.
   B: OK, now I get it. Thanks!
   A: No problem!

3 A: Do you have the time?
   B: Yeah. Look, there's my phone, on

the table.

A: But it's switched off.
B: Just press that button on the side.
A: Which one? This one?
B: Yes, that's it.
A: Great! Hey, I like that – my phone doesn't do that!
B: So what time is it?
A: Oh, no, ten to six. I'd better go! I don't want to be late!

🔊 11.2, *p. 119, Ex 2*

A new survey out today says that the five happiest professions in the UK are hairdressers, chefs, priests, plumbers and mechanics. And the five unhappiest are office workers, architects, secretaries, estate agents and bankers. It appears that hairdressers, chefs, priests, plumbers and mechanics have one important thing in common: They make people feel good – or help them solve an important problem – quickly! Which might explain why architects are more unhappy – because it takes a long time to see the results of their work. It can take many years to finish a building, but a haircut or bowl of pasta takes just a few minutes!

🔊 11.3, *p. 120, Ex 1*

P = Phil   T = Toni

P: Welcome to Job Search – the radio programme that helps you find your ideal job. Toni, what have you got for us today?

T: Well, Phil, I just saw this incredible job advert on an Australian website. This has to be the best job ever!

P: What is it?

T: Well, the Queensland Tourism Authority is looking for someone to be a caretaker on a tropical island off the coast of Australia – in addition to a fantastic salary of 150,000 Australian dollars…

P: One hundred and fifty thousand?

T: Yes! The caretaker will get 150,000 dollars for a six-month contract. And, in addition to the salary, the caretaker will live rent free – that's right, they won't pay any rent – in a three-bedroom beach-side villa … with a swimming pool!

P: Wow! That really is the best job ever … but what will the caretaker need to do?

T: Very little! He or she will work about 12 hours a month.

P: A month? Not a day?

T: No, a month. He or she will collect

the mail – you know, letters and packages and things – for the island, and look after some of the hundreds of different fish that live in the sea around the island.

P: Is that it? Are you sure that's all? There's nothing else they need to do?

T: Well, yes … the caretaker will also write a blog about his or her life on the island. He or she will take photos and videos of all the wonderful beaches and fantastic things to do on the island – and all the other tropical islands around.

P: Ah, I see…

T: That will really be the most important part of the job – they want to attract more visitors to these beautiful islands.

P: So, what kind of person are they looking for?

T: Well, the successful candidate will need to know how to swim, snorkel, dive and sail. And, of course, he or she will need to know how to use a computer…

P: And how to take good photos!

T: Yes, and write a good blog!

P: Well, I'll be interested to see who gets the job of the blogging island caretaker!

T: Me, too!

12.3, p.129, Ex 1

H = Hanna   R = Renata   S = Stephen

H: …I hate these lists…

R: Why? I think they're interesting…

H: Come on, I mean, life isn't a list … it's how you live from day to day that's important – who you are, not the number of things you do. This is just a list of expensive holiday experiences … just another thing to consume.

R: Consume? What do you mean?

H: Well, it's a list of things to spend money on – things you can buy – isn't it? You know, an exotic holiday or skydiving. All these 'before you die' lists say you haven't had a good life – a full life – if you don't do all these exotic – and expensive! – things. And I think that's wrong.

S: Hanna has a point … and this list is a bit stupid. I mean, drive a Formula One car! That's just for kids! Some people think that life is just about driving fast cars, obviously…

H: I know, that's exactly what I mean. But then, looking again, there are some good things on the list, too. I'd love to go whale-watching, for example.

S: Me too!

R: I did that in Argentina a few years ago. It was brilliant.

S: And I've been to Antarctica.

R: Seriously?

S: Yeah, I went last summer. It was amazing. And I'd love to see the Northern Lights. Hanna, you've lived in Finland, haven't you? Have you ever seen the Northern Lights?

H: No, I haven't. We went up to the north once, but we didn't see the lights. I've seen the midnight sun, though … but then, that isn't on the list, is it? So, I suppose it doesn't count!

12.4, p. 131, Ex 1

1 **Gus**
I've never been to Scandinavia. I've always wanted to go there, so Copenhagen could be interesting to visit, sure. But everybody tells me it's very expensive there … though that obviously doesn't worry the magazine … maybe the journalists have a lot of money! It looks beautiful in the photo, so clean, and the air so fresh, not like where I live. I went to Munich last summer … I wonder if it's similar. I don't know if the cultural life in Copenhagen is so good, but I like the fact that the people are liberal there – they have open minds. So, yes, I would like to go … one day!

2 **Maria**
Well, I don't know why it's this magazine's number one city. I went to Zurich a few years ago, but I didn't like it much. I didn't have a very good time there. It's a very beautiful place and everything runs on time, like the transport, as they say. But it's not a very friendly place … maybe it's just too efficient. I like cities which have more life, more chaos … for me, the atmosphere on the street is the most important thing, and the cultural life. I don't think it's so great in Zurich. I've been to other cities in Europe which I like more … Berlin, for example.

12.7, p. 132, Ex 4

I = interviewer   K = Klaus

I: Well, Klaus, we've just heard the news. You're going to represent Munich at this year's Ironman World Championship in Hawaii!

K: I can't really believe it, to tell you the truth! I'm very excited indeed.

I: How did you get the place?

K: I was very lucky! It's a lottery – that's the only way they can limit the number of people in the race. To be in the lottery, you need to do a half Ironman event somewhere in the world, that's all.

I: So, some people think you need to be crazy to do this. Is that right?

K: Well, maybe, yes – I'm sure it helps! I started with normal triathlons, like a lot of people, and I realised that I was quite good. I began as a swimmer, really – I swam in competitions when I was a kid. Then some friends told me about triathlons. I did my first one here in Munich five years ago.

I: Which is your favourite of the three sports?

K: I think it's swimming, that's my best sport. Cycling is the worst one, I sometimes get very tired!

I: So, what are your plans now, Klaus? How are you going to prepare for this event?

K: Good question! The training is very difficult. For the next six months, I'm going to follow a very strict programme. On Tuesdays and Thursdays, I swim about 3 km in my local pool. On Fridays I swim another 2.5 km, and I try and swim in open sea, if I can, but that's not easy here in Munich. On Wednesdays, I usually go for a short run, around 10 to 12 km. On Saturdays, I usually do a long bike ride, which right now is about 120 km! Then, on Sundays, I run a longer distance, about 20 km … but all those distances will start to increase. Mondays are usually my day off!

I: What about the climate in Hawaii?

K: That's a problem. Here in Munich it's very cold, but in Hawaii the weather will be hot – and it can be windy, too. I need to be careful! Right now, I'm running with lots of clothes on to prepare myself for the heat.

I: What about the rules?

K: There are a lot! You can't receive help from anyone in the race, except the officials, who can give you food and drink. Also, there's a new rule for the swimming … you can't wear swimsuits made from certain material because they give you an advantage – they help you swim faster.

I: Well, thanks, Klaus, for telling us about the preparations for the race. Good luck and congratulations!

K: Congratulations?! Let's hope I finish first!

IRREGULAR VERBS

INFINITIVE	PAST SIMPLE	PAST PARTICIPLE
be	was, were	been
become	became	become
begin	began	begun
break	broke	broken
bring	brought	brought
build	built	built
buy	bought	bought
choose	chose	chosen
come	came	come
cost	cost	cost
do	did	done
drink	drank	drunk
eat	ate	eaten
fall	fell	fallen
feel	felt	felt
find	found	found
fly	flew	flown
forget	forgot	forgotten
get	got	got
give	gave	given
go	went	gone, been
have	had	had
hear	heard	heard
hold	held	held
keep	kept	kept
know	knew	known
learn	learnt/learned	learnt/learned
leave	left	left
lose	lost	lost

INFINITIVE	PAST SIMPLE	PAST PARTICIPLE
make	made	made
meet	met	met
pay	paid	paid
put	put	put
read /riːd/	read /red/	read /red/
ride	rode	ridden
ring	rang	rung
run	ran	run
say	said	said
see	saw	seen
sell	sold	sold
send	sent	sent
show	showed	shown
sing	sang	sung
sit	sat	sat
sleep	slept	slept
speak	spoke	spoken
spend	spent	spent
stand	stood	stood
swim	swam	swum
take	took	taken
teach	taught	taught
tell	told	told
think	thought	thought
throw	threw	thrown
wake	woke	woken
wear	wore	worn
win	won	won
write	wrote	written